Mimi Kwa has been an Australian journalist and television newsreader on the ABC and Nine Network for twenty years and has appeared in commercials and FOXTEL, STAN and ABC TV series. She and her partner, John, live in Melbourne, with their four children, two dogs and a cat. Mimi loves to paint and write. This memoir is her first book.

mimitv.com.au

@mimikwatv

@mimi.kwa.writes

Praise for *House of Kwa*

'*House of Kwa* enchants and enthrals like the best kind of sweeping, dynastic fiction, but it rattles the bones and breaks the heart with the pure facts of Mimi Kwa's extraordinary story. Revelatory and remarkable storytelling.' **Trent Dalton**

'An astonishing true tale that leaps across centuries and cultures to land with a thump in your heart.' **Lisa Millar**

'A startling tale of the past, its terrible grip on the present, and the battle to set yourself free. Full of scenes that hover between tragedy and farce, *House of Kwa* is one of the most compelling stories you'll read this year. Memorable and vividly told, this is a book for anybody forced to survive their own parents.' **Richard Glover**

'From the back streets of China to war-torn Hong Kong to suburban Australia, this is a heroic saga that reveals just some of the stories behind the multicultural nation we are today.' **Mike Munro AO**

'This is a charming and compelling story, an insight into a deeply traditional Chinese family in times when China was undergoing internally and externally induced upheaval.' *South China Morning Post*

'A rich and riveting read which heralds a new chapter in Kwa's life as a writer. The spirited tiger, full of life and driven to achieve, has many stories to tell yet.' *The Weekend Australian*

'*House of Kwa* answers the question of how one should write about one's family with generosity and love – to read it is to experience Kwa's wonder at the strength and resilience of her family, as well as the intimacy of her relationships with them. Traversing the boundaries of a traditional memoir, *House of Kwa* is the biography of a family that explores the way our lives are shaped by the past we can and cannot remember.' *Kill Your Darlings*

'If you're a fan of the book *Educated* by Tara Westover, as I am, and most readers I know are, then you have to read this.' **Joan McKenzie, Joan's Picks, Whitcoulls**

'Mimi's narrative about their family life is heart-breaking, hilarious and often unbelievable.' **Magic Talk FM**

'An exotic journey that takes readers through the contributions Chinese immigrants have made to multicultural Australia.' **ABC Nightlife**

'Kwa is an engaging storyteller.' *Asian Review of Books*

HOUSE OF KWA

MIMI KWA

ABC
BOOKS

The ABC 'Wave' device is a trademark of the
Australian Broadcasting Corporation and is used
under licence by HarperCollins*Publishers* Australia.

HarperCollins*Publishers*
Australia • Brazil • Canada • France • Germany • Holland • India
Italy • Japan • Mexico • New Zealand • Poland • Spain • Sweden
Switzerland • United Kingdom • United States of America

HarperCollins acknowledges the Traditional Custodians
of the lands upon which we live and work, and pays respect
to Elders past and present.

First published on Gadigal Country in Australia in 2021
by HarperCollinsPublishers Australia Pty Limited
ABN 36 009 913 517
harpercollins.com.au

A catalogue record for this book is available from the National Library of Australia.

ISBN 978 0 7333 4352 0 (paperback)
ISBN 978 1 4607 1289 4 (ebook)

Cover design by Andy Warren, HarperCollins Design Studio
Cover images by shutterstock.com and istockphoto.com
Typeset in Bembo Std Regular by Kirby Jones
Photograph of Mimi Kwa (on page i) by Rachael Dere
Photograph of Mimi Kwa and her family (on the seventh page of the picture section)
  by Jesper Nielsen

Printed and bound by CPI Group (UK) Ltd, Croydon, CR0 4YY

For John and our children,
Royston, Mason, Harper and Berry

In memory of Aunty

AUTHOR'S NOTE

You know that feeling when you've been burned by someone you love and you think you can only save yourself from the flames by walking away? When that someone is your family, there are, as I see it, three options: estrangement, obligation, or forgiveness and gratitude. There's no right answer, and the path will always be complex.

When you join me in my story, please remind yourself that the lens of a child is not the one I look through now. As an adult I can see other points of view – right or wrong, good or bad – that weren't available to me then. Delving into my past to bring fractures of time into focus has uncovered my story through a kaleidoscope of experiences. Here on these pages I seek to make the brushstrokes of my family portrait dance to life.

Today, I reach into my trove of painting implements and pass to my own child an heirloom, handed down for a thousand years. Accepting it tentatively, she examines its soft grey bristles – shaped like a turnip bulb into a point. She weighs and turns the decorated bamboo stem in her small hands. 'You are holding an ancient Chinese calligraphy brush,' I say. 'Imagine how many artworks this brush has painted, how many stories it has told, how many hands have held it, and how much more it has to say.' She hesitantly hovers the tip of the brush over a petite porcelain well. 'Now, dip the brush into the ink, and daub it gently from point to base, pulling it downwards lightly before quickly lifting. There, you've made your first stroke.'

As she wields the brush, I see the hands of our ancestors gripping its shaft, wrestling with its handle to bring the most vivid images into view, the black pigment bleeding into flax paper to create shadows and shade. I speak to my child of a dragon and a tiger, and tilting my head towards her mark on the page, I watch her confidence grow as she makes another. 'You see, my love, this is who you are. This brush will tell you a thousand tales, and in the end you will use it to paint your own. Because this is a story that began millennia ago and has no end. This, my darling, is the brush of Kwa.'

PROLOGUE

GREY HAIR, LIKE MARIE ANTOINETTE. IT CAN'T REALLY BE possible, but as I examine the phenomenon in the bathroom mirror, there's no denying I went to bed without any grey hairs and now a brittle, coarse sprig of them is right there on my scalp.

The cause is a letter from my father, the latest of several he'd sent recently. After finding it in the mailbox, I had ignored it for days, on the kitchen bench, the piano or the dresser, or shoved under the stairs on a stool next to the schoolbags. Then, finally, last night, when the kids were asleep and my husband was watching TV, I opened it.

> THE SUPREME COURT
> OF WESTERN AUSTRALIA
> Kwa v Kwa

I had no words. All the strangeness in my life, the past I'd tried to put behind me, it kept coming back, smoke wisps around my feet: the dragon.

Dad was suing me.

Now, as I stare into the mirror, I have flashes of my child self, from age ten, proofreading Dad's legal letters and court documents. They would stream through a dot-matrix printer, perforated paper swallowing every available space in his home office. I would catch the pages as they spewed out and guide them into neat, concertinaed stacks. Dad was always suing someone, and as late as one in the morning he would come into my room and ask me to check his letters.

'Excuse me, Mi. I need to get this off tomorrow.' He'd hand me a wad of legalese that I'd scour with my pen, returning it to him after I'd applied my system of placing an 'x' in the margin at the end of the line to indicate a correction.

If only I'd spent as much time studying as I had working for Dad. At least he prepared me for fighting him in this latest legal tussle. His combative spirit is perhaps natural for a man who has been through so much, but all the same – why would he do this to his own child? *Kwa v Kwa* is something I never dreamed could happen.

Cortisol and adrenalin surge through me, a survival response triggered since childhood, a response passed down from my ancestors. My very existence, the very Kwa of me, is under siege, this time in the unfamiliar territory of the courtroom, which is Dad's patch, his dragon stomping ground. I'm a tiger running towards a fire, leaping into the flames while I look behind me – as far back as I can, to ancient China, near the Emperor's palace in Beijing.

The sky opens, and the shaman's almanac, which he uses to predict all things, shows clearly beneath my Wood Tiger stars that it was always my destiny to be trapped in a battle with a dragon.

And then the book closes, and all that remains are tendrils of smoke from Great-Grandfather's pipe and Grandmother's cigarettes. There are whispers of 'you are Kwa, you are Kwa' – for even in visions, my family members repeat themselves. I am

4

surrounded by their stories, flooding through windows and under doors, House of Kwa tales curling round the leg of my chair, clinging to my curtains like Aunt Theresa's brushstrokes on silk.

I watch a tree grow from my table, branches and twigs rapidly filling the room, blossoms blooming in sharp bursts of spring colour, like fireworks, like bombs: our family. From all the tragedy, silken threads weave together into a picture of survival, a banner of hope. Then a dragon flies from the tree and, without warning, engulfs the branches in flames. As the tree burns, the dragon disappears, but for his eyes lingering in the sky among the stars that said I would always be exactly here, that we cannot escape what is already written.

Of course, a tiger cannot help but stop to look at her reflection as she passes by water under a burning tree, beneath dragon eyes in the sky. This image of her and what she's endured may show her how she became so fierce ...

OLD KWA

龍的傳人

Descendants of the dragon

OPIUM AND SILK

'I AM A DIRECT DESCENDANT OF THE EMPEROR OF CHINA,' Great-Grandfather hollers. 'How dare you hide from me.'

It's the Year of the Wood Monkey, 1884. My great-grandfather is looking for his servant Chen She.

'Where is he?' spits Great-Grandfather in his best nineteenth-century Mandarin, arms outstretched and laden with layers of soft glossy silk. He warms his hands on a heating pipe as ladies of the elite bustle across his courtyard in their own silken finery, the sheets of vibrant thread dancing in the gentle rays of spring sunshine.

'Gossiping, always gossiping,' Great-Grandfather mutters resentfully before turning to scream across the decadent compound. 'Chen She!'

Great-Grandfather's voice carries through a lace wooden window embedded with tessellations of rectangles and squares, a honeycomb of shapes protecting the privacy of the many stone rooms interconnected with terracotta roofs, garden walkways and broad internal corridors: hard to see in, easy to see out.

Great-Grandfather steps out of a door into the courtyard and leans on a post encircled with etchings of dragons ascending to heaven. He heaves a frustrated sigh and shouts, 'Must I find my own opium pipe?' His fury replenished, his best Mandarin slips, giving way to an enraged common dialect. A timber lantern swings in the gusts of his temper. 'Must I stoke my own pipe?'

The two stone lions at the compound gate bristle with alarm. Up on the roof ridges, terracotta dragons turn to one another in panic.

'Must I light my own pipe?' Great-Grandfather's rage sweeps the dry earthen paths and blasts the stone pillars of the bridge over the koi pond; the water ripples.

Most others in the courtyard have fled to their rooms or are trying desperately to blend in with the manicured hedges.

Two young concubines huddling by a heating pipe in an adjacent room are alert at the yelling and quite possibly alarmed. They turn to Wife Number One, as she glides in from a corridor, calm as ever, her bound feet causing no apparent pain. She is both admired and feared.

'He has never lit his own pipe,' she says. 'He wouldn't even know where to find it.' She claps her eyes on a Ming vase, which sits atop a cabinet lavishly adorned with mother-of-pearl, and she remembers the time Great-Grandfather smashed its mate. Then she cocks her head to one side. 'Must I find my own opium pipe? Must I stoke my own pipe? Must I light my own pipe?' She mimics Great-Grandfather quite well but is sure to keep her voice at a rasp – it is in no one's interest to enrage him further. She glares around the room, imitating his wrath, sweeping the air with her wide silk sleeves as the two concubines exchange a glance and stifle giggles. First Mother can be funny sometimes; so long as she doesn't feel threatened by the younger women of the house, she can be quite a lark.

With a thud and all the drama of an overacted Chinese opera, Chen She falls through the door, landing on his knees, head bowed, hands splayed. 'Master, Master! I beg your forgiveness.'

The concubines and First Mother turn to stare in disdain at the familiar dishevelled figure.

'You fool, Chen She,' First Mother hisses. 'Grand Master is next door in the ancestors' room.' She rolls her eyes. 'Idiot.'

The girls stifle giggles again, and poor old Chen She pulls himself together, dusts off his robes and prepares to go through his routine a second time. He is, however, beaten to the punch, quite literally, when Great-Grandfather enters the room and wallops him across the head.

The concubines rise to flee. Where Great-Grandfather's temper will hit its mark, only the gods can predict. The girls stoop, duck and weave, covering their heads in anticipation of his lack of both coordination and discrimination. Like dragon fury, he tears through the compound while women, children and servants rush to hide.

By afternoon, Great-Grandfather is worshipping at his Confucian altar. He tells the ancestral tablets and statues what a heavy disappointment everyone else in the compound is, and he confides his deep regret at employing, marrying and spawning such insolence. 'I am twenty-first generation firstborn Kwa,' he says indignantly as he places a joss stick in a bowl of sand at the feet of the cast figure of his father, the twentieth generation firstborn Kwa. 'Do they have no respect?'

Great-Grandfather now has his pipe in his hand and Chen She to stoke and light it. The servant knows better than to stray far again, at least until next time. Great-Grandfather draws the white smoke up the blackened pipe stem engraved with tiny horses, and the opiate streams into his lungs, filling every blood vessel with sweet poison. He holds his breath until a cough forces its way out. With each exhale he instructs in meticulous detail, according to unquestionable tradition, how Chen She must prepare an opium pipe and silk bag for Number Three Son's eighth birthday tomorrow; although the boy isn't a firstborn from any wife, a pipe will be a fitting gift for him.

A morphine haze envelopes Great-Grandfather; his black lashes flutter, his eyes roll upward and a stupor sets in. The compound is peaceful. Cooks are cooking, rickshaw drivers are resting, children are finishing homework since private tutors have made tracks for the night. A nursemaid breastfeeds a baby – not hers, of course – and two concubines wash before bed in preparation for the possibility of a late visit from Great-Grandfather. Moonlight reveals the swollen expectant belly of one consort, a child herself, recently turned fourteen.

'Father.' First Son of Third Wife, Ying Kam, stands at the door to the ancestors' room, trying to bring Great-Grandfather out of his tete-a-tete with his forebears. 'Father, may I talk with you?'

Great-Grandfather looks up as if seeing his son for the first time and rearranges himself into a more dignified pose befitting a prominent trader of the elite class of Beijing.

'Father, I am sixteen; I should be married by now.' This is the law – sixteen for boys, fourteen for girls. 'Most of my friends have wed. Why will you not marry me off?'

Great-Grandfather looks to his ancestors for strength. Why don't children just do as they're told? 'It is in the stars and the ancient almanac that you must wait until the fourth moon of the new sun and marry a girl born in the golden pig.'

'Father, I know all that. You've been telling me that since I could walk. Second Brother from First Mother is married *twice*, with Wife Number Two already expecting his first child. Even First Brother from Third Mother is married.' Ying Kam pauses, exasperated. He cannot keep his voice from rising, but he grits his teeth and holds back his tears. 'Why not me?'

'I have told you, son, it is not yet in your stars to marry.'

'But the matchmaker has arranged a bride.'

'You must be patient. We wait on the fortune-teller to determine when the time is right.'

'Father, I am born a Yellow Earth Dragon, the most powerful of all the zodiac, can I not decide on my own wedding? I will leave and find my bride myself if you will not set a date.'

Ying Kam's shame – of being the only unmarried boy among his rich and privileged friends – bubbles up like the thick black mushroom soup the family cook would force him to eat when he was younger, saying it would ward off *Yaoguai*, demoted gods who became monsters, relegated to earth for breaking the laws of heaven. Just like his brothers, boys his own age from all six of Great-Grandfather's wives and concubines combined, he is ready to forge his way in elite Chinese society and, most of all, to be a man.

But the stone carvings, ancestors, heating pipes and lanterns of the compound know that this argument can only end one way.

'There are contemporary thinkings, Father. We don't have to follow every word of the fortune-teller. Father, Ping Ma is to be my bride – make it so, now.'

'I will no longer tolerate your insolence, boy. Go. You behave as though you know better than your superior. And in front of your ancestors.' He looks to the altar apologetically. 'You bring shame to this family.'

Great-Grandfather slaps his son across the cheek, and a red welt sears the boy's tender skin. Tears well in his eyes. He turns and runs from the ancestral room, his silks trailing behind him like watercolour brushstrokes, across the courtyard to a room he shares with his unmarried younger brothers. He holds a grief so heavy he cannot let it go lest it may crush him, so instead he packs it up with all his worldly possessions.

Ying Kam opens chests and flings silk garments into cloth rolls as two younger boys – mouths open and faces pale with disbelief – dare not utter a squeak. Best to feign sleep than to be complicit in this crime taking place. Reaching into a hole in his mattress, Ying Kam removes the savings he's squirrelled away since he was nine, the year his father gave him an opium pipe – another gripe he has: receiving his pipe at a later age than some of his brothers.

He cups the face of Eighth Brother in his hands and whispers a tacit warning not to alert the household to his escape, '*Shan shui you xiang feng.* Mountain water will meet again,' and stops to take in the room one last time.

Ying Kam stands in the darkened courtyard and looks in through a window to see Great-Grandfather cavorting with a concubine, smoking opium and laughing. Ying Kam tiptoes to a study at the end of a passage, where he opens a desk drawer to reveal an ivory abacus and a stack of black leather-bound notebooks. On top of the desk there is a heavier version: a ledger. But this is not what Ying Kam is looking for. He has spent years sitting by his father's side and knows to open a compartment hiding under inkwells and fountain pens.

Mountain water will meet again. Two graves, he thinks, *we will meet again in heaven,* and places a dense journal, the size of two hands, in a fold of his coat, caressing the smooth leather and patting his pocket.

A wife younger than Ying Kam comes in giggling with intoxication, smelling like poppy juice.

'Shhhh,' he says. 'Get out.'

'Shhhh. Get out.' She mimics him in a high whisper, sways in an attempt at enticing him, then loses her balance and grips a heating pipe for support. Her dainty lotus flower feet cannot hold her up, although she is accustomed to the great pretence afflicting all girls and women of her status: that bound feet cause no bother.

'Come,' Ying Kam says to Lotus Flower, his nickname for her. 'Come with me now.'

The laughter in her eyes drains away as she realises he is not kidding.

Lotus Flower is Great-Grandfather's fourth wife and has not yet blessed him with children. She came from a village in the Eastern Coastal Zhejiang Province when she was fourteen, and now she is fifteen there are suspicions she is barren. As if to remind her of this shame, a baby cries on the other side of the compound.

'Come,' Ying Kam insists. 'Come now.'

He has no love for Lotus Flower but a companion will provide the necessary reassurance to set aside the violent inner tussle over what he is about to do.

Great-Grandfather roars with laughter in the next room as Ying Kam prepares to abscond with Fourth Mother and the leather-bound book that holds the key to their future. It is November but the brittle sunset air will not deter him. The French navy has recently attacked Foochow on China's coast, bolstering numbers heading south, and while war and starvation are the common reason for migration – not thwarted betrothal – the Yellow Earth Dragon, Ying Kam, is resolute. The Ottoman Empire blocked trade along the Silk Road four centuries ago but Kwa has used alternate silk routes by land and sea ever since. And there is no better port for trade or travel overseas, than Swatow.

'I will pay you well,' Ying Kam tells his favourite driver. 'You will be my second-in-command. What is there for you here? A life of endlessly pulling the rich in rickshaws – with a horse one day, if the gods bestow mercy?'

Lotus Flower's face pokes around Ying Kam's shoulder as he crouches beside the straw mattress of Storm Boy, his nickname for the driver – although driver barely describes the manpower Storm Boy must harness to run along cobblestones and dirt with a carriage at his back, or to ride the family's bicycle-drawn shaw on his luckier days. Storm Boy has been Ying Kam's confidant since he was young. They have grown up together, the driver little more than three years Ying Kam's senior.

Storm Boy's mattress lies on the soil floor of the rickshaw stable. As Ying Kam shakes him awake, speaking low and soft, it dawns on Storm Boy this could indeed be his chance for emancipation. Swatow is the Western name for Shantou on Guangdong's east coast, and Storm Boy has heard of many thousands of Chinese establishing great fortune there.

The bronze serpent door-knocker whispers adventure, as the stone lions stand alert at the gate. Terracotta roof dragons exchange hopeful glances. The three fugitives may yet escape, before they are killed.

When the driver agrees, there is nothing more that needs to be said between friends.

Ying Kam and Lotus Flower climb into the rickshaw, and Storm Boy sweeps them off towards the outside world. Great-Grandfather's laughter fades as they wheel past the stone lions and a sleeping guard at his post. No one sees First Mother watching from her window or witnesses her tears.

My grandfather Ying Kam creates distance from his beginnings, propelling himself closer to a new life. House of Kwa splinters. Click–click–click go the rickshaw wheels. A family diaspora catches a north wind. Over cobblestones and dirt, steep terrain and wooded bush, the rickshaw rides. *Whoosh*, the dragon's tail. *Snap*, the branch of a tree. *Tap, grind*, a claw sharpening on teeth.

RICKSHAW AND GOLD

YING KAM AND LOTUS FLOWER HAVE NEVER BEEN BEYOND the Beijing principality before, and now they are as far down the map as Guangdong province. When Ying Kam pats his pocket, he's comforted by the shape of the black book. The long journey has been arduous, with the travellers fearful of wolves and plagued by bandits, giving them no choice but to cross hungry palms with silver bullion for smooth passage to the mouth of the powerful Han River, and Swatow.

Lotus Flower turns to Ying Kam in the rickshaw. 'How much further?'

Storm Boy pedals through yet another bustling town, dodging swarms of bicycles carting textiles in rolls alongside bundles that shroud cases of opium. Opium to relieve a peasant's long day slaving for landowners, as well as for an elite bothered by the stresses of managing peasants. Opium for children and wives. Opium for teachers, officials and holy men. It is the shame of a greatly artistic and deeply spiritual people now living in a country sedated.

Ying Kam fixes his eyes on Lotus Flower.

'How much further?' she repeats. This is by far the greatest distance any of the trio has ever ventured, except in Ying

Kam's dreams where he flies on the backs of dragons to far kingdoms, and then all of a sudden he *is* the dragon, breathing fire and brimstone on villages below, more like the stories he has heard of Western dragons on the attack. Then he is a boy again, steering a winged reptile home, away from the burning rooftops, and he cannot decide who he prefers to be.

'It can't be far now.' Ying Kam squeezes Lotus Flower's hand.

The three pass through tropical forests of bats and dragonfly swarms. A butterfly alights on Ying Kam's shoulder. '*Oh look.*' Lotus Flower reaches out to touch its wing and it flies away. This is the place where tigers once roamed. Past mountain and bamboo grove they have glimpses of the South China Sea, and finally the runaways have arrived in Swatow. Their rickshaw ambles along streets of two- and four-storey neoclassic-inspired Qilou architecture forming shaded footpath corridors and balconies with French windows. They can go no further south now that their silver bullion has washed away down cracks in the floors of rented rooms and into the pockets of bandits.

Storm Boy is skin and bone, and although Ying Kam feeds him and Lotus Flower dresses his wounds and massages his legs, his soul is in his eyes, pleading. No one could be more relieved than the skeletal rickshaw driver to arrive in Swatow and hear the words, 'We are here.'

Ying Kam and Storm Boy unload a chest from the floor of the carriage. It's bereft of coins yet laden with valuable currency, and Ying Kam sets about finding buyers for these rare silks, which will attract great intrigue here in Swatow where pigments differ from those in the more Imperial prefectures. Within each province, the design of cloths and garments is subtly nuanced to recognise the most popular styles of local noble craftsmen.

As Lotus Flower wanders the fish market, the long flowing robe of her *Hanfu* gown, designed after the style of the ancient

Han people predating the Qing Dynasty, reveals her foreign status in the art of belting at the waist and the crossover of scarves at her bodice. But something else instantly gives her away as an outsider: her lilting dialect. Although the Kwas have learned both their native Mandarin as well as some Cantonese, there are many obvious differences. Communication between speakers of the two languages is said to be *ji tong ya jiang*, like a chicken talking to a duck.

Ying Kam takes the black book from his pocket, sending a shot of excitement through his body. The contacts in the book are a gift from heaven, sure to make moving the priceless fabric easy. A collaborator surfaces within the hour, then another and another, until Ying Kam assembles a team.

Soon he will have a fully fledged trading operation as he paves his way into networks of wolves. Ying Kam is a wolf of sorts himself, a merchant by blood. And he knows the richest trade routes well from sitting beside Great-Grandfather, hearing the stories and tracing his finger along expansive maps: 'By the same path as silk, goes opium.' China's new silk routes move opium, silk, gold, tea and spices abroad and Ying Kam is about to learn the way of Swatow's own great sea port to the West. He and Lotus Flower watch the sun bounce on the water. The ancient fisher folk here would never have dreamed of the cargo heaving in and out on the sea today, where their narrow boats once moored with nets full of large-mouth bass. Ying Kam buys some fish rice brine and fish balls, and hands Lotus Flower a pair of chopsticks.

A room for the night evolves into a Swatow house for rent. Ying Kam is seventeen now, the long journey having aged him in more ways than one, and as Lotus Flower is fifteen, the couple decide it is high time they wed. The ceremony is low-key with no betrothal letters, gifts or dowry, and no wedding party or guests visiting their home. They are married in a local temple by a shaman who wonders if such a union should take place before the gods without the extended family present, but he takes their silver and sets aside his concern. For Ying Kam and Lotus Flower, having no family or friends in the district means no need for traditions such as disinviting people born in the Year of the Tiger to avoid bad luck or serving tea to elders. However, there is one ancient tradition for good fortune that Lotus Flower is loath to disregard: the practice of crying.

The louder a bride cries on her wedding day the better the luck, so Lotus Flower wails from dawn, pinching herself to make the tears come harder, stabbing needles into her thighs to bring them faster. She conjures such miserable thoughts that the sobs pour out and the luck, presumably, pours in. Then, wiping her face and drying her eyes, Lotus Flower pulls down an ornate lace veil of scarlet and gold to hide her blotchy, swollen complexion, and calls to Ying Kam, who has been waiting in the tiny front courtyard for her to finish. 'We may be late for our own ceremony,' his bride scolds, still sniffing after the hours-long assault on her sinuses. 'Hurry, Ying Kam, where is Storm Boy?' she snaps, and almost trips on her shimmering embroidered gown, deliberately designed with no pockets so she will not be able to steal her father-in-law's luck or wealth. Great-Grandfather is technically her first husband, but no matter, tradition is tradition.

As Ying Kam's enduring servant, friend and business manager – a recent promotion – Storm Boy is the closest person to witness the nuptials. After the service the newlyweds each cut a lock of their hair, tie them together in a knot, and slip it into a silk bag to demonstrate oneness of flesh and blood, an earthly and heavenly connection that can never be broken.

Once they have completed all the religious and traditional obligations possible, it is time for the most important objective of any good Chinese marriage: to beget heirs and therefore a continuation of this new strand of Kwa.

Ying Kam and Lotus Flower build an altar to worship their ancestors and pray to the gods for a child. The sun rises and sets, a dragon circles and withdraws, but no baby comes. Prosperity arrives in silver bullion for the trading of silk, yet still no offspring. Another Kwa compound rises from the dust, a new House of Kwa. It is the largest residence in the village, with half the rooms and halls of Ying Kam's Beijing home but not even a small fraction of its life. The new courtyard remains bereft of infant wails, toddler stumbles and busy household bustle.

News of the barren couple travels fast throughout the local community, down lanes, through marketplaces, over the hills and into villages. Lotus Flower's sorrow-stricken face and flat belly betray her, sending an open invitation to parents of would-be brides to line up and impatiently wait in the wings. Whenever Ying Kam passes by, eager mothers and fathers wring their hands and straighten *Hanfu* outfits on teenage daughters. The parents wrench on headpieces and slap their girls' tender faces to encourage an appearance of fertility.

TINY FEET AND MUDFISH

LOTUS FLOWER FOLLOWS A THREAD OF GOSSIP INTO MARKET and out again to arrive at the door of another of the district's revered shamans, Reputable Wu Master, an unparalleled aficionado, according to the whispers, of ancient folklore to predict and evoke luck. Lotus Flower tells him she is hoping for a child, and he agrees to visit the Kwa compound. She is only weeks shy of turning twenty-three, and Ying Kam is now twenty five.

The couple waits with silver at the ready for the shaman's arrival. Ying Kam is pacing when Reputable Wu Master enters with a theatrical upward motion of his hand, his sleeves fanning out and rippling with all the exaggeration of Chinese theatre. His palm assumes a pose of refusal, indicating money is of no importance, but the pair insists on paying despite his humility – in fact, it's required that they do. The shaman shakes his head in pity at the young lovers' simple earthly ways and his robe swallows their silver.

A Buddhist holy monk is soon to arrive, and with Reputable Wu Master's elaborate performance pushing things past schedule, Ying Kam is keen to move proceedings along. He thrusts out an empty palm for the shaman to read, and Lotus

Flower follows suit. 'Why have we borne no fruit?' she asks and quickly adds, 'Oh, one of wisdom.'

The shaman straightens his back. He enjoys the adulation and wishes it would continue, but as Ying Kam seems hurried, it is with disappointment, Reputable Wu Master skips his usual chant and dance and accelerates his routine by accepting the offered palms. He shakes his head and furrows his brow, repeating these actions until Ying Kam says impatiently, 'What is it?'

The shaman looks grave, shaking and furrowing one last time for effect. 'No child will be born to this house.'

There is a stunned silence. Ying Kam and Lotus Flower drain of colour, grief-stricken.

Holy Monk is waiting outside, tapping his foot. When Reputable Wu Master leaves, he slips a coin into Holy Monk's open palm as they exchange a passing greeting.

'No child will be born to this house,' Holy Monk also predicts. Ying Kam and Lotus Flower can hardly bear it, for they are certain the core of existence is to bring about children. 'But for a price.' Holy Monk looks grave and shifts his eyes from side to side to demonstrate the degree of confidence he is about to impart. 'Yes, for a price I will get you your child.'

Ying Kam instantly regrets his impatient, ignorant demands that he be married off young. 'Father was right about almanacs and superstition.' The young man hears Great-Grandfather's voice: *The holy men foretell truth. Listen and heed their warnings.* The image of his father evaporates, leaving a heightened sense of determination in Ying Kam. He resolves, then and there, to take control of Kwa destiny and dynasty.

So, on the advice of Holy Monk, Ying Kam buys a baby boy. The twenty-third generation Kwa firstborn son is adopted. The house is blessed and there is much celebration, with Holy Monk and Reputable Wu Master invited to enjoy a feast in honour of the new arrival. As they gorge on pork and dumplings, they forget to tell Ying Kam what will happen next: he will be blessed with thirty-one more children.

As the first of these babies arrives, the two wise men, replete from many banquets around town, have an explanation for the deviation from their prediction. 'The good stewardship you have displayed with your adopted son has caused the gods to bless you for your faith.' A thirty-one child blessing.

Ying Kam and Lotus Flower didn't see the impoverished home their adopted son came from – not the bed of straw in the lean-to dwelling, or the birth mother scrounging for scraps to feed her toddler. They know nothing of her heart shredded with grief from watching her husband die, aged twenty, from a lung complaint she will never know the name of. The most basic treatment was beyond her financial reach.

By comparison, Ying Kam and Lotus Flower are millionaires. They name their baby Tak Wai. No one knows what his birth mother called him before he was taken from her in exchange for a few coins.

The year Tak Wai turns three, Year of the Water Snake, 1894, Ying Kam hits his professional stride, business swells to proportions worthy of red lanterns all year round, and his seed finally takes root.

To the couple's surprise Lotus Flower bears Ying Kam a son. Two years later – twin girls, although one doesn't survive the winter, dying of an ailment of no name and probably the will of demon gods. At the turn of the century, Lotus Flower is expecting another child and although there are concubines at his beck and call, Ying Kam decides to take another bride to further the Kwa lineage. She is fourteen, and his nickname for her is Happy Shadow. She bows low as she enters the compound, her parents following cautiously while also bowing low out of respect for the grand master Ying Kam must be.

After all, he has his own compound with a courtyard and koi pond, and even his own drivers.

'He must be a rich man indeed,' they told their daughter when she begged them not to send her away. 'Be grateful the matchmaker has found you a good husband.' Her mother lifted a silk cloth from the dowry chest Ying Kam had sent and was so mesmerised by its shine, she seemed not to notice her daughter was there. At that moment, a sliver of the child bride's heart turned to stone.

Now the family has arrived from a village, far beyond the Swatow border, with what the parents insist to Ying Kam is a modest gift – their daughter – in return for his most gracious generosity. After a ceremony of tea and some festivities, Ying Kam's new in-laws, whom the Kwa family will likely never see again, bid a tearful Happy Shadow goodbye.

With now two wives, Ying Kam works his silk trade and sets his sights on Hong Kong, 175 miles away and, since 1841 during the Anglo-Chinese opium war, under British rule. He has the idea of opening a shop there to increase visibility for international customers, so he travels to the territory frequently to investigate, leaving his family behind for weeks on end.

Lotus Flower is Number One Wife, but rather than feeling empowered by her upper-status role, she is irritated at having competition. She becomes a snapdragon – with the slightest squeeze, her pretty jaws close. She campaigns vigilantly to protect her sovereignty and reminds all in the compound and village of her superiority, in every way, to Happy Shadow. 'I am first and I am senior. Am I not more beautiful, more charming and pleasing than Second Wife?' No one can deny Lotus Flower's attractive qualities; however, that she has been surpassed in all of them by the younger girl, no one dares say to her face.

In her first marriage Lotus Flower was an excellent student, watching and learning from the older wives as she trained to serve Great-Grandfather. She was beaten and laughed at, consoled and beaten again. Now she is high in rank she brings lessons from the old family compound to the new. But the shiny serpent door-knocker and freshly carved lions know she will do well to hide her jealousy, as such vanity will surely attract a beating from Ying Kam when he returns this time. Her abuse must be considered and cunning. *Ruo rou qiang shi. The weak are prey to the strong*, she thinks. Lotus Flower, who did not come down in the last rainfall, realises that Happy Shadow – having also been exiled from her family to endure a life of broken feet and broken dreams – may be prone to her own ideas.

And she is right. With no doubt of her worthiness of first place in the heart of her husband and in his household, Happy Shadow takes to the town with her own campaign. 'Why does her husband need a second wife if the first is so good?' she whispers to a fishmonger as she collects her order. 'Would you not rather look upon me than her?' Happy Shadow asks in a teashop, as she reaches to select Ying Kam's leaves of choice, seductively revealing a slim ankle as she gently sweeps her cape aside.

The village does love gossip.

'It's true, Second Wife is younger and prettier than First Wife.'

'Perhaps she is also a stronger type than First Wife.'

Stories spread like silken sheets on a freshly made bed and loyalties shift like bitter beans in a bowl of fragrant rice. According to who is speaking and with whom, villagers make sweet and sour alliances; like golden pheasants they watch and wait for more gossip on the Kwas. In between Hong Kong expeditions, honourable husband Ying Kam visits Happy Shadow in her bed. The low lantern and smell of musk and wild honey is more inviting than the worn-out mattress and dull clove odour of First Wife, and Ying Kam has grown weary of her constant insecure posturing. Besides, her body has borne so many progeny for him, it is beginning to sag and lacks the lustre of his nubile new wife's form.

'All Lotus Flower does is nag and complain.' Happy Shadow self-assuredly assesses her appearance in a long mirror framed with phoenix tail wood. 'I will be all my husband needs from now on.'

She blesses House of Kwa with one child, and then another, determined her birthrate will surpass that of Lotus Flower, and that she will hang on to her figure.

'That will teach First Wife,' the villagers whisper. 'She should not have fixed her glance behind but rather looked in front.' They are right: Lotus Flower's jealousy evokes the slow unravelling of her silken belts like snakes uncoiling and slithering towards her throat.

On his next trip away Ying Kam opens a shop at number 16 Pedder Street, a thoroughfare on the North Shore of Hong Kong Island, and calls it Swatow Lace. His half-brother Eng Lee, first son of Great-Grandfather's replacement Number Four Wife is already living in Hong Kong and, during Ying Kam's frequent visits to the territory, the two have reunited over yuenyeung yinyeung, a mixture of three parts coffee and seven parts milk tea, overlooking the harbour. Eng Lee brings to the business his advanced accounting and bookkeeping know-how. He's a Kwa on the ground, eyes and ears for Ying Kam.

With the population burgeoning under the one Kwa roof, in Swatow, it becomes apparent that adopted first son, Tak Wai, has served his purpose.

'Tak Wai is not Kwa blood,' says Reputable Wu Master, after claiming to have received a sign from the gods. 'Tak Wai must leave the family. His job is done.'

Immediately Tak Wai is demoted from Number One ranking and, not daring to challenge the will of the gods, he follows his beloved father Ying Kam's order, 'You must go.'

His adopted family bids a tearful farewell, and Tak Wai, his silk pockets lined with silver, and his heart painted in shame, returns to his peasant mother.

'He would have married soon,' Ying Kam reflects, turning his back on Tak Wai's departing rickshaw. The sandals of the driver and wooden carriage wheels sluice dust from cobblestones to form puffs of grey cloud behind them. 'But his children would not have been true Kwa.'

The vehicle turns a corner and disappears and Tak Wai is erased from the Kwa family portrait.

Happy Shadow has aged past thirty when, in the lucky year of the Fire Dragon 1916, another child bride appears with bound feet. Ying Kam is tired of nicknames and calls her by her birth name, plain and simple, Ng Yuk. She speaks only Cantonese. She is steely, no-nonsense, and positively terrified by the knowledge her job as Third Wife will be 'utterly impossible', 'probably undoable' and 'the lowest honour of all', almost everyone has told her. And yet it's an honour her family can hardly refuse, given their poor circumstances.

She wanders on painfully folded feet to the marketplace down the hill from her new home. The fish barrels whisper, 'Always better to be first,' while the fruit carts moan, 'She's more like concubine than wife.'

Ying Kam is handsome and quite capable of kindness. But *you qi fu, bi you qi zi*, like father like son, he is prone to dragon outbursts and his temper has him reaching for his stick. He isn't himself when he gets like this, the dreamer boy travelling on dragon hide to become the dragon itself. Sometimes he doesn't know who he is. Servants cower, and wives use their wiles, but no matter their status or number all meet with blows from time to time.

The villagers regard Ying Kam with reverence for his many wives, children and accomplishments. The three women are famous in Swatow for their rivalry, and Ying Kam for his temper; stories of the Kwas are passed down as cautionary tales.

A musician plucks and strokes erhu strings on a street corner and the folk song 'Paoma Liuliude Shanshang' drenches the stiff air within the Kwa compound walls as the town vocalist paces the cobblestones outside, a dizi flautist trailing behind. The song is about being unable to resist loving all the beautiful girls in the world, and the fierce male competition for their hands because even the moon and stars woo maiden beauty.

Ng Yuk births her first son in the year of the Earth Goat. Babies continue to come forth from the wombs of first and second wives too, sometimes two at a time or dead on arrival – stillborn and cursed or making it through the night to die the next day, cursed too. This is the Chinese condition. But, despite sinister celestial forces bent on preventing their healthy passage, many Kwa infants cling successfully to life. The compound brims with children's laughter – the peels of Ng Yuk's firstborn among them.

Twenty-third generation Kwa is firmly rooted in Swatow, Japan has seized pockets once belonging to Germany, along China's coast, and the Emperor has sent 140,000 labourers to help the British and French WWII effort. There has been a series of battles with Japan during the past few decades, and Ying Kam is only too aware of their effects on trade, but until now silk routes have been good to him. He counts his gold, imagining it is molten lava circling a giant dragon nest, hardening into a brilliant glow, and protecting the eggs inside. Kwa children line up to collect their weekly allowance, jostling and laughing.

The next morning, an unforgivingly cold January wind sets in and Ying Kam rushes past a dormant flame tree, on his way to an appointment with a long-time customer. When he arrives he warms his hands against a smouldering plate of hot stones in a paved entrance hall to wait for his contact. Moments later, the flame tree watches him hike determinedly past again. Bad news weighs on his handsome features.

England's agreement to stop sending opium to China is affecting Kwa trade. The India–China trafficking heyday is over. 'And now' – Ying Kam twists and pulls a silk belt agressively in his hands as he faces Storm Boy – 'now there are no British profits from selling opium to buy my silk.'

The gods close the tap and the Kwa rush of gold slows to a trickle. A molten bar of the precious metal slips from Ying Kam's grasp, smashes to dust and disappears in a breath of wind whispering, 'Hong Kong!' Week by week, year by year, the pocket money dwindles, until there is none. The Japanese military seem always to be posturing towards China's north east. 'The Japanese are coming, run,' the wind whispers again. 'Hong Kong.' Children jostling gives way to solemn foot shuffling, laughter to lip biting.

After his key man Storm Boy defects, Ying Kam's syndicate of traders is undercut by competitors. He has spent sixteen years cultivating business relationships in his father's shadow, and now they crumble into an abyss. Formerly loyal staff go unpaid and resign in favour of greener pastures.

Rumours circulate in Swatow. With so many Kwa mouths to feed and so much face to save, Ying Kam walks his compound corridors in a dense shroud of unhappiness. For Lotus Flower, Happy Shadow and Ng Yuk, a bitterness wends its way over their tiny feet and up their legs, green tendons wrapping around their bodies until they feel they will suffocate.

For years, ever since they reunited in brotherhood and business, Eng Lee has been encouraging Ying Kam to contact their father. It's the last thing Ying Kam imagined himself doing, but Kwa blood is thick so he forms beseeching character strokes on calf-skin parchment. But Ying Kam's words fall on deaf ears and blind eyes. Undeterred by the silence, he sends information to assist his father's merchant activities, and finally the two find cooperation. '*Nuren he shagua yong bu yuanliang.* Women and fools never forgive.' Great-Grandfather is far from the fool, appreciating the benefit of another set of eyes and ears in the sea port of Hong Kong. '*Buyao jiang ni de haizi xianzhi zai ziji de xuexi zhong. Tamen chusheng zai ling yige nian dai.* Do not confine your children to your own learning. They were born in another time.' Great-Grandfather writes back to his son, wishing him well and agreeing to work with him. Ying Kam is pleased yet cautious and, refraining from asking his father for money, he writes to his brother instead.

Circumstances plummet to the point Ying Kam takes up work as a rickshaw driver, cycling day and night to keep the household, while he waits on his brother's help. He chauffeurs former peers and friends, who look upon his sweat-soaked back with a mixture of pity and fear, thinking, *That could be me next.*

The wives quarrel over fish in the market. The villagers are accustomed to the Kwa women fighting, but now it is over scraps. The prestigious knife fish of the Yangtze River is no longer within their means; instead the Kwas eat local cyprinidae, full of mud.

Still, villagers relish this fodder for idle gossip. '*Jia jia you ben nan nian de jing.* There is a skeleton in every house. Every family has a problem it cannot solve.' They speculate over the fall of the House of Kwa. '*Fu bu guo san dai.* Wealth does not sustain beyond three generations.'

Three wives stick close together. Three wives exist far apart. With three heads held high, denying three hearts scorched with shame, three stride towards survival, though their tiny feet can barely hold them up.

'*Meiyou renhe sunshi de ren shi fuyou de.* He who has nothing to lose is rich.' The enviable life of Kwa has vanished. There is no way Ying Kam and his wives can disguise this financial distress by dressing it in silk and calling it success – no, they must bear witness to its exposed skeleton. If a penny goes unaccounted for, servants, wives and children are beaten. Squandered food? Same penalty applies. Ying Kam runs a tight ship, *Houseboat of Kwa*, buffeted by a threatening tide of destitution; tossed by a storm of merchants, peddlers and thieves. He scans the horizon, searching for a life raft to save his family.

One floats into view. Ying Kam's brother replies to his letter with the promise of money to relocate.

Ying Kam calls in his wives. To Happy Shadow and Ng Yuk, he says, 'Pack all belongings and unwedded children.' He turns the parchment over in his hands and is grateful to his brother. 'Number One Wife, you will stay. Today we move to Hong Kong.'

'How can honourable husband Ying Kam leave me?' Lotus Flower asks. 'I am Number One. I'm the only one responsible enough to look after the family – the only one to be trusted.' Although bitterness has marred the sheen of her silks for years, she is struggling to make sense of her abandonment.

'It is simply too far and too expensive for you to join the family in Hong Kong,' Ying Kam reasons. 'You will be safe and looked after here.' But not by him: Lotus Flower's children are obliged to support her into old age. They are already adults, married with children themselves.

She looks at Ying Kam, whom she has served by bearing him offspring he believed he would never have, and by absconding from her lowly fourth wife post with his father and pledging her life to him. Ying Kam exiled Tak Wai after he had served his purpose, and now as Lotus Flower looks at her useless feet, she realises she has served her purpose too.

Ying Kam is by no means without a heavy heart but chooses to follow his head. '*Kongzhi ni de qingxu, fouze tamen hui kong zhi ni.* Control your emotions or they will control you.' Happy

Shadow, Ng Yuk and a dozen children make the pilgrimage with him to Hong Kong. Most of these children are too young to fend for themselves, while others are old enough to work but too young to leave the nest. 'They will help support the family,' says Ying Kam.

BABIES AND DRAGON

HOUSE OF KWA IS SMOKE FROM AN OPIUM PIPE, GENTLY coiling around a cherry tree. As the smoke envelops the tree, a baby dragon soars into view. He curls up at the base of the tree and watches vibrant blossoms open. Some thrive while others lose their hue and shape, wilting and floating to the ground. The young dragon falls sound asleep, awaiting his own birth as a blossom on the tree.

That's my dad, the sleeping dragon. Sometimes the days preceding our time on earth say more about us than the days we are here, and although he is not yet born, his constellation has glowed for centuries.

The baby dragon stirs. His snores gently shake the family tree. A cherry blossom tumbles, leaving space for a fresh bud to appear.

With the help of Great-Grandfather's money, as promised in his letter to Ying Kam, the Kwas take up residence at 183 Wu Hu Street, Hung Hom, Hong Kong. To expats 'Wu Hu' sounds like a party; a lot of Chinese names seem funny to the mainly British foreigners living in the city. The Kwas' new home is inland at one end of Wu Hu Street. At the tip of the other end, on the west coast of Kowloon Bay, is Whampoa Dock, one of the biggest dockyards in all of Asia. Ying Kam and his brother are in the perfect place to reinvigorate their business in textiles: Swatow Lace. Very soon, their sewing rooms filled with women bent over machines multiply into factory floors that become entire factory buildings. Ying Kam can afford to ride in rickshaws again. He and his brother work hard to rebuild a Kwa Empire, and now as well as a head office in Hong Kong, there are branches in Peiping, Shanghai and Swatow.

Happy Shadow readies her children for life in Hong Kong. She lives on the second floor of the Kwa building, the only concrete two-storey complex on the entire street, in the industrial district near Hung Hom Bay and Whampoa Dock. Relieved by the return to House of Kwa trappings, she returns to competitive wifely traditions and scolds Ng Yuk, who has taken up residence downstairs, with more vigour than before. Then Happy Shadow promotes herself to First Wife status — what Lotus Flower doesn't know won't hurt her.

Ng Yuk has grown thinner with worry this past year. She has had a string of miscarriages, and she smokes more and more to cope with each loss. When she becomes pregnant again, Ying Kam calls upon a local fortune-teller to find out if this baby will survive. He is told it will and celebrates the news with long black tea and opium.

Two months too soon, Ng Yuk is rushed to hospital when she begins to contract. Preferring a homebirth, the old way, she protested but was dragged here anyway, into an alien world of linoleum and beeping machines, strange nurses and doctors.

She is giving birth to triplets, a blessing the fortune-teller did not predict. The searing pain of not one but three babies entering the world in close succession is almost too much for her tiny frame. In her terror and delirium, she tries to imagine this is just a bad dream. A milk nurse on hand becomes a blurred apparition that Ng Yuk tries desperately to bring into focus, but she's struck back down, eyes to the sky, to push again.

As the medical staff fight to keep the three boys alive, a Buddhist and a shaman are called in, along with, for good measure, a Catholic priest. Ying Kam does not care which god saves his sons, but it seems the gods are preoccupied playing mahjong somewhere in the clouds.

Ng Yuk shakes, her blood loss left unattended as the newborns take priority over their mother, being boys after all. They are tiny and thin with distended bellies and amidst the frantic grasps at the infants' lives, their three small souls leave their tiny bodies to lie lifeless and exposed. The first turns out to be stillborn, the second holds on for an hour, and the third and last hope struggles and is gone by sunrise. 'The brain damage will be terrible,' the doctors say, lowering their instruments. 'It is best not to fight anymore.' Nurses wrap the brothers in cotton swaddling to hide their yellow skin as it begins to turn grey.

Still neglected and bloodied, Ng Yuk is weeping and smoking when Ying Kam comes to the door. 'You have cursed the family.' He lurches towards her. 'My three sons.' His eyes are red with the immeasurable pain of lost progeny.

A doctor follows Ying Kam out of the cold, stale room, whispering deliberately loud enough for Ng Yuk to hear. 'Such shame.'

A proverb springs to Ng Yuk's mind as she draws deeply on her cigarette: '*Yige bu hao de gongzuo zhe zhize ta de gongju*. A bad workman blames his tools.' Splinters of bitterness embed in Ng Yuk's heart. The blood between her thighs has dried, and scorn and grief pour out of her, filling the room.

Back in the House of Kwa, her emotions course over the floors, down corridors and stairs, across beds and tables. For days, despair laps at the concrete walls.

Before long, though, Ng Yuk is with child again, this time, as before, only one heartbeat is detected and she hopes that this time there really is only one baby. Her grit restored, she lights a cigarette and settles in for gestation, even managing a smile that her purpose in life has not ended. She slaps a maid and yells for supper, just like her old self again. A sigh of relief can be heard in rafters and rugs, bone china and ivory, crystal and lace. 'Third Wife is back,' mahogany chairs and Persian tapestries cry. However, Ng Yuk latches on to bottomless dissatisfaction, constant complaining and endless criticism, addictive like the cigarettes she is seldom seen without. Her madness deepens as the Kwa children watch on.

The shame of the curse of lost male triplets plagues Ying Kam's thoughts for some time, but he finds solace enough in prayer – since converting to Christianity, another layer to the family's history of Buddhist, Taoist and Confucian beliefs – and work, providing for his family through Swatow Lace, and getting life back on track. Second Wife Happy Shadow immerses herself in embroidery work and painting, and unlike Ng Yuk, she doesn't smoke to pass the time, nor does she have pregnancy or babies to occupy her these days. Ying Kam bursts through the door of the upstairs apartment to call her to the latest birth below, to sit by Ng Yuk while the girl servants and midwives attend to her. It's an Earth Dragon Boy, destined, predicts the fortune-teller, to be lucky, warm-hearted and full of blazing energy.

Two years on, in the spring of 1930, a new blossom falls from the Kwa family tree and a fresh bud appears. Ng Yuk gives birth to a baby girl. Number Four Daughter Wai Ching Kwa is hoisted high. She has plump cherry cheeks and a permanently inquisitive look about her, an old soul in taut rosy skin. Eighteen months later, in the mild November heat, Ng Yuk has another baby girl, this one with bright eyes and a shock of lustrous black hair; Wai Mui Kwa has a beguiling smile.

In line with Chinese naming custom, each Kwa child is bestowed with the same first character of their two-character names – Wai for the girls and Tak for the boys, although Ying Kam takes the liberty of deviating from this tradition, in accordance with modern thinking, or simply when he feels like it.

Great-Grandfather writes, *Japan has invaded North-East China. I've heard that Hong Kong is swamped by a hundred thousand refugees.* Japan's invasion of Manchuria is so far north-east, Ying Kam pays little attention to rumours spilling over his factory floor, or in smoking dens, about Emperor Hirohito's militaristic ambitions for China, let alone Hong Kong.

His household is once more filled with the joy of healthy dumpling babies, and while Ying Kam would prefer a small army of boys to swell the family ranks, these girls will help in the home and perhaps fetch fine dowries one day. In truth, the girls of Ng Yuk have an enchanting way of capturing his heart. Perhaps he is softening with age. They are Kwa and the youngest of his blossoms.

News travels to Hong Kong about the Japanese invaders still on the long march from China's north, swallowing up villages as they head south. Rumour falls on the marketplace and stumbles over oranges and melons, rearing up between rice bags and carrot barrels.

'They commit heinous acts of depravity,' a fishmonger says.

'They are under orders to kill boy children,' a flower seller cries.

'They kick in doors, terrorise families and do unthinkable things,' a herbalist whispers.

Ng Yuk will take no chances. Her triplets are dead and, if rumour is to be believed, Japanese soldiers are killing newborn boys. Fortune-tellers and midwives confirm Ng Yuk is carrying a boy this time, and when she calls on a shaman to look at her palms, and he frowns, nods and frowns again, she knows she'll need to play a clever tile in order to outwit fate.

'Trick both the gods and the invaders,' the wise man says. 'It is the only way your son will live.'

In the depths of night on 30 May 1935, the auspicious Year of the Wood Pig, a cry from the healthy lungs of a fat baby boy heralds a new heir. My dad, Wing Nin, is born into the House of Kwa. The hospital birth was disastrous luck for the triplets, so Ng Yuk's insistence on a homebirth held sway this time.

Exclamations of 'Lang Loi!' ring out to fool gods in the sky and demons on earth. Lang Loi means 'beautiful girl'. Ying Kam forces a diamond earring with a solid gold stem through Wing Nin's earlobe; it bleeds, and the baby suckles his wet nurse harder. 'This will protect him. It will confuse immortal gods and human defilers.' Ying Kam takes Wing Nin from the nurse and brings his son to his shoulder. He looks to the heavens and then to his son and whispers, 'You are Kwa.'

The Buddhist, shaman and priest are back with their palms open for silver before a procession through the house to deliver blessings from every god.

Neighbours are told: 'It's a girl! No name yet. "Lang Loi" for now.'

Ng Yuk imagines that if Japanese soldiers tear through the house and happen upon Wing Nin swaddled in the arms of a nursemaid, Ng Yuk will stay calm and ask them, 'This beautiful girl, Lang Loi, is she not truly just like a Japanese blossom?' The soldiers will then turn to leave without checking if the baby is a girl or not. Ng Yuk lies awake at night and frequently rises to ensure the nurse never takes her eyes off Wing Nin.

When the child turns one in 1936, the Kwas feel it is safe to stop calling him a girl in public, although Lang Loi remains his nickname at home. The shaman is again summoned and paid handsomely for his wisdom. 'This boy must have a new name so the gods will never know they have been tricked,' the shaman advises with a stern flourish. 'So they cannot trace him.' He taps a metal bowl with a small wooden stump, and a mesmerising chime rings throughout the house.

Ying Kam and Ng Yuk visit Hong Kong's Births, Deaths and Marriages Office and change Wing Nin's name to Tak Lau. An earnest young man sits very straight and still behind the service desk. Proficient in English and Cantonese, he moves his mouth without expression, encouraging Ying Kam and Ng Yuk to give their son and other children Western names as well. 'After all, the British are here to stay.'

My grandparents sign the paperwork for 'Theresa' Wai Ching and 'Clara' Wai Mui. They settle on two new names for Wing Nin in English and Cantonese. The boy's name is Francis Tak Lau Kwa. The girls will go by their English names, while Wing Nin will now go by Tak Lau.

Treachery cannot reach Francis now; curses cannot touch him. Dad's flower bud blooms on the cherry tree that was always waiting for him to arrive. The baby dragon grows fat and full of adventure.

BOY AND WRENCH

IN 1937, TWO YEARS AFTER FRANCIS TAK LAU IS BORN, Japanese troops capture Nanking. The systematic rape of the city rages for over a month, resulting in a massacre of mammoth proportions. Japanese soldiers conduct door-to-door searches for women and girls to brutally defile. Between two and three hundred thousand defenceless adults and children are murdered. Precise numbers depend on who's counting – the Japanese say less; the Chinese say more. Happy Shadow surprisingly gives birth to another child, a boy Ying Kam names Wing Tai before changing it to Patrick Tak Yeung. Inexplicably he is not called 'girl' even though the enemy is closer than ever.

The invaders move south and within days take Guangdong. The Hong Kong Kwas did well to get out years ahead of the sweep. There is no way of knowing what has happened to Lotus Flower, her children and grandchildren, with mail routes currently suspended and foot messengers suddenly scarce. No town in the Japanese military's path is left unharmed as the march of destruction ploughs the coast. Ng Yuk delivers another baby girl: Mary Wai Choy, who has irresistibly plump cheeks.

By 1939, Shenzhen is under attack, and Hong Kong is so near that bombs 'accidentally' fall on the British territory; the Japanese seem to be having new ideas.

'But I want to build my tower.' Five-year-old Tak Lau slaps away the hand of a maid. It is February and cold; with his rosy cheeks, Tak Lau looks like a doll wrapped in layers of wool. He will turn six next month.

The maid rubs her hand and looks to a more senior maid, but she only shoots her a sharp expression and shakes her head, dismissing any idea that the younger maid should reprimand young master.

'I am the boss – you don't tell me what to do.' Tak Lau hits the young maid with flailing fists as she attempts to clear up his collection of tin and wood and wire.

The little boy has been fashioning these oddments into something from his imagination, maybe a rocket or a ship. *Surely not a tower*, the maid thinks.

As if he can read her mind, Tak Lau shouts, 'This' – he holds his contraption aloft – 'is the key to the … the …' He hesitates and looks around.

He can see his father, Ying Kam, in the front room beyond a short corridor, talking with another man. They are speaking so softly Tak Lau cannot work out what they are saying. This is one of the men he must call 'Uncle', he knows that much – oh boy, does he ever.

Distracted by this new thought, he shrieks, 'I *have* to call everyone Uncle!' and slams his contraption onto the Persian carpet. His frustration makes his hands tremble. 'They can't all be my uncle, can they?'

His father and the man are shaking their heads, and his father strokes a wisp of beard.

Tak Lau turns back to the maid, who sees no choice but to

sit patiently through his little episode as he points again at his creation.

Ng Yuk hobbles in on tiny feet. To keep her balance, she holds on to the arm of a servant girl who is around fourteen, the same age Ng Yuk was when she married Ying Kam.

Tak Lau sees no similarities between the women. The big feet of maids are only good for helping them follow orders. But one maid had grown on him. Like all the other servants, she had not been allowed to use her real name in the house; she had to answer to whatever name Ng Yuk decided on her first day when she arrived for work. '"Puddle", I will call you. Like dirty water on the ground.' It was meant as an insult, of course, but Tak Lau liked the friendly sound of it. He has always loved jumping in puddles; when splashes end and ripples still, he can see his reflection and that of the sky, and he imagines himself as a dragon soaring through it. *Splash*, the image disappears.

His mother cast Puddle out on the street with nothing more than a few days' pay – that was 'compassionate', Ng Yuk said. When Tak Lau cried because his favourite maid had been dismissed, his mother screamed at him that the girl had a 'baby inside her' and 'the devil put it there to put shame on our house'.

Ng Yuk told her son to stop crying. And then she slapped him. 'Puddle was stupid anyway. You're all stupid.' She glared at the two maids who stood in the doorway, hanging their heads, and took a deep breath to compose herself. 'Now help me to my feet, to the bathroom.'

There is contempt mixed with pride and shame whenever Ng Yuk has to call for assistance to carry out this most rudimentary bodily function, the situation always seeming worse when she's mid-rant and then has a sudden urge. She scolds her helpers all the way to the toilet bowl, relieves herself and scolds them all the way back.

Since Puddle left him, Tak Lau has not let another maid get close. Not even the ones whose eyes crinkle with laughter or hold a hint of fun. Not kind ones or clever ones, and certainly not dour or miserable ones. There is one reason, and one reason only, for these big-footed females and that is to serve him.

'Tak Lau, darling boy,' Ng Yuk says, snapping her son out of his reverie. She croons, high on nicotine and black tea, 'What have we here?'

Tak Lau raises the metal model towards Ng Yuk's face as a maid lowers her into a chair. She has days when her feet are so uncooperative she can hardly walk – this is one of those – but on other days she can hold her head up proudly and carry herself unassisted into the marketplace throng. On those days she swats away the helpful maids accompanying her. 'You're a nuisance,' she scolds. 'Leave me alone.' One of the maids then has no choice but to follow at a safe distance, just in case, because Ng Yuk sometimes loses her balance or needs to rest.

She takes the object from her son and turns it over in her sinewy hands as he waits eagerly for her appraisal. 'The key to the bomb that will defeat the Japanese, is it? Well, let's see what your father thinks of such a thing.'

Tak Lau smiles, but Ng Yuk's face darkens. 'You've been wasting time on this. It is not mathematics!'

Tak Lau's bottom lip trembles, but he knows better than to cry. It can be like this: one minute she is full of praise and encouragement and the next, filled with rage.

'Can't you teach him even the simplest maths?' she screams at the two young maids. 'Well?' Her demeanour betrays the dignified Chinese furniture and modern wallpaper. 'You are incompetent!' She slams her hand down on the arm of the polished branch chair.

While his mother berates the servants, Tak Lau backs out of the room – straight into a pair of legs, which turn out to be attached to the indomitable figure of his father. The tall man hardly ever sees his son.

'Ng Yuk,' Ying Kam interrupts her, and her cascade of insults freezes midair as though Chinese characters are suspended in the centre of the room. 'Ng Yuk, I have just finished speaking with the commander. If all of our suspicions are right, we haven't got a lot of time.' He sits down and explains. Ng Yuk watches his whiskery chin move up and down as he speaks. She nods, but what he's telling her is almost incomprehensible. 'Under international law they are supposed to make a formal declaration of war on Hong Kong. But who knows what they'll do?' He stands to leave. 'We have little choice but to begin preparations.' He goes upstairs to have the same conversation with Happy Shadow in her apartment.

Over the following few weeks, Tak Lau shadows the workers who go in and out of the house, while he marvels at all the hammers and chisels dangling from leather loops on their belts. He sneaks out onto the street to visit hardware stores – to him, living in an industrial area is heaven. He runs his hands over the holy grails of building tools and appliances. The shops are narrow and deep, crowded and overflowing with nails and screws, wire coils and pipes, mallets and planks. A handyman's paradise.

To the boy's further delight back at home, a worker says the very words he has been waiting to hear: 'Pass me the two-inch wrench.' Tak Lau silently does a little fist pump. 'Sure,' he replies casually and reaches into an open bag, so eager to find the correct tool a bead of sweat trickles past his ear. The worker's head and shoulders are barely visible as he leans on all fours to reach behind a timber partition. He is adjusting the heavy-duty steel hinges on a new false wall – hinges that allow the wall to pivot open, revealing a hidden room.

All of Hong Kong seems to be busy reinforcing false floors and walls, hiding valuables and battening down the hatches in advance of the feared onslaught. Tak Lau has been visiting construction sites since he was three with whoever he could coerce to take him – usually a maid or Elder Brother from Third Mother, seven years his senior. Lately, though, he's been preoccupied with all the building going on at home. And next door. And next door to next door. The activity right here in his neighbourhood gives him so much joy that he goes to bed each night with images of axes and anvils dancing in his head like sugarplums. In his dreams he rides a dragon through the clouds. Both he and the dragon are wearing tool belts.

'Aha!' Tak Lau finds the two-inch wrench just in time to put it in the worker's right hand as it gestures from the end of an outstretched arm. The boy places the wrench in the man's palm with such satisfaction, it may as well be the heart of a tiger he has hunted and killed. 'Can I look behind there?' he asks.

The worker pokes his head out from the other side. 'Yes, boy, crawl round here and I'll show you how to fix a hinge.' The man smiles at the earnest determination of this little boy from a distinguished household, always dressed in his Sunday best, completely enamoured with dusty building materials and heavy tools.

'You've made a mistake here,' Tak Lau calls from inside a cavity in the wall as he passes out a nut that had been loose. 'Shall I fix it?'

The worker shakes his head in disbelief and, smiling again, hands the boy a wrench.

JIGSAW AND JEWELLERY

HOUSE OF KWA HAS BEEN IN DISARRAY FOR MONTHS NOW, ever since that man in military uniform met with Tak Lau's father. To the little boy, the low voices of men in the front room sound like how he imagines the rumble of tanks and horses coming over the hills for battle. He's heard of such things in stories and in snippets of conversations on street corners.

He knows that his family is having an underground bunker constructed in forested land at the base of the hill where Chatham Road meets the end of Wu Hu Street. It's a source of great fascination for Tak Lau as he watches teams of poorly paid men excavate the plot with shovels. The bunker has been marked out beneath trees among tropical shrubbery, and the itinerant workers, brought in from China, are sworn to secrecy and threatened with the might of Kwa should they disclose details of the project or its location. 'When we survive this,' they are told, their mothers, sisters and daughters can come to work at Kwa factories in prize jobs for a poor underclass.

In the house on Wu Hu Street, a builder finally loses his patience with Tak Lau and shoos him away from his tools, so the boy wanders down the hall to his father's study. 'Why are we building these things and changing our house?' Tak Lau asks Ying Kam.

Adjustments have been made to floorboards and ceiling spaces as well. Undetectable trapdoors have appeared under rugs, while a section of the wall, here in his father's study, has been refashioned to contain a safe. The desk sits slightly out towards the middle of the room to allow the fresh decorative paper to set. Tak Lau remembers how his mother screamed at the design consultants that she didn't care about the pattern of the new wallpaper, so they rapidly rolled up the samples they had unfurled for her consideration. She had wanted to hit one of them, Tak Lau could see that. He can always read her temper.

Father pauses over his ledger, on which he has been writing long lines of numbers Tak Lau does not understand. 'Boy, we once called you "girl" to save you from the enemy. Now they truly come.' When he places a hand on Tak Lau's shoulder, dust collected on the boy's clothing – from his adventures fossicking among construction rubbish – forms a small cloud and disappears. 'Being a boy will be a good thing this time.'

Tak Lau stares at his father, not understanding the logic.

'If you cannot fight them, then go along with them until you can. If you can't beat them join them.' Tak Lau has heard this expression before. 'When they come, and they will, our small territory cannot defend itself with only three aeroplanes for an air force.' Father refers to the pitiful defence the British have left Hong Kong with; it's so underwhelming, the colony may as well give up now. Under the oldest monarchy in the world, ruled from Japan's Chrysanthemum Throne, the attacking forces have every resource imaginable, while this British outpost is completely underprepared. 'We must take care of your sisters. The work we're doing will help them. It will help us all.'

Tak Lau is confused. *If we are joining the enemy*, he thinks, *why must we hide my sisters?* He nods anyway.

Ying Kam is tired. The boy is too young for the truth, so he smiles and pats his son on the back before handing him a fistful of bills and coins. 'Go buy me a small black notebook like this one.' He points to a leather-bound journal on his desk and sends Tak Lau away.

The boy needn't be asked twice – he stashes the money in his pocket. The youngest boy of thirty-two siblings tears off down the hall on a mission for the most important man he knows.

A sullen maid emerges from a bedroom off the passage way. 'Where are *you* going?' She can tell he's headed for the front door, wearing a cap thrown on in his haste to leave on his father's errand. 'I'll get in trouble if you go out without a chaperone,' she snaps.

Tak Lau sighs. He is often out on his own; the servants don't seem to care once he's beyond view. He has never actually witnessed his maids on the rough end of Ng Yuk's beatings when he goes missing, so he doesn't understand why this maid would want to stop him. He shrugs and puts his hands in his pockets. Then his eyes light up with an idea.

Tak Lau hands the maid a bill from his trousers; she looks around nervously and it disappears into the folds of her shabby oversized pinafore. He has just learned something about maids: they can be manipulated with beatings *and* money – except that one maid, Puddle. She was different.

The boy looks past the sullen maid to see his little sister Mary in the arms of a wet nurse. He thinks the nurse looks sour too. 'Sour milk,' he mutters, and laughs quietly at his own joke. Mary is almost two, so she will be completely weaned soon. Tak Lau thinks she is the sweetest thing on earth but would never admit it. 'What a baby.' He rolls his eyes and races down the hall to the relative freedom of Hong Kong's streets.

Peril is on its way to engulf the territory, but Tak Lau is full of excitement as he picks up his pace.

* * *

The best part of a year has passed since the Kwas went on high alert. They decide to relax, as yet another year may go by before war is officially declared, or perhaps it won't happen after all.

However, the Kwas and all of Hong Kong are taken by surprise on 8 December 1941. Tak Lau is six, and Japan has attacked Pearl Harbor. As the world scrambles to process that news, Japanese troops storm Hong Kong. Enemy bombs rain down on the British colony while soldiers swarm over the border from mainland China focused first on taking the Kowloon side, where Wu Hu Street is, and then the Island. On the same day, Japan wages coordinated attacks on the Philippines, British Malaya and Thailand.

Hong Kong is in utter chaos, a war zone of mortars and grenades. The deafening sound of high-speed shells sends people running onto the streets. Everyone but the Kwas.

'It's too dangerous to attempt to make it to the bomb shelter,' Ying Kam tells his family. Their house, the most structurally sound on the street, may just be strong enough to withstand the assault. The Kwas stay inside and take their chances.

Buildings crumble nearby. Homes are ransacked. Shops are looted. The shelling of civilian houses goes on for days in a relentless pulverising of Hong Kong, and all that families can do is struggle to hide wives, daughters, sisters and mothers.

Tak Lau and his siblings slip through newly installed trapdoors and hide under floors in their home whenever troops march by, while Ying Kam, Happy Shadow, Ng Yuk and their servants pray, giving the ancestral joss sticks a workout like never before.

They are all Kwas and look out for one another. The competition between Second and Third Wife is still stiff, but since Ying Kam left First Wife in China, they keep their squabbles between themselves, not wishing to be old nags to their husband and bear the consequences.

House of Kwa hangs on for a miracle.

Tak Lau's sister Theresa, five years his senior, wraps an arm around him. The two of them are hidden in a cavity beneath a trapdoor, while the other Kwa children are concealed elsewhere around the house. Since birth, Theresa has retained her old soul demeanour and avid curiosity, and she has acquired a protective maternal instinct.

The daily Japanese military march along the Kwas' street towards the docks and back again has finished, but soldiers are known to splinter off suddenly on a spree of killing civilians and taking prisoners. So far, the House of Kwa remains untouched as if cloaked by a force field.

The children have been playing games to distract themselves. Theresa has shown the others how to thread beads onto string to make a necklace, and they do the same jigsaw puzzles over and over again.

A distinctive knock followed by a chair scraping the floorboards signals it is safe for the siblings to come out. Theresa whispers, 'Are you ready?' Tak Lau nods. Together they push against the wooden door above them until a crack appears, enough for Father to wrap his fingers around the edge and pull it up.

He reaches down to help Theresa and Tak Lau out, their small hands in his.

'The Japanese have taken the Island,' Ying Kam says.

The children stare at their father, knowing from his expression this can't be good news.

It's 18 December. The Kwa family has survived ten days since the Battle of Hong Kong began.

* * *

As many as ten thousand women and girls have already been raped; their families have been murdered or are powerless to help. Refugees are fleeing. Even disease-ridden, famine-distressed areas of mainland China offer more appealing prospects than here in Hong Kong.

The Kwas are growing hungry, but they don't know when to risk venturing out for supplies or where to obtain them. At least they still have water, if only for a few unpredictable hours a day. In the beginning their well-stocked pantry was a blessing, but for a large family and staff it only went so far. Western treats such as honey and jam were shared and savoured by the quarter teaspoon as the Kwas huddled around a gas lantern in a boarded-up room. Luckily, one of the maids had purchased a large sack of sugar before the battle; it had been hard to get, with everyone panicking and stocking up. Sweet sugar tea was such a treat, but then they ran out. The maids were too terrified to go out since then and besides could not be trusted with the mission of buying provisions anymore, so by day ten Ying Kam was forced to forage under cover of darkness for anything edible he could find, and tree foliage was better than nothing. Now the family is managing on food scraps mixed with leaves and bark, topped with weeds and berries: strange grey broths of no distinct flavour.

But the whole family has survived so far, along with their house, while most buildings on Wu Hu Street are either unrecognisable or razed to the ground. While any remaining neighbours flee or scramble to rebuild and repair, against the odds, the House of Kwa lives and breathes.

Surprisingly, the family knows of only two places near the Hong Kong shoreline that have been spared any structural damage at all: their home and the central financial district, which the Japanese avoid attacking. The enemy forces are careful not to destroy the commercial centres because they want to *take* Hong Kong, not obliterate it.

Ying Kam knows it's no accident that the House of Kwa is untouched. 'It's fate and the will of the gods,' he says to himself, venturing a glimpse outside from a top-floor window. He sees scorched streets and mangled corpses on neighbouring lots, and he knows there will be some way to go before he and his family can come out of this unscathed.

Few neighbours remain on Wu Hu Street. Most have fled to join the hordes of refugees fleeing across the border to China. Those who stay lie low to rake through the rubble of their homes for lost loved ones and clutch at the dust for missing valuables. All the while they keep checking the coast is clear – Japanese soldiers sometimes burst into what's left of Wu Hu homes, ripping jewellery from ears and necks and chopping off fingers when rings can't be effortlessly removed. Horror and fear blanket a city under siege.

'You cannot be too careful,' whispers Ng Yuk to no one in particular as she crouches and rocks to soothe herself while she listens to screams drift in through her window.

CHRISTMAS AND HOLLOW PIPES

AFTER SEVENTEEN DAYS OF TERROR, IT'S CHRISTMAS. JAPANESE soldiers set upon a hospital, bayoneting injured Allied military men in their beds, while nurses are raped and murdered.

A few hours later, on the third floor of the Peninsula Hotel at the corner of Nathan and Salisbury roads, British officials surrender to Japanese authority and a new occupation of Hong Kong begins. Today is Black Christmas.

Tak Lau wonders if the deal with the enemy means he and his family will be able to eat a proper meal again, and to see the sky.

From now on, the Japanese will demand identification papers at checkpoints. Enemy civilians – mainly British ex-pat men, women and children – will be forced from their homes, relocated to camps, starved and beaten indiscriminately. Gazes will be lowered. Shoulders hunched. Ordinary native Hong Kong people will be given ration cards and risk life and limb to bring even the most meagre amount of food to the family table. Commerce and industry will grind almost to a halt. Schools will shut. Children will have nowhere to play. And the eldest

House of Kwa girls will be hidden. 'The sky will wait for you, child,' Father tells Theresa. Then he closes the partition wall to her room with Clara.

Upstairs, many of Happy Shadow's children have long moved out to start families of their own. She sits silently with her remaining teenage sons and her youngest boy, Patrick. Her two daughters, nineteen and twenty-one, go to their room and lock the door. Happy Shadow places her hands over her ears to block out the Japanese shouting and Cantonese pleas for mercy drifting past the outside of the building.

The two sons of Ng Yuk, six-year-old Tak Lau and thirteen-year-old Elder Brother, step off the porch and survey the carnage. Their mother didn't want her boys to go out, but there was little choice with the whole family starving. Because the servants were all female, they might be raped or killed and not come back. Food is now only available in rations, which the boys will try to collect from a local bakery.

Fifty paces down the road, the boys pass a man crouching in a doorway with an injured, bleeding child in his arms. A door, half a facade and a few ground-floor rooms are all that's left of this home. The man rocks silently; the child, listless and still, must be dead. Tak Lau and Elder Brother avert their eyes just as a pair of Japanese soldiers approach on horseback.

From his position in the saddle, one soldier catches Elder Brother's temple with the butt of his rifle. No provocation is needed for any act of Japanese violence against Hong Kong Chinese. The other soldier says something in Japanese, and the assailant brings his gun to rest against his pommel. The boys fall to the ground, kneeling and covering their heads. Elder Brother's scalp begins to bleed from the blow. The soldiers jeer and ride off, probably returning to base; a number of Japanese troops have set up residence in the theatre on Bulkeley Street around the corner.

The brothers slip along alleyways, exploring their changed city. A face peers through balcony shutters on a third floor, but when Tak Lau looks up it disappears. Most streets are deserted.

There's a long line outside the bakery. Everyone in the queue has downcast eyes; no one wishes to stand out. A Japanese soldier barks in a dialect none of the locals understands and marches alongside them. He pulls one man out of the line, flings him to the ground and kicks him in the stomach before taking a document from the writhing man's jacket, holding it high and shouting again. The Chinese people get the idea now and pull identity papers from their pockets, so the boys do too.

Last night and the night before, a van with a megaphone drove through the streets declaring in Cantonese that the colony had surrendered to Japan. But no one needed to be told the news – they'd known the moment the sounds of gunfire and shelling stopped.

The Allies decide that if they cannot hold Hong Kong, they will at least make life difficult for the Japanese. In October and November 1942, the US conducts four air raids, shelling the city in an attempt to drive out the occupiers. Over the following two years, they will attack more than twenty-four times. Before the end of World War II, the number of Allied air assaults on Hong Kong will be fifty-one.

House of Kwa is deep in among it, watching B-25s and P-40s soaring directly overhead. Mostly the targets are Japanese cargo ships in Victoria Harbour at Whampoa Dock at the end of Wu Hu Street.

The floating targets are obvious, but occasionally bombs go astray. The closer you live to the docks, the higher the risk. The Kwas begin a ritualistic rush back and forth between their bomb shelter and home. They didn't make it there during the Battle of Hong Kong, but the dugout in the hills near Hung Hom was a good decision after all.

* * *

Through the doorway in the darkness, Tak Lau can just make out the shapes of maids as they scurry up and down a corridor, carrying blankets and bread. *Probably stale*, he thinks. He hasn't had fresh bread in weeks.

'Children,' says Father, fixing his eyes on Theresa before his gaze bores into Tak Lau. 'The bombs are coming closer tonight.' He holds a candle up to his face. The distant sounds of soaring followed by thunderous explosions then earth tremors do seem more powerful than usual. 'The US and British are bombing the water again to try and save us.'

Tak Lau's eyes light up. 'Are they are aiming at Japanese ships on the harbour again, Baba?'

'Yes, but as I've told you, sometimes they miss.' Ying Kam leads the family to the door. 'We are not safe tonight.'

The Kwas huddle in pairs or groups of three, taking turns to slip out into an alleyway at the rear of the house. The night air is warm and humid. Three-year-old Mary, the youngest Kwa, lets out a squeal as she trips on a cobblestone. 'Shh,' twelve-year-old Theresa says abruptly, scanning the road. Her eyes are adjusting to the moonlight; she can only see the shadows of Father and several men the children call Uncle. The tall figures have positioned themselves at lookout points along a route to the bunker. Ying Kam has invited as many people as the shelter can hold, so other families are headed in the same direction. The Japanese tend to stay away from this area after dark, knowing how vulnerable it is to stray Allied bombs. But nevertheless, as everyone in Hong Kong now knows, you can never be too careful. Theresa picks up Mary, who continues to complain about her grazed knee.

Tak Lau falls into step with two friends – even in darkness he would know his street football playmates anywhere. Sometimes they roam the territory together too. They are older boys by perhaps two or three years, and he feels grown up being around them. Whenever Elder Brother grows tired of playing Tak Lau's childish games, these are the boys he turns to.

Before the darkness of occupation, the boys even rode the light rail once without paying. They leaped off from the far door as an angry conductor made his way after them through the crowded tram carriage. The bigger boys had jumped first, then they called to Tak Lau to jump too, arms outstretched and shouting, goading him on. Adrenalin coursed through his body and Tak Lau leaped. He stumbled, but one of the boys grabbed his hand to steady him and they ran down an alley without looking back. The face of a beggar, curled up on the corner with an empty bowl, had crinkled with laughter to see such mischief. The boys ran laughing too, all the way home.

The walk to the bunker is supposed to be a sombre one, but a friend of Tak Lau has a twinkle in his eye. Everyone calls him Einstein because of his crazy hair. He is always on the lookout for adventure, and tonight is no exception. 'C'mon,' he says, motioning to Tak Lau and their other friend. 'Look, the Bogies.'

The Bogie Boys is a gang known for its Humphrey Bogart hairstyles and tough image – so far as eight- to twelve-year-olds go. They are never unfriendly to Tak Lau and his friends. He enjoys catching up with them; he's lucky that there's always someone to play with in his neighbourhood, and they rarely comment on his upper-class wardrobe.

'I went to the top of the hill with them last time.' Einstein sounds excited. 'To see the lightshow.'

The friends catch up to the three Bogie Boys, and together the six of them walk in moonlight towards the communal bunker the Kwas have funded. Their closest neighbours and friends have priority after the family. Then it's just whoever else can squeeze in.

As they start the climb, Tak Lau realises he and the boys aren't headed for the bunker. He sees the silhouettes of his sisters being ushered into the cavernous hole in the ground. Other families crowd in. He knows the drill well. They will be in total darkness until a large barn-like door has been pulled shut by the strongest men. Only then will it be safe to light an oil lamp. They will sit shoulder to shoulder in the damp, cramped room until Father says it's okay to come out. It isn't airless in there because builders have installed hollow pipes to various surface points; they are covered in mesh to stop debris falling in and are large enough for a small child to climb through to safety if the door becomes blocked. An outsider in the know could even roll down food and provisions if things got really dire. *It's not airless in there*, Tak Lau thinks. *But it does feel like you'll suffocate.*

In the dark clamber to safety, it's no wonder Tak Lau's family haven't noticed he's missing. He is already well away, hiking up the hill. The six boys wade through tropical shrubbery, pushing swathes of long wet leaves aside. The only way is up, but just as they near a small plateau, Tak Lau stumbles; he feels blood trickling down his shin and touches his wounded knee. 'Don't look down. Don't look down.' He thinks of Mary's grazed knee and how Theresa kept her quiet.

The boys emerge beneath the stars at the top of their ascent. From this vantage point, they see Hong Kong Island and Victoria Harbour, moonlight striking the water and rooftops. There are no lights on in the buildings or any bustling of people in the Jade Market in Jordan. No streetlights illuminate the footpaths leading to unsavoury haunts down alleyways towards Kowloon, and there's no one shopping on Tsim Sha Tsui's main streets. Hong Kong has been quiet for an hour now. It is as if the Allies drop warning bombs to give civilians a chance to get away before unleashing the full force of their *friendly* fire.

Hong Kong is silent and dark. She waits.

Tak Lau sits shoulder to shoulder with his friends, hoping the Bogie Boy who is chewing gum will break up his packet into small pieces and share it around. When he does, Tak Lau chews enthusiastically and alternates between looking up at the sky and down at the magnificent harbour. It is difficult to know which is the better view. His eyes rest on the bottom of the hill where the bunker must be – where his family is huddled in the dark.

And then it happens. Planes soar and cut through the inky cloth of the sky, blades of steel that are blacker than the rich thick night. They are black as death, these US bombers sent by Roosevelt to help Churchill eject the Japanese. Every time they appear, it seems they come from outer space then disappear into a black hole until they are summoned again.

Tak Lau watches as each fuselage releases its bombs, birthing them into the humid air, raining them onto the water. Three, four, five, six, seven. Falling, whistling. The vibrations are accompanied by violent explosions. Some shells hit their targets, smashing Japanese vessels to smithereens. Some miss and fall to the depths of the harbour or connect with buildings near the shore. An untouched Japanese vessel rocks violently in the storm of its life. Another target explodes, and the boys cheer. The lightshow continues.

'We know about the bombs before London does,' one boy says. He is wearing horn-rimmed glasses and still chewing gum even though it must have lost its flavour by now.

'We know about the bombs before the world,' another boy shouts over the next explosion.

At the edge of Tak Lau's peripheral vision, a row of houses is taken out on Wu Hu Street. Before he has time to think about it, a bomb pounds the area near to where the family bunker must be.

'I'm so clever.' Tak Lau nudges his friend with boyish bravado. 'My whole family might be dead down there. Up here I am alive.'

Bombs keep coming, and six boys cheer and holler on top of a hill. At one stage, to the group's delight, Tak Lau does a little dance mimicking a Japanese soldier looking up in terror at a descending bomb before it pulverises him. Tak Lau flounders on the uneven earth, flailing his arms and legs.

The boys take a break from clowning around to see if there is a better viewing platform. The previous air raid lasted around two hours, so they have plenty of time to gad about. After Tak Lau points to a good spot, the boys congregate there on a broad rock that fits them all. Tak Lau has prime position. His eyes widen, the reflection of the fires making his pupils glow.

Japanese aircraft fly onto the scene, ducking and weaving, intercepting the US B-25s and P-40 Warhawks.

'We must be pretty special,' Tak Lau says, almost drowned out by the rumble. 'Everyone is fighting over us!' he shouts louder as the other boys laugh.

Tak Lau turns his back on the airshow and holds up a piece of paper so that it catches light from below. It's a diagram clipped from the newspaper of six warplanes, including the three in the sky right now. Whenever he can, he tears out pictures of mechanical things he fancies. The paper is crumpled from being incessantly studied, and for the hundredth time Tak Lau traces the printed shapes on it with his fingers. He can barely make out any labelled parts anymore, but that doesn't matter, he's memorised them; he keeps the news clipping for reassurance.

Now the news is right here in front of him. Planes fire and fly at one another, spitting, twisting and diving. As a vessel tacks towards shore, an Australian naval mine explodes beneath it. Above, US bullets tear the wing from a Japanese aircraft, and its fuselage dips, the relentless shots a jagged burst of fire against the oily backdrop. There's a lull, then a splash. Tak Lau watches the burning Japanese fighter spin into the water. It sinks slowly until it disappears.

EGGS AND COMICS

BY LATE 1943 THE FACADE OF THE HOUSE AT 183 WU HU Street shows signs of the violent reverberations of bomb assaults, the kind of crumbling and distress that weather would take centuries to achieve.

After the first time Tak Lau disappeared up the hill during a raid, he was severely reprimanded by Mother and Father, but they later had a change of heart.

Ying Kam said to Ng Yuk, 'Remember the humble farmers who took a basket of eggs to the Emperor?'

She did remember the tale. The eggs had been laid by the world's finest rare hen, and after the farmers took them on a long and treacherous journey to the Imperial Palace gates, they were completely unharmed. But as the farmers approached the throne, one of them tripped, and the eggs tumbled out of the basket and broke. Even as a Cantonese speaker Ng Yuk knows the Mandarin expression is *Bie ba quanbu de jidan fangzai yige lanzi li*: now they are afraid of putting all their eggs in one basket again.

'No royal family ever travels altogether,' Ying Kam insisted.

Ng Yuk agreed, and from that point on the Kwas have split up during Allied attacks: Tak Lau and Elder Brother go to the top of the hill, and the remainder of the family to the shelter at the bottom.

All except Theresa, who stays and prays in the house. The concrete building has held out against friend and foe so far, and it may end up being the Kwas' best chance. As she is only a girl, Theresa cannot pass on the family name, but she has always been the family's good luck charm for her dexterous ability on an abacus and for her maternal and thoughtful ways with all her siblings. During the air raids she waits patiently for the shelling to end and the family to return, never once complaining other than to say, 'But what if you need my help out there?' To which Father replies, 'You will help by digging us out of the ground.'

'The shelter can be closed in by a bomb, and everyone inside will be buried alive,' Tak Lau tells Elder Brother like a broken record. 'Being on the hill is much safer because the planes will not be shooting at us.' No matter how many times he says this, the idea of surviving their family gives neither brother comfort. Tak Lau reassures his brother with a grin, 'At least we get free fireworks.' He doesn't feel quite so brazen as the first time he watched the bombs drop, but even after so many air raids, the spectacle never gets old.

'Haha,' Tak Lau shouts over the din breaking his own reverie. 'We are so clever. We know where the US drop the bombs before the news broadcast.'

US aircrafts avoid the central business district and even errant bombs land clear of essential commercial buildings, but the Hung Hom shipyard is heavily shelled several times. One missile destroys five houses in a row, very close to the House of Kwa, and embeds in a concrete slab, its tail visible among the rubble. This is a stark reminder of how Hong Kong exists on a precipice: no one is safe in the path of deadly friendly fire.

Tak Lau peers over the balcony. He feels like theirs is the only house left standing, that this latest onslaught completes the flattening of homes on Wu Hu Street. Ramshackle dwellings have been erected in their dozens where buildings once stood; this is all the living can do to stake a claim to their land, the only thing they have left. The House of Kwa is like a shrine of hope to the locals, who have a kind of reverence for the Kwa family as a result.

The Kwas count themselves lucky and raise lit joss sticks to the gods, tapping the red incense vigorously three times before pushing it into dishes of sand. They could be far worse off. Their home, at the far end of Wu Hu Street from Whampoa Dock, enjoys proximity to a park with trees near enough to brush Ng Yuk's upper-storey windows. They have the immense privilege of breathing clean air from a rooftop terrace above Happy Shadow's place. Even so, for months a sickening smell hovers near the Kwa home, reaching under doors and windows, wrapping itself around furniture: a reminder of the rotting bodies caught beneath rubble nearby. Locals bring wheelbarrows and shovels, digging into the night to bring up the corpses. They load them onto carts: ten, twenty, fifty – Tak Lau loses count. Locals who passed in the street a few years ago without so much as a nod are now pulling one another from under twisted roofs and fallen walls, an awful intimacy that leaves survivors guilty and hollow. There is no proper burial for these neighbours and friends. Their bodies are carted to trucks on a path to one of the civilian burial grounds in the countryside, to be lain to rest often unidentified and nameless.

Weeks wear on with air raids occurring so unpredictably that everyone lives in a heightened state of fear. Kwa luck sustains, though. Not only are they all still alive, but they are also fortunate not to be among the thousands of civilians held in internment camps, let alone the POW British, Indian and Canadian soldiers here and in Japan – subjected to inhumane and horrific conditions. The Kwas are of Chinese descent, and there are no Chinese in confinement. They are simply captives at home, and at least have the freedom to take their chances in bunkers and houses or on hills.

Tak Lau and Elder Brother roam streets and lanes; every way the boys turn, people are dying of starvation. Hong Kong is on its knees. Japanese ships continue to blockade Victoria Harbour and control all the territory's supplies.

The malnourished Kwa boys make their daily scrounge for scraps before joining a queue for rice, along with hundreds more anxiously awaiting their allocation. After an hour the Kwa boys reach the front, and Elder Brother stands behind Tak Lau, shielding him from view as the little boy scoops extra rice into his pockets.

A Japanese soldier paces up and down the line of people deliriously focused on the heavy sacks of grain. As one bag empties, the soldier prods a poorly dressed middle-aged man to return to the truck to replenish supplies; his filthy half-buttoned shirt and full-length trousers rolled to three-quarters may have once been part of a suit.

Elder Brother leans forward as if to assist his younger sibling, just as Tak Lau spills some rice on the ground. The two hold their breaths. The soldier stops and looks down his nose at the boys. Then he walks on.

Tak Lau and Elder Brother hurry home, passing corpses in doorways, starving orphans huddled under cardboard-box lean-tos, and beggars pleading for 'just one small morsel, please, sir'. Tak Lau keeps his arms awkwardly by his sides to hide his full pockets, while Elder Brother carries a decorative ceramic mug full of the official rice ration; he holds his right hand over the lid to keep it steady.

Death leans on buildings and stalks alleyways, couples hold each other for the last time, and parents cling to their dying young. Morgues overflow, and mass graves fill before another must be dug, over and over. King's Park is host to routine beheadings, along with Japanese soldiers carrying out shooting and bayonet practice on civilians as targets.

Tak Lau and Elder Brother walk on, now eight and fifteen years old.

The life the Kwas knew before the occupation is a distant apparition. Yen is the currency now. Bankers and brokers are locked in small hotels, forced to trade, and Japan has taken ownership of the Kwa factories, everything Ying Kam and his brother Eng Lee have worked for. Japanese firms are established in Hong Kong, and factory production across every industry is suspended, stopped and started according to the unpredictable whim of the new masters.

The House of Kwa buys additional rationed rice, oil, flour, salt and sugar with the pittance Ying Kam has saved from his Swatow Lace shop while the factories of his own sweat and blood lay dormant.

Tak Lau's infant school has been turned into a military hospital; another local school, it's rumoured, has become an execution headquarters. In fact, there seem to be no normal Hong Kong schools left.

The authorities tell the Kwas that Tak Lau and Elder Brother must attend a Japanese language class at a recently abandoned shopping complex. Each local family is represented by either a child or children, who are expected to return home to teach their parents and grandparents their new 'mother tongue'.

Their way to the class is littered with evidence of looting. Roller doors and concertina panels have been buckled by force, and there is nothing of any value to see. As they approach their destination, Tak Lau and Elder Brother automatically bow their heads at a Japanese guard wearing an oversized soldier's cap. He looks them up and down. He's holding a rifle across his chest in a lazy, disinterested fashion and doesn't seem much older than Elder Brother.

The boys take the stairs to a second storey. Smooth tiles gleam, perhaps from the sweat of an old man who is hard at work, charged with mopping the floor before classes begin each day. 'The enemy may be torturing and killing in our school buildings, but they do like a clean classroom,' Elder Brother whispers to Tak Lau.

The skin of the janitor's crinkled hands is like leather. Gripping the mop, he methodically passes it over the surface, almost mesmerised by his task. He wears a brown buttoned shirt and matching brown shorts, his hair dishevelled and his left eye bloody and bruised. There are bruises on his legs too. He lowers his head as the boys pass.

'Get back to work!' the juvenile Japanese soldier screams from a landing below, and the old man resumes mopping the sparkling floor.

Tak Lau ventures a glance at what used to be one of his favourite stores. Trinkets and comic books are haphazardly heaped in a corner, their charred and burned pages like a black moss engulfing a hill. *Someone must have lit a fire then changed their mind and stamped it out*, the boy thinks. One of the rules is that all English and Chinese reading material must be destroyed – everything must be printed in Japanese from now on. This is a real blow to Tak Lau: he has only just got a grasp on Cantonese characters, and he enjoys reading English, though he can hardly speak it.

Something catches his attention. There is a counter with an empty open cash register on top. A *Sanmao* comic book pokes out from under it as though his favourite character has been waiting especially for him. The cartoon boy, Sanmao, was born the same year as Tak Lau, and living in poverty against a backdrop of colonisation and war just like him, the famous manhua illustration is a survivor.

The Japanese guard is lecturing the old cleaner about a missed tile. People are killed for random things these days, so Tak Lau can understand why the cleaner falls to his knees, begging for mercy. With the guard distracted, Tak Lau takes his chance. Before Elder Brother can hiss, *What are you doing? Get back here*, Tak Lau scoots inside the shop and slides the *Sanmao* book out from under the bench. The orphan boy on the cover, with his trademark three strands of hair, gives him an encouraging wink. He quickly scours the floor for any of the ancient hero books he also loves, without any luck, and slips the comic inside his shorts, so it flattens against his back. The guard looks away from the apologetic janitor in time to see the Kwa boys disappear around a corner to their classroom.

The language lessons take place in a large shop that was once a record store, the jewel in the crown of the shopping centre. Now stands of gramophone records have been shoved along the edges of the room – miraculously, though, they seem relatively untouched. Tak Lau wonders if he can bring any more souvenirs home. It won't be long before all Chinese and English language music is destroyed along with the reading material. Radio stations are shut or used to spout Japanese propaganda, with both new announcers and old favourite media stars proclaiming, 'How wonderful it is to be living under the most holy rule of the Japanese Emperor of the Chrysanthemum Throne.'

A hand slaps Elder Brother's left cheek, abruptly snapping Tak Lau back to earth in the makeshift classroom. 'Sit down!' a soldier-turned-teacher screams.

It is as though Japanese people don't know how to talk, thinks Tak Lau. *Do they believe we are deaf?*

He watches his brother rub his reddened face, then the boys take their places on school furniture at the very back of the class.

Local teachers who have not been executed are at a camp for re-education about Japanese customs and values, and, most importantly, Japanese language. 'Teachers have three months to pass an exam in Japanese,' Ng Yuk told Tak Lau. 'If they pass, they will come back to teach you. If they don't, they will be killed or sent to China.' While Tak Lau and the rest of Hong Kong's children wait for their teachers to return from being indoctrinated, they are stuck with soldiers for tutors.

An older Japanese figure with a commanding look sits in the corner. *Maybe he's a captain*, Tak Lau thinks, *or a colonel*. The boy has learned every military term he's ever come across, along with the names of weapons and land, sea and air vehicles.

'If you are late again,' Soldier Teacher screams in broken English, 'I will shoot you!' He pulls a pistol from his belt and points it at a boy near the front who was not late. 'And' – he scans the eyes of the class for dramatic effect – 'I will shoot your classmate.'

Tak Lau and Elder Brother bow their heads. The roomful of boys – six to sixteen years old – holds its breath.

Soldier Teacher returns his gun to its holster. 'Time to begin,' he shouts.

Tak Lau wriggles in his seat. The comic book digs into his back, making his spine tingle.

AXES AND STEAK

AFTER A FEW MONTHS, THE STRICT LANGUAGE LESSON requirements are relaxed. Teachers return and a few schools reopen, but everything is unrecognisable from the signage to the curriculum. Everything is in Japanese. Posters of Emperor Hirohito are pasted on walls and lockers, while his framed regal portrait is hung in classrooms and offices to show that Japan's Imperial House has an eye on everyone.

Far fewer schools are needed than before with so many children having died or been sent to China, often rounded up onto buses without the supervision of parents or guardians. Tak Lau's old school is among those to remain shut; for all he knows according to the whispers it is still a death and torture camp, and the nearly nine-year-old Kwa hasn't been assigned a new place for his education.

'Perhaps they are satisfied with the course you did at the shopping centre,' Ng Yuk says over the sound of hammering next door as neighbours attempt to rebuild their home.

'Perhaps they have forgotten us,' Ying Kam says hopefully, knowing full well the Kwas are not forgotten.

'Collaborate or die' is the clear message everywhere, on the streets and at kitchen tables. Ying Kam has endured countless 'meetings' with senior Japanese soldiers over the handover of his factories, and he must bow to them as though they are royalty before and after they meet. But the occupiers are careful not to antagonise or kill a golden goose. Kwa factories produce embroidered fabrics sold the world over, and the Japanese understand they must tread delicately so as not to compromise production any more than they already have – a maimed or dead director of enterprise is not in the interest of Imperialism.

Before the occupation, Hong Kong's population was 1.6 million, but there are fewer than half that number now. The Kwas can provide value to the Japanese, and this might be their only way to survive. 'Collaborate or die,' Tak Lau hears his mother mutter as she picks at a pale-yellow stalk floating in grey broth. She has been feeding most of her share of rice to her sons for weeks and is growing thinner.

With no school to attend, Tak Lau fixates on finding a job. He is tall and well built for his age. His mother and older sisters give him and his brother bigger portions to keep them robust enough to support the family. Apart from visiting the blessed rooftop, Theresa and Clara haven't been outside in sunlight for years; they cannot work, so Ng Yuk orders that they give part of their meals to those who can. If only First Son were here to help, but he is twenty-five and long married, so Ng Yuk must rely on her two younger boys to supplement whatever Ying Kam can bring in. His brother Eng Lee has been stranded with three of his children in Shanghai since the occupation began and Eng Lee's wife has been holding the fort – looking after their own remaining sons and daughters, as well as the Swatow Lace shop when it's open.

'The Japanese are taking girls and raping them. Mrs Wong down the street is dying of sorrow.' It is another day, and Ng Yuk is worrying into another bowl of grey broth. 'She rubbed dirt on her daughter's cheeks. She told them that little Yip Niya was stained and dirty and a horrid child, that taking her would curse them.' Her voice becomes desperate. 'Mrs Wong held Yip Niya so tight. Then they dragged her away from her mother.' There is horror in Ng Yuk's eyes. 'She was only ten. We must not let them find our girls.'

Lately Ng Yuk has taken to rocking back and forth muttering worries, mostly to herself or to Ying Kam if he is there, or just into her soup. She slaps a maid who rises from massaging her gnarled feet. 'If you so much as breathe a word about my girls,' she says with a scowl.

The maid is provided with just enough food to stay of service. Where would she go anyway? It hadn't crossed her mind to disclose the location of the children to the occupiers; she has barely the strength to think, let alone to conspire. *The mistress is growing madder*, she realises.

'Now take me to relieve myself,' Ng Yuk orders.

Tak Lau has an opportunity to join his family at work in the factory, but constant military surveillance at the business makes it far less enticing than his dream occupation of working with metal. He begs the local blacksmith, Mr Soon Tun, for a job. The man's business remains intact: he repairs carriage wheel fixtures and household iron decorations, as well as carrying out industrial repairs, and soldering, pressing, bending and folding iron under extreme heat then hammering it into shape. He doubles as a pawnbroker of metal, either selling it on as is to a factory, where it's melted down and repurposed, or refashioning it for wholesale to one of the many trinket shop owners with whom he regularly does business.

Since the occupation, under duress, Soon Tun has expanded his business to include work on gun barrels, axe heads and bayonet spikes. The original Kwa family name is Ke, which is written with the same character as Kwa. It's pronounced Ke by Mandarin speakers in the north of China and Kwa by Cantonese speakers in the south. Ke and Kwa both mean 'handle of an axe'. Tak Lau's fascination with flattening and folding iron is therefore connected to the legacy of his family name.

'I'm strong,' the boy says, flexing a scrawny arm, 'I can follow instruction' – he does a mock salute – 'and I am a hard worker.' He screws up his face in a fiercely determined expression. '*Please.*'

'I can only pay you in rice.' Soon Tun places his large calloused hands on the crevassed benchtop and examines the neatly dressed boy before him. 'The soldiers take all my Hong Kong dollars and give me back half the value in yen.' The blacksmith pulls on his right earlobe out of habit. 'Then they tax what's left.'

His hair is greyer than the last time Tak Lau saw him, before the occupation, during one of the boy's missions to appraise hardware stores in the area. He would always stop at the blacksmith shop and sit on the step at the broad front entrance, watching customers come and go with all manner of iron and other metal for repair. It was thrilling to see.

'How much rice?' Tak Lau asks astutely.

'I have an extra ration card. I can pay you 2.4 ounces of rice per day.'

Tak Lau can't contain his excitement – a broad grin emerges with the marvellous realisation he has a job. A whole extra allowance of rice, every day!

'You can start tomorrow,' Soon Tun says. 'Tell your parents you won't be touching the furnace.'

Tak Lau is a little disappointed about that last point, but he skips home anyway, and the next day he flies over the cobblestones leading to Soon Tun's workshop. Excitement courses through him; he can finally take his obsession with twisting and bending wire and tin to the next level. He is a working boy now.

Mr Soon Tun looks up from a bayonet he is working on to see Tak Lau bound in. The blacksmith waves a muscular arm in greeting. *His hand is like a steak*, the boy thinks. *His fingers are sausages.*

Tak Lau hangs a small lunch satchel and a hat on a black iron hook. The rough timber wall is covered in hooks; opposite, a grey brick wall holds hundreds of smaller ones pressed into the mortar, laden with tools and loops of wire and rope. Tak Lau's lunch stays warm in a round tin container tucked in his bag; it is his umpteenth day in a row of cooked rice and a few vegetables. No wonder Soon Tun's blackened, greasy hand looks delectable.

By day three Tak Lau has learned the names of all Soon Tun's tools, and he quickly develops the ability to predict which instrument is needed before the master reaches for it. When the crew of adult workers are forging by the dozen with sledgehammers on anvils, Tak Lau manages to assist everyone. He is becoming indispensable. Weeks of metalwork bliss bring extra rice for Mother and the girls to eat their complete share again, and Tak Lau's heart is full at the knowledge they are returning to health thanks to him. On occasion Ng Yuk sends a few morsels upstairs to Happy Shadow, who returns the favour when she can.

Flames from the furnace reflect in Tak Lau's eyes, and for a moment he is mesmerised as he imagines taking over the blacksmith business one day, standing at the helm, his own large, calloused hands on the counter. There's often talk of succession in the House of Kwa, as naturally boys will inherit the Swatow Lace family business. There will be more than enough contenders to take over. Although Ying Kam founded the shop, Eng Lee took charge before leaving for Shanghai, coinciding with President Sun Yat-sen himself appointing the Kwa to a committee overseeing the entire Chinese districts of Chiuchow and Mei-hsien. 'A *significant* honour,' the adults tell Tak Lau. 'Your uncle, *very* important man.' He is the arbiter for the business now. But silk and embroidery are not Tak Lau's thing anyway so he pays no mind to these grown-up concepts – he's much more at home here with tools and fire.

While the boy's mind wanders, Soon Tun holds out a meaty hand in search of the axe he needs. Tak Lau is meant to be standing by. He snaps out of his daydream and hastily reaches for the handle, knocking the axe off the wall. The blade slices his hand, and he yelps then bites the inside of his lip to hold back tears.

A worker wraps a filthy rag around the bloody wound. To Tak Lau, the shame of his miscalculation far outweighs the pain. Embarrassed, he leaves without his portion of rice and walks home nursing his pride.

Ng Yuk is furious their food supply has been compromised, and Tak Lau cries as Theresa cleans the cut, winds cloth around it and whispers – so as not to upset Mother further – reassurances to him. 'It will need stitches, Mother,' Theresa looks up to say, so Ng Yuk sends Elder Brother to find a doctor.

All the British doctors are imprisoned in internment camps. They surface only to work in military hospitals to operate on Japanese soldiers injured in accidents or Japanese naval workers who've caught the fire of an air raid, but they don't tend to the local population anymore. Elder Brother returns with a Chinese man, Dr Huang.

'Bite this.' He hands Tak Lau a dry cotton washcloth, rolled up so the boy can fit his mouth around it. Theresa moves her chair closer and places an arm tightly around her little brother's shoulders as Dr Huang disinfects the wound with alcohol. He begins stitching as calmly as if the skin were a swathe of silk at a Kwa factory.

Tak Lau is delirious with pain. He can't tell which is worse: the burning alcohol or the sting each time the needle punctures his skin. Then, of course, there's the drag and cut of Dr Huang pulling the thread taut.

'Leave it a week at least,' he tells Ng Yuk. 'After that he can return to usual duties.' The doctor shakes his head to refuse the small bag of rice she offers him before he leaves.

The next day Ng Yuk makes the short journey, on her tiny lotus feet, to the blacksmith shop. Her traditional silk-draped elegance is striking amid the blackened, greasy men in filthy singlets.

'Thank you for employing my son.' Ng Yuk flashes a bewitching smile at Soon Tun who takes one hand off the counter to pull on his earlobe.

She notices a boy behind him trying to reach a tool high above. *Stupid boy*, she thinks. *Why doesn't he just use the stool next to him to climb up?*

She faces Soon Tun, who has noticed her noticing his new employee. 'It would be terrible' – she lowers her gaze – 'if anyone were to find out you deliberately harmed a child. Punishing him like that with an axe.' Ng Yuk is living up to her reputation: she is not a woman to be messed with. 'Tak Lau looks forward to returning to work with you once he has recovered.' The diminutive woman stares the large sooty man squarely in the eye.

Everyone knows Ng Yuk is a flagrant collaborator. Soon Tun has heard stories about her welcoming Japanese soldiers into her home – inviting them! He nods, and she turns to leave. Then he takes a parting shot. 'You'd send your son down a coalmine if it meant more food for you.'

'Isn't that exactly what this is?' Ng Yuk asks, casting her eyes theatrically around the grimy workshop before exiting as elegantly as she entered.

MAHJONG AND BARRELS

On her way home Ng Yuk runs into Mr Chung, the Japanese warrant officer in charge of the Kwas' borough. He picked up some Cantonese during his time as a Japanese spy in Hong Kong pre-occupation, and Ng Yuk has been helping him to improve his fluency. Knowledge of Cantonese is an advantage when communicating with the Chinese population, though few occupiers will admit it; the political line is to use English and Japanese only.

'I will see you upon the hour for mahjong,' Mr Chung says, nodding respectfully as Ng Yuk bows as low as her balance will allow.

'I very much look forward to seeing you and any other warrant officers or sergeants who wish to play today.' She smiles, taking her leave.

Mr Chung is most respectful and bows his head again, rather taken with Ng Yuk and her graceful ways. She gestures like a Chinese opera singer, her silks making every movement more dramatic. He watches her disappear around a corner.

Once she's out of sight, Ng Yuk leans against a wall – her feet are killing her. She looks up at the clear blue sky and hopes her good mahjong skills will help save her family.

Her *Hanfu* silks conceal a swelling belly. Another baby grows inside her: a child to be born into the occupation.

That afternoon, Tak Lau is at the kitchen table nursing his stitches when three soldiers enter without knocking. Mr Chung greets the boy in Cantonese, and the other two nod before all three make their way out onto the large tiled balcony. A round table has been set up for mahjong with branch chairs at its north, east, south and west. The officers remove pistols from their holsters and place them on spare branch chairs at the balcony's edge, then lean their rifles against a wall. A maid pours Chinese tea.

Ng Yuk emerges looking every bit the lady of the house, having changed her outfit since that morning. She and Mr Chung conduct a serious mahjong conversation in Cantonese, while the two other officers find it difficult to keep up.

'Our army is on a recruitment drive,' Mr Chung mentions just as, at Ng Yuk's behest, all four pairs of hands reach in to shuffle the 144 tiles in the middle of the table. 'Will you be dealer?' he asks her.

She nods. 'Help me build the walls.' She gently raises the sleeve of her garment to reveal her dainty wrist, a tantalising gesture of Japanese geishas. As they stack the tiles into four walls, Ng Yuk continues in Cantonese, 'Now choose thirteen tiles.' Mr Chung has played many times with Ng Yuk; her explanation is for the benefit of the other officers, who are here to learn the language as they play the game.

To begin, she turns over an extra tile. She starts to explain the chow, pung and kong suits to the bewildered men when Mr Chung interrupts. 'Might your son be interested in joining our ranks? He can begin by helping out in the army barracks.'

Ng Yuk looks over at the kitchen table, but Tak Lau is no longer there. Mr Chung gestures with his head to the corner of the balcony behind her; the boy is crouched over a rifle, running his hand across the cool metal barrel. 'You'll be able to have one of those when we're finished with you, boy.' Mr Chung directs this at Tak Lau but smiles at Ng Yuk.

Collaborate or die, she thinks as she returns the smile with a nod.

On Tak Lau's first day there are none of the formalities one might expect of a military induction. He simply fronts up to the old cinema building as Mr Chung has instructed. The boy waits on his own for only a few minutes before the warrant officer arrives and appraises him, nodding with approval. The boy is turned out in the miniature uniform delivered to the House of Kwa last night, and to Mr Chung's great satisfaction, Tak Lau remembers to bow low. *The boy learns fast*, Mr Chung thinks.

Tak Lau follows the warrant officer into the barracks. What strikes the boy at first is the almost convivial atmosphere: calm, relaxed and so very unlike the chaos wreaked by these soldiers in the streets and homes of Hong Kong – beatings, executions, rapes and humiliations. It's not always like that, of course, but when it's all that people speak of, it feels as though the terror never rests. Here, the soldiers smile and give almost imperceptible nods, acknowledging Tak Lau as Mr Chung leads him down a corridor. The boy has seen what these men are capable of, but despite the horror they have visited upon his life, he puts his fear aside. He is a spy on a mission: a child in a classified domain with access to all areas. Fascinated by how the new ruling class lives, he is thrilled to be taken under its wing.

'You can begin by polishing the boots,' Mr Chung says.

Tak Lau takes in a huge hall containing rows of stretcher beds and tatami mats, some with sleeping bodies in them, presumably the night shift. Hoarded items of furniture and art are stacked along the walls, and stolen personal items such as coats and scarves are stuffed into crevices. This is the theatre complex Tak Lau used to sneak into with Elder Brother to watch national defence films about China resisting Japan's invasion, and now he is joining that very enemy. Rows of chairs are piled against a long wall to the right of the cavernous hall, the decorative vaulted ceiling making the barrack beds seem diminutive.

Mr Chung asks a subordinate to help Tak Lau set up a place to shine shoes. Once word circulates, the boy is polishing boots all day.

'The barracks even have a sauna, Mama,' he tells Ng Yuk excitedly as he walks in the door. He dumps a parcel of fish on the kitchen table, puffing out his chest.

Mother acts disinterested. 'Go clean yourself, you make the whole house smell like boot polish.'

When Tak Lau is gone, she unwraps the fish. It stinks. She is about to shout something about rotten fish, but a maid slides the package to the other side of the table. 'Shall I cook it now?' she asks, and Ng Yuk gives a brusque nod.

After dark the family gathers round to hear about Tak Lau's adventure. There is an ongoing curfew for the Hong Kong Chinese. White bankers are still locked up in a hotel, while civilian expats who haven't been killed remain in the internment camp at St Stephen's College in Stanley, at the southern end of the Island: 2800 men, women and children.

Theresa and Clara join the others around the table. Mother puts a bowl of grey broth under Theresa's nose, and she crinkles it up at the smell – something unfamiliar is floating in it. 'Fish,' says Mother. Like the rest of the family, Theresa hasn't eaten meat, let alone fish, in months. She scoops up the rancid morsel cautiously in an embellished green ceramic spoon, then brings it to her lips.

'And Mr Chung says he'll have other jobs for me tomorrow,' Tak Lau says, chewing enthusiastically.

* * *

Soon enough, Tak Lau is a trusted messenger for the Japanese officers as well as their shoe-shiner. He returns to his position at the blacksmith shop as well. With no school to attend, he works hard juggling his two jobs. Each day he slaps a parcel of rotten fish and an extra cup of rice on the kitchen table. He watches his mother's face glow with pride, then almost instantly she appears disinterested again. He has seen her vote of confidence, though, and it makes him feel like a man of the house. Father is gone long hours at the factories, which he says are no longer his, and Tak Lau daydreams about rising through the ranks of the Japanese Army, taking back Swatow Lace and bringing the enemy to its knees.

Mr Chung observes that Tak Lau is a good runner and hard worker. He knows the boy has a keen interest in mechanics, always finding something to pull apart so he can investigate its internal organs. In military lockdown in the middle of wartime occupation, Tak Lau is anything but bored.

'Today you graduate from boots and errands to weapons.' Mr Chung gestures for Tak Lau to sit opposite him at a table in the barracks.

Every handheld Japanese military weapon the boy can imagine is laid out: a combat knife bayonet, two different side-arm pistols, a Type 38 bolt-action carbine rifle and even a machine gun. Tak Lau thinks about shooting all the Japanese soldiers like in the last Chinese movie he watched with Elder Brother in the building where he now sits facing the enemy. 'Collaborate or die,' Mother can be heard muttering more frequently these days.

Tak Lau keeps staring at the arsenal of weapons. 'Behind this door, there are many more.' Mr Chung points at a steel door to his left where the theatre projectionist would have stored large reels of film; the segmented steel shelves are perfect for gun storage. 'This is our junior armoury. I want you to clean all these. Then start again.' Mr Chung smiles and proceeds to instruct Tak Lau on how to dismantle the unloaded weapons, his hands caressing each of them in turn as though he knows them inside out and backwards. 'Once you have tended to a thousand weapons, you will be ready to use one.'

A steady stream of 'customers' line up for Tak Lau's work, from warrant officers – Mr Chung's equivalents – right down the ranks to privates. They mostly require the boy to clean their weapons, sometimes to polish their boots; they are familiar with him being around and don't hold back on jobs for him to do. He memorises uniform insignia so he can tell whose jobs to prioritise, but because many of them walk around off-duty wearing only a singlet and trousers, it's tricky to tell exactly who outranks who. Delivering messages between soldiers makes knowing who's who much easier with clear titles supplied on the notes or the Japanese reading the names out loud when he can't decipher the kanji.

After a few months, Mr Chung decides to introduce Tak Lau higher up the chain: a serious spy-game promotion.

The people of Hong Kong no longer receive rations and are left to fend for themselves in alleyway marketplaces where rats have burgeoned in number thanks to the neglect of waste-management systems under the Japanese. Coal supplies are dwindling too; households must restrict lighting to one room after dark, if they have any power at all. But the cross-cultural mahjong summits in the House of Kwa and Tak Lau's outward enthusiasm for the Japanese not only shield the family from further deprivation, but garner special treatment.

Ng Yuk sends her maid with some food upstairs to Happy Shadow and her Kwa offspring. The two wives barely exchange words these days, and Ying Kam sometimes stays away all night, forced to manage his own factory floor for the Japanese who bank the profits. Eng Lee has still not returned so his wife continues to retain the shop and keeps the columns of the books under Japanese control.

Tak Lau dashes past a heavily scarred, emaciated elderly man who sits crouched with his knees up around his chin. He rattles an empty bowl against a step, hoping for money or food. This stranger would once smile and tousle Tak Lau's hair when he was a toddler. The boy tosses a Hong Kong coin into the stranger's bowl; it's virtually worthless now that yen has taken over, but it's all he has to give.

Tak Lau keeps running. Mr Chung is taking him to meet a big official today, and he mustn't be late. He stops to catch his breath when he reaches the gate to the barracks.

Mr Chung takes Tak Lau in a rickshaw up town to Mr Yamagata's residence, where they are served sugar black tea. Tak Lau sips it slowly, savouring the sweetness on his tongue. His eyes widen at talk of his important part in helping to shape the new Hong Kong – to do the will of ancestors, Buddha and of God by supporting its transition to a fully fledged Japanese state. Mr Chung translates what Japanese Tak Lau cannot understand, and the boy tries to listen intently.

Weighing on his mind is the grandfather clock that stands behind Mr Yamagata. It's showing the wrong time, the pendulum having frozen, but no one aside from Tak Lau seems the least bit bothered by it.

Mr Yamagata drones on. The house belonged to a British academic and his family, who are now either dead or in an internment camp. Mr Yamagata sits on their settee and uses their possessions as if this all belongs to him. He sips from a Wedgwood cup with a silver rim and elaborate leaf design.

Tak Lau resists an urge to tinker with the clock. Its detailed golden spandrel and elaborate moon-dial are begging to be touched. The sun is frozen in a partially eclipsed position, almost obscured by a row of marching-band instruments, followed by a moon and clouds etched on a brass plane that would move if only the clock would start ticking again.

The clock is like Hong Kong: stuck in an hour of darkness, in need of repair. Tak Lau sips his delicious tea, nods along with a look of serious concern, and thinks with delight of the grandfather clock, its cogs and spindles, coils and springs.

Mr Chung is pleased with his recruit's apparent attentiveness. In the rickshaw on the way back, he reminds Tak Lau that he will now be a trusted errand boy between the barracks and officials' homes. 'This is a step up from running messages between soldiers on the street, in the field and within the barracks.' Mr Chung pauses. 'You will be invited into homes like Mr Yamagata's and be asked to wait if a response is required to be written. If so, you will return with the reply to the original sender.' Mr Chung is fond of the Kwas – Tak Lau and Ng Yuk in particular – but he sees his duty to Japan as paramount. 'If you break this trust, and disrespect this honour,' he adds, 'I will kill your family.'

Tak Lau is still for a moment, his eyes fixed on Mr Chung's. Now the boy is like an ancient hero in his comic books, keeping his adventures secret to protect the lives of his family: a dragon protecting his lair. 'Thank you, Warrant Officer Chung, sir.' Tak Lau gets out of the rickshaw and salutes. 'I won't disappoint you.'

TRAPDOOR AND TROUSERS

For almost two years, since the family stopped taking her with them to hide in the bunker, Theresa has stayed indoors, stealing sunlight and sky on the balcony and through windows, and sleeping in the room concealed behind the custom-made partition wall Tak Lau likes to think he helped build. She spends most of her days in the main house when the coast is clear, but the hidden room is only moments away. Clara retreats there with Theresa during military marches down Wu Hu Street, in case of a spontaneous raid; she is getting too big for the cramped spaces in the floor and ceiling.

Theresa and Clara are under family-imposed house arrest for their own safety. At first, isolation from the outside world tormented the girls, but their fear has always outweighed any desire to go outside, and they gather mental strength and maintain their spirits by painting and writing. Theresa also reads everything she can get her hands on and is fast becoming fluent in English, even passable in Japanese.

She sits late at night in her windowless room, studying beneath the glow of a kerosene lamp hanging from a hook on the side of her bedhead. There is only room for a bed and small table, the edge of which overhangs the mattress, so Theresa sleeps curled up with her back against the wall. The benefit of this arrangement is that the bed doubles as a seat when she works at the desk. At night when she lies down to read, she transfers the lamp from her desk to the hook. She isn't concerned about the restriction on electric lights – no one can see in. An air vent near the base of the partition ensures she won't suffocate if she is forced to stay hidden for long periods. And there is a trapdoor in the ceiling; she can get onto the roof through there if something happened to the family and she was somehow barricaded in.

Theresa is fourteen; Clara, eighteen months younger. The older Clara gets, the more eager Mother and Father are to shut her away with her sister. 'I hate my chest growing,' she complains to Theresa as they huddle together on the bed. 'Mother has been making the maids bind it like her feet. They've wrapped me in bandages – look.' She lifts her silk shirt to reveal her bound chest.

Theresa glances up from her book. 'She only wants you to stay looking like a child so you don't attract unwanted attention. She tried to do that to me too, but it was too late.'

'Well, I'm not a child anymore. I may as well stay locked up with you all the time. Look at you, you're allowed to be a woman.' Clara jabs the side of Theresa's left breast.

'Aya! Ouch.' The thought of spending every day in a room with her beloved sister makes Theresa grimace – every now and then is enough.

'Maybe,' Clara giggles, 'we should make two of the soldiers fall in love with us. Then we could live in an aristocratic house on The Peak and drink tea like the expat ladies used to.'

Theresa sighs. 'You know it doesn't work like that. The Japanese are brutal with Hong Kong women.'

Clara crosses her legs and turns her back to Theresa, who picks up her Mason Pearson and brushes her little sister's hair. 'Mother married when she was fourteen,' Clara says defiantly.

'Yes,' Theresa responds, pulling the bristles through a knot in Clara's mane. 'And look how miserable she is. Baby after baby and another on its way. And for what? To hide us? To barely feed us? Her damaged feet can't walk ten minutes.'

Now it's Clara's turn to say 'Aya!' as her sister finds more knots. 'Okay, stupid idea,' Clara concedes.

'Yes, Wai Mui' – Theresa uses Clara's Chinese name – 'a very dumb idea.'

The brush glides through Clara's hair easily now. The strands shine in a pool of lamplight.

'*Sister*,' says Theresa, putting down the brush and wrapping her arms around Clara, 'you will marry someone much more grand than a Japanese soldier. One day we'll be free, and you will take your pick of all the men.' The girls giggle some more.

Even with the immunity Mr Chung provides House of Kwa, two of Ying Kam and Happy Shadow's daughters, older than Theresa and Clara, and women now, are dragged off the street by Japanese soldiers. When they stagger home, their mother sobs until the unmarried two assure her they have not been sullied. Bloodied blouses can be laundered; bruised faces will heal. Luckily a group of children came around the corner during the assault, they tell their mother, and interrupted the soldiers as they were unbuckling their trousers. Instead of raping the women, the men beat them – ostensibly as punishment for being out without a chaperone.

Ying Kam wants to rage through the streets and tear apart the men who did this to his daughters, but instead he retreats silently to his study, knowing that even dragons must withdraw from battle when they are outmatched. He must protect his entire family from being killed. *Our captors cannot be trusted*, he thinks, *no matter how convincing their smiles or how much rotten fish they give us.*

The Kwas have hidden their most precious possessions: paintings, jade, gold, silver, ivory, silk, diamonds, pearls, Tak

Lau's diamond earring and, most precious of all, Theresa. Ying Kam admits to himself that she is guarded more jealously than his other girls. He cannot explain his daughter's gift on the abacus or gracious ability to manage both staff and family from a young age, but she is the only one of his daughters for whom he would consider breaking tradition by allowing a woman to inherit his share of Swatow Lace. Perhaps she really is an old soul. He plans to ask a shaman about this once the war is over.

The Japanese would kill all the Kwas if they learned of the trapdoors and partition walls. Ying Kam thanks his ancestors and the gods that the soldiers never do more than poke their heads into bedrooms for a cursory glance around.

Ng Yuk gives birth to a half-term baby, stillborn into the occupation. She has been pregnant twice since Black Christmas, and neither infant survived. She lights a cigarette and inhales deeply as Dr Huang wraps the tiny body in a blanket, covering its lifeless face. One of the maids, who held Ng Yuk as she screamed and pushed, carries the bundle out. 'A girl,' Dr Huang says and turns to leave. Ng Yuk exhales a heartbroken plume of smoke. It coils up and around the corner of her mahogany bedhead, then down to caress the silk pillowslip before it slowly vanishes. 'Like the last one,' he adds before disappearing from the room.

Ng Yuk touches the bloodied sheets between her legs with her free hand and brings the cigarette back to her lips. 'What is in this world for another girl, anyway?'

There will not even be a funeral, and it will be as if the infant never existed. Mr Chung has no idea about the pregnancy; neither does her husband. He is too preoccupied at the factory or upstairs with Second Wife. Ng Yuk exhales. Her wealth and the little freedom she had were stripped away when the Japanese dropped their first bomb on Hong Kong. She waves her hand erratically through the smoky air. A pall of grief forms above her and disperses into the blankets and curtains.

'Clean this up,' she shouts to the maids. 'Before Master returns.'

Days later Ng Yuk has one of her help bind her stomach to rid her body of excess fluid after labour. The idea is that this will quickly return her figure to its youthful glory. She drapes and ties a finishing touch to her outfit then emerges from her room.

It is a mahjong day, and Ng Yuk is late in her preparations. Clara looks up from her writing at the kitchen table. With brush and ink, she is copying Japanese characters from a book. They are a version of writing not far from Chinese, since Japan borrowed and built on them seventeen hundred years ago. 'This is incredibly difficult to get right, Mama,' Clara complains. She finds the subtle nuances between the writing systems excruciating and the Japanese pronunciations impossible.

'Your sister can do it.'

Clara rolls her eyes, scrunches up her nose and purses her lips at the comparison to her sibling. She intensifies her focus on her brushstroke.

'You call this finished?' Ng Yuk shouts at the servants. 'This is not clean!'

A maid moves quickly to attend to an imaginary mess, and Ng Yuk pulls violently on her hair. In the old days, before the occupation, Ng Yuk would have smashed a dish by this stage – but these are harder times, and she is careful to spare the crockery.

Clara retreats to her room, where a doll on her bed has hardly any hair from all the pulling when she flies into a rage.

Mary cries out from the nursery. Because there is no baby to take her place, the girl has occupied that room since she was born four and a half years ago. 'Aya! Aya! Aya!' She has slipped and fallen from a windowsill that she climbed up to watch a nest of tailorbirds wedged into the pipes running down the building. She has been trying to imitate their trills like Snow

White. Before the occupation she watched the cartoon at the cinema with her brothers and sisters, and although she was only two she still remembers the girl and the birds.

Mary is doted on by her older siblings and the household help. Theresa, especially, finds her rosy, chubby cheeks a joy to squeeze.

Mary's cries sail down to Theresa's room. The partition is open, and no one else goes to check on the youngest child, so Theresa slides out from behind her desk, walks down the passage and picks her baby sister up off the ground. 'It's just a bruise. There, there, Mary.'

The little girl wails as Theresa feels her arm to test if it's broken. It doesn't seem to be. Mary throws her limbs around her big sister's neck and waist, and Theresa carries her to the kitchen where she can inspect the injured arm under a better light.

In the commotion caused by the harsh words of Ng Yuk and the howls of Mary, no one notices as Mr Chung knocks and walks through the door.

That is when he sees Theresa for the first time, consoling Mary in the middle of a chaotic kitchen scene. He is taken aback by the teenager's radiant youthful beauty. She looks up in alarm. Ng Yuk shoos her away, but it's too late – such a girl cannot be unseen.

'You have another daughter,' Mr Chung says as a statement rather than a question. Ng Yuk nods, and he continues, 'She is very beautiful. It is understandable that you try to protect her from those who may wish her harm.' His expression is difficult to read.

Theresa takes Mary's hand to lead her back to her room. The little girl looks over her shoulder at the tall man and beams at him, her tear-stained face suddenly like the sun.

Ng Yuk calls Theresa back, and she obediently steps into the room with her head bowed. 'This,' Ng Yuk tells her, 'is Mr Chung,'

Theresa smiles disarmingly.

'Mr Chung, please meet my daughter, Wai Ching.'

'I am Theresa.' She curtsies. 'How do you do?'

Once Mr Chung recognises Theresa's language and bookkeeping skills, she is recruited to assist the occupiers. She is unassuming and sweet, canny and sharp, and her skills on the abacus are well honed from years sitting beside Ying Kam at Swatow Lace and nights at his ledger clacking the ivory beads.

Four is not a lucky number for the Chinese because the word for four, *si* in Mandarin or *sei* in Cantonese, sounds similar to the word for death, in both languages. They are only one tone apart, but Number Four Daughter doesn't care about that. Theresa Wai Ching Kwa is about to prove how lucky she is.

Food far tastier than rotten fish and standard rice rations appears – fruit and dried meat from official quarters. For the first time in years, House of Kwa feasts.

Theresa is asked to tag along to meetings with dignitaries, academics, deposed lawyers and judges. Her Japanese and English are proficient enough, while her looks and charm are what truly get her by. She translates high-level cultural exchanges at only fourteen. In China she would be eligible to marry.

POISON AND FIRE

TODAY IS 6 AUGUST 1945, A MONDAY. WORLD WAR II HAS been raging for six years, and Hong Kong has been under Japanese rule for three and a half. It's just after 8 am, twenty degrees Celsius and humid as it always is this time of year. Tak Lau runs down to his job at the blacksmith shop. Theresa gets ready to accompany Ying Kam to the factory.

America's B-29 Bomber the *Enola Gay* drops an atomic bomb on Japan. Its nickname is Little Boy, and it kills eighty thousand people in Hiroshima; sixty thousand more will die by Christmas from fallout. Ninety thousand buildings will be destroyed, leaving fewer than a third of that number standing.

Theresa walks with her father along the factory floor aisle between lines of workers hunched over sewing machines.

Three days later, on 9 August, it's another warm, humid morning in Hong Kong. Theresa sits by Ying Kam helping him with calculations on the abacus.

The US atomic bomb Fat Man wreaks hell on Nagasaki. Eighty thousand people, including POWs, will be dead by Christmas. There is immeasurable horror on earth, bodies haemorrhaging, skin embedded with glass, and limbs crushed by debris. Unspeakable suffering. That same day, the Russians push back Japanese forces in China.

Ying Kam switches on the wireless to find that there is only a Japanese language station on air today with no update on the situation in Japan at all. That's strange – most rebel stations were found out and their operators executed months ago, but he still expected to find the Japanese-sanctioned Cantonese station disseminating basic news and propaganda. At least there's still word of mouth.

At home Ying Kam, his two wives and their children await whatever will come next.

Happy Shadow has had three more children during the occupation, two girls and a boy. Ng Yuk curses her womb and reaches for a slim lacquered box containing three cigarette holders in porcelain, ivory and wood. She selects one and drags on her Double Happiness tobacco. 'What do I have to show for the war? Two more dead babies, only five alive.' She exhales and tries not to tune in to the cry of a Second Wife baby upstairs. 'Younger and more beautiful,' Ng Yuk mutters bitterly about herself. 'But not enough to produce more children.'

She shuffles her ivory mahjong pieces, sliding them around on the balcony table. It has been weeks since her last game with the occupiers. The tiles face down, and Ng Yuk flips one over with her left hand: Red Dragon. Then another: North Wind. Next: Plum Blossom.

Theresa has been watching her mother from the balcony door. Ng Yuk stares at the upturned trio of tiles as if they speak to her. She draws in another nicotine hit and watches paper and leaf smoulder. Theresa pulls up a chair next to her mother and places her right hand on Ng Yuk's left. And, on this rare occasion, Ng Yuk does not pull away.

* * *

As a last act of defiance towards the West, the Japanese execute as many remaining British citizens in their camps as they can before the armies of liberation have a chance to take over. They set fire to Hong Kong homes and industrial workplaces. Over their dead bodies will they surrender, with many committing harakiri to avoid the shame of capture.

Fierce dragon flames envelop the second storey of one of the Kwa factories. Ying Kam runs out of his burning building, and workers stream onto the street, coughing and spluttering, blackened by the inferno. Ying Kam faces the carnage, unable to speak, watching fire devour his dreams as the flames flicker in his eyes.

Japanese soldiers retreat in military vessels and cargo ships, chartering whole suicide boats full of soldiers towards Commonwealth aircraft carriers. They take with them Hong Kong's food supplies, specifically to leave the population to starve. Some of the Japanese will churn the rough waters home to their mother country if they think they can avoid capture, while others choose to sink to a watery grave in communal shame.

Whatever law and order existed under occupation is now out to sea.

Before Britain has a chance to reclaim the colony, Ying Kam steals away from his family for a moment alone. He sits in his den, the many brutalities and sorrows of the occupation whirl through his mind. Heaving a sigh, he is sixty years in the past on his journey from the Kwa compound in Beijing after stealing his father's concubine; his mighty House of Kwa in Swatow and its fall; and its rise again in Hong Kong. Only – he heaves another sigh – to fall once more. He apologises to his ancestors then shakes his fists at the gods.

Lifting a vial to his lips, he transports himself out of his body and swallows. It is a fast-acting poison. The vial has been hidden beneath a floorboard for years: a parting purchase from the local shaman before he was publicly executed by Japanese officers in the early days of the occupation, when unlucky families and their children were dragged down to the park and forced to watch.

In his last moments, Ying Kam prays for his family. They have a few riches and one another. With three wives he has sired thirty-two children. Of course he knows about Ng Yuk's two recent stillbirths – Dr Huang could not keep such information from a husband. There has been no word from First Wife in China, given all outside communication has been cut off or intercepted since the occupation began three years and eight months ago. All Ying Kam can hope is that the survivors of his thirty-two children will remain alive as his legacy. He is the twenty-second firstborn son of the firstborn son of Kwa.

He scrawls lines of characters down a page, convulses and falls to the floor, holding his chest.

A maid finds Ying Kam's body. It is carried down the hill in a coffin draped in silks and taken directly for cremation to avoid overburdened morgues and mass graves.

Ng Yuk and Happy Shadow tell their children and people they know, 'He died of a broken heart.'

When Lotus Flower, who is still living in Swatow, receives word her husband is dead, she weeps and remembers when she fled with him from his father's compound to build a new life. She releases any hope he would one day come back for her and cries into the night.

Theresa goes into her father's study and sits at his desk, running her hand over the last page he touched. She reads his calligraphy as though he is right there speaking the words.

哀莫大于心死. 活着是更好的出路.

The saddest thing is death of the heart.

The remedy for dying is living.

* * *

Theresa places the paper into the pages of a black ledger that Ying Kam saved from the factory fire. 'The remedy for dying is living,' she whispers. She smooths her cheongsam against her thighs and traces a finger over an embroidered plum blossom wending its way across her breast to her collar. Then she stands up and walks out.

SILVER AND ASH

It's been two weeks since the Japanese retreated, and Hong Kong is starving. Tak Lau slips through a wire fence around the old barracks at the theatre complex he knows so well. Scavenging for rice and food scraps here should be easy.

He fills a bag with provisions for his family. There are abandoned pocket knives, belts, ammunition cases, boardgame pieces and even a watch. The ten-year-old feels light and full of adventure. With the conquerors gone, he wanders and explores freely, collecting abandoned objects to examine, restore, swap or sell.

At home, Tak Lau drops off the heavy bag. His sisters call after him to stay and eat, but he shakes his head and runs out again, not looking back. Father is gone, so the boys must now provide for House of Kwa. He runs down Wu Hu Street towards Whampoa Dock.

Structures along the wharves show significant signs of the Allied air raids. Broken cranes and ruined warehouses occupy rearranged chunks of shoreline, while expat homes Tak Lau remembers from before the occupation are damaged, in ruins or no longer there. He slips through a gap in a fence and runs towards the waterfront homes. The sunshine is brilliant in his eyes, making him squint. This is where British dock managers lived with their families. He steps inside the first home he comes to, through a doorway that looks to have been battered by axes. There are bullet holes in the walls and splash marks of dried blood on expensive linen wallpaper. Skulls and other human remains litter the floor. Rugs are stained crimson. These people must have been butchered in the early days of the attack.

Tak Lau steps from room to room, from house to house. Houses of horror with groupings of skeletal remains, sometimes a single skeleton near a back door or curled up in a bloodstained closet, like the preserved bodies of Pompeii, telling a story of failed escapes. An emaciated rat scuttles over a dusty mantel – not even slim pickings are left for it.

After searching through wardrobes for a bag, Tak Lau makes do with a dusty pillowcase. He fills it with silverware and then, satisfied there is nothing else of value to take, he runs onto the beach and vomits up what little is in his stomach. He sits up and tries to polish the tarnished silver with sand. The granules damage the fine surfaces. He rubs harder, his shirt abrading the metal, before he realises what he has done and bursts into tears.

Alone on the beach beside scenes of unspeakable atrocities, he doubles over and sobs. He cannot understand what emotion he just experienced but is too filled with shame to take the ruined silver home to his mother. Instead he visits his old boss to sell his find as scrap metal. It fetches a small price, and Tak Lau is crestfallen he has so little to show for his efforts.

Soon Tun rubs his thick steak-and-sausage hands together. He will melt the utensils down and turn the transaction around once the economy picks up again. Banks will pay good ransom for solid silver.

Ying Kam's younger brother Eng Lee absorbs any control of the business Ying Kam may have had left. With the registration already in his name and with no known agreement otherwise,

Swatow Lace is now entirely his. Most of his own Kwa family and fortune have been preserved thanks to his wife, who kept the shop at 16 Pedder Street going while he was stuck in Shanghai for four years.

Tak Lau watches his uncle's car pull up outside the Wu Hu Street house and remembers Ng Yuk scolding Ying Kam that his brother was 'squeezing him out'. Uncle Eng Lee lives in a wealthier part of Hong Kong than Hung Hom; he has driven over to take Theresa to work with him, where she will help manage the books just as she once did for her father.

All the way to the factory, Eng Lee complains to his niece that the road where she lives is too rough for his Mercedes-Benz. Theresa is unsure if he is fully aware of what the family endured in his absence, when his wife and brother were responsible for maintaining the business under extreme duress.

'You should feel proud to live in the only concrete building on the street,' Uncle tells her. 'And proud it is the only one left standing – that you are still standing.' He presses his car horn to hurry along a shirtless man. 'But,' he adds, 'you must aspire to greater heights. Your father did not die for you to wallow.'

The man on the road wears a rice-paddy hat and loincloth, with a wooden pole across the back of his neck pulling down his skinny shoulders. At either end, ropes hold up baskets filled with mounds of cement dust. The cavity under his ribs gives way to the skinny curve of his stomach, probably bloated with air. Cheap labour rebuilding the city.

'You could aim to live at The Peak, perhaps,' Uncle suggests, referring to the most valuable real estate on the Island side of the city, where he lives. 'Chinese weren't allowed to live there before, but now the Brits give us new freedoms.' He presses his horn again. 'Have you heard? We can even visit the "whites only" beaches now.'

The skin of the emaciated worker is dark from the sun, and he moves out of the way without looking up.

At the factory, Theresa click-clacks the ivory abacus Ying Kam left behind. He made no will, but it was obvious this should be hers.

The factory bustles with workers, and Eng Lee is pleased with progress: his phoenix from the ashes. The damage from the fire wasn't as bad as Ying Kam thought. *Brother, you leaped to conclusions.* Eng Lee opens Ying Kam's black ledger, the one that belonged to their father, my great-grandfather, and vows eternal thanks to his brother for rescuing it from the inferno. 'Out of the fire,' he says. 'Ashes into the grave.'

Before the Japanese occupation, under British rule the children's English names were favoured over their Chinese ones, especially outside the house. Under the Japanese, English was officially banned on the streets, and it was a kind of comfort to revert to traditional Asian monikers. Now the terror has ended, Theresa Wai Ching, Clara Wai Mui and Mary Wai Choy go mostly by their English names again to suit their Western clothes. Tak Lau takes the opportunity to reinvent himself too: he uses Francis now.

It's a new era, a new life. Hong Kong is recovering at an astonishing pace now the free market is open again. But the reprieve from loss is short-lived for the Wu Hu Street Kwas.

Francis is eleven when word finds its way into number 183 from a local market, past the old bunker and rebuilt homes, through the front door and up the stairs; eighteen-year-old Elder Brother is in hospital.

By the time Ng Yuk arrives at his bedside, the doctors tell her there is nothing to be done. Her eyes and heart hollow, she cradles her boy. 'It will be alright, it will be alright.' She blankets him in her sorrow and rocks him in her grief. 'Father waits for you. Brothers and sisters wait for you – the triplets and the sisters you never met. You'll join Kwa on the other side, my boy. I will see you there too one day.'

Elder Brother dies in her arms, blood dribbling from his mouth. He had been unconscious for hours. His insides were shredded by broken glass in a bowl of noodles, the doctors tell Ng Yuk. Intestinal injuries, terrible suffering, a fever above forty-three.

Francis is at home by a window, holding his knees against his small chest, waiting and pining for Elder Brother, the favourite of all his siblings, his idol and confidant. But their mother returns alone, her cracked voice breaking the news although her tears and bloodied blouse already tell the story.

Francis runs from the house and keeps going into the darkness, flying down Wu Hu Street, not stopping until he reaches the Whampoa Dock and the houses he ransacked at the end of the war. The international port is fully operational again, as though nothing happened. Cranes are lifting cargo from vessels at the wharf, while teams of men dig and build, working around the clock to make Kowloon not only restored but bigger, better and stronger after the great darkness.

Ghosts rise up and chase Francis home.

Despite all the death Francis has witnessed, Ng Yuk tells him that he is too young to attend Elder Brother's funeral. She needs her servants with her today, so Francis must care for Mary. He knows better than to argue with his mother, particularly at a time of bereavement.

Francis watched the meagre family procession carry his father's casket past his home and down the hill to a crematorium. Now he will watch his brother's funeral procession go by.

Before the family leaves to attend Elder Brother's open casket, Francis crouches on the floor of his room and peers through a keyhole to get a good view of preparations. Theresa brushes Clara's hair; a maid smooths Ng Yuk's coat and takes her arm.

An hour later, Mary has fallen asleep and Francis watches alone as the closed coffin, draped in religious silks and embroidered fabric from Swatow Lace, wends its way down the hill on the shoulders of uncles and cousins.

Theresa looks up from the procession and sees Francis's tiny face at the window. She runs up the road and takes the stairs, two at a time. Her little brother is still fixated on the procession when she slips into the room and places her hand gently on his shoulder, breaking a spell. He turns towards his sister and flings his arms around her neck, sobbing and longing for the sadness, which has stretched out over years, to end. She holds him close.

PEBBLES AND CANE

EACH MORNING, SIXTEEN-YEAR-OLD THERESA WAKES UP IN her room in her family home on Wu Hu Street, just as she has done for most of her life. It is bigger now the false wall is gone, and she is no longer sharing with Clara. Theresa has gone through a metamorphosis, and so has Hong Kong – now they are both spreading their wings to fly.

Change happens quickly. There's already a new metal street sign at the end of Wu Hu, in English letters with Chinese characters below. Local sign factories are inundated with lists of street and building names to reinstate as well as neon and hand-painted signs. This is just one small part of the work to do to start again, but Hong Kong's survivors are ready.

Theresa and her family are among the 600,000 residents remaining. During the occupation, hundreds of thousands of refugees fled or were forced over the border to China. At least ten thousand Hong Kong locals were arbitrarily executed, while hundreds of expats died in camps. Now, finally, there's no risk of being shot dead for crossing a road or looking the wrong way, or just for being there. Although with such horrific memories comes lingering pain.

On 30 September 1946, General Takashi Sakai is executed in China by a firing squad on charges of war crimes committed when he led the invasion and served as Hong Kong's governor at the start of the occupation. The man who presided over the beginning of the terror is dead, a clear message that Hong Kong's dark days are over.

With characteristic determination and industriousness, Chinese citizens resuscitate hospitals, businesses and schools. Expats and refugees trickle back, and some of the freed civilian POWs return to their Hong Kong homes. Optimism resurfaces and, on the face of it, the colony is the picture of post-war resilience as the world dusts itself off from the trauma of conflict.

Theresa is still working at the factory with Uncle Eng Lee. Now that Ying Kam and Elder Brother are dead, the lion's share of responsibility to provide for Third Wife's part of the family has fallen to her.

The death of their father has further separated Happy Shadow and Ng Yuk's broods, along with the women themselves. Their estimation of each other has never been outstanding; now they are widows, there is barely even a sense of obligation between them.

House of Kwa moves into a new phase of survival, splintering again from the top of the tree.

Theresa has become as invaluable to Swatow Lace as she was to Japanese meetings with Hong Kong Brits. She stays in contact with some of the captives who survived, and they are still grateful for her diplomacy in the meetings they were forced to attend during the occupation. She had a knack of making confrontational content gracious in translation. No one can be sure she translated everything accurately, but she kept the peace and may have saved their skin. Gratitude comes from high places and Theresa attends multicultural academic and diplomatic events. Soon Clara is old enough to come as her guest.

'You can't dress like that!' Ng Yuk shrieks. 'What will people think of us?' She watches her two oldest girls brazenly head out the door in high heels and Western outfits, stunning young women turning heads wherever they go.

Although Ng Yuk is cross, she knows that Theresa always holds Clara tightly under her wing. No harm will ever come to her siblings – she'll see to that.

Theresa's unwavering loyalty to House of Kwa gives Ng Yuk a silvery glimmer of hope to line the cloud of smoke that hangs above her. She rests her cigarette at the edge of a speckled brown ashtray and exhales, a mother dragon releasing her fledglings.

Today, Clara is on a date with a British policeman, so at Government House, Theresa swans through the gates alone. It's a strictly guest-list only affair and she shows her identification to two guards at a sentry box. They check it against their list even though they remember her from last time – no one forgets Theresa.

Her participation as a junior interlocutor under the Japanese has won her an invitation to tea from the reinstated administration. Three hundred or so guests congregate in the ballroom, all of them invited here as an acknowledgement of their various civilian efforts during the dark days of occupation. The building was significantly renovated by the Japanese into a hybrid of oriental and neoclassical design: one of many marks left by the enemy that will never be erased.

There are speeches from dignitaries about the honour and valour of resistance but also of the need to collaborate when there is no other option.

While the crowd applauds, Theresa turns and locks eyes with a young Englishman. He's about twenty-five and quite handsome.

After the formalities he walks over to greet her. 'How do you do? Jolly terrible business you lot have been through. What brings you to Government House?'

Theresa curtsies, and they have an animated conversation during which she mentions, 'I am most keen to improve my English pronunciation.'

He replies that her good looks and command of three languages should already be enough to ingratiate her to princes and paupers, but he agrees to introduce her to a man in the crowd who may be able to help: a professor of linguistics and self-proclaimed master of elocution.

Theresa begins weekly visits to the professor's home in the affluent Mid-Levels, located between the coveted Peak and central business district. '*How* n-*ow* said the br-*ow*-n c-*ow*.' She is a good student, making steady progress.

One day the professor holds out his hand to reveal a rather extraordinary elocution tool. In his palm are half a dozen small stones. 'The pebbles of Demosthenes, the greatest orator in all of ancient Greece.'

Theresa is puzzled. What is she to do with these stones? And what does the greatest orator in all of ancient Greece have to do with her?

'Put them in your mouth and they will help you to prrrrrronounce yourrrr Rrrrrrs.' The professor makes a flourish with his hand.

Theresa is dubious. *Surely he doesn't actually expect me to put them in my mouth.*

The professor embarks on a tale. He often tells stories to illustrate a point; they are usually too long for Theresa's liking, but she is always too polite to say so. This one is about a young man in Athens with a speech impediment who used stones to make him force out the sounds. 'It improved his speech,' the professor concludes.

Theresa acquiesces and does as told. 'Around the rugged rocks the ragged rascal rrrrrran,' she repeats after her tutor. The stones rattle around uncomfortably against her teeth and tongue, and she has to be careful not to swallow one or choke.

She wonders if this is such a good idea after all. The professor tells her that as well as using the pebbles, Demosthenes ran along a beach, shouting over the roar of the waves in order to improve his projection. Theresa would much prefer a beach to these stones. For all the practice she does, as soon as she removes the pebbles her Rs – or lack thereof – are back to normal. *I can hardly walk about with stones in my mouth all day,* she thinks. *How silly.*

Theresa is determined not to allow shortcomings in the elocution department to hold her back. Grace, charm and diplomacy are her strongest personal attributes, so she embraces her beauty and hones her social smarts; she learns how to use her best qualities to 'really go places', as she likes to put it. The curse that relegated her to hiding for much of the occupation is fast becoming a guiding gift. The pageant of Theresa's life is about to begin.

For Francis, the next few years are a combination of study and part-time work. He is trying to catch up on missing four years of formal education. The post-war population has more than tripled, and school places are in hot demand. Francis was expelled from St Mary's due to poor grades; because of his age and size they made him skip the years he missed, as if war was no excuse for having fallen behind.

'What is this?' Mother waves a report card at Francis, who is now in his teens. 'Ds and Fs. Are you trying to ruin us?!' La Salle College only took him on after First Brother from First Mother Lotus Flower moved to Hong Kong and condensed years of academics into a few intense months of private tutoring. Theresa also wrote to the school with glowing accounts of Francis's war effort, working for extra rations, and the family pedigree. Ng Yuk slaps his face. 'Where's my cane?' she screams at a maid. 'Get me my cane.'

Since Ying Kam died, Ng Yuk has had to take on dishing out discipline. Francis shakes but doesn't cry as the wooden cane cuts the palm of his hand.

A dragon stirs within him. He has learned foreign languages, collaborated with an enemy, worked and supported his family, lived through war and deprivation – all to be humiliated with another caning from his mother for bad grades. His class is crammed with new migrants, and they sit in the seats of the dead or deported, and study in halls where atrocities occurred.

Francis does something he has never done before. He hits his mother back, swift and sharp. It happens so fast that she topples over, her tiny feet sliding out from under her slight frame. She holds her red face in her hand, looking up at her son from the kitchen floor. In an instant he is gone, running to Whampoa Dock, to the sea, wishing himself far away.

Back home, Francis packs his bags. Kai Tak Airport is only a few kilometres from Wu Hu Street, and he has money saved, enough for a ticket somewhere, anywhere. He doesn't really have a plan, but he catches a rickshaw to the airport regardless.

Clara witnessed the whole commotion – Mother at it again. But Fifth Sister has never seen Francis so upset. She follows him at a distance and takes a rickshaw of her own. Dark skin and sweat; the spin of bicycle and carriage wheels; skinny legs, sinew and muscle.

Two siblings sit side by side on a bench, the sign 'Kai Tak International' behind them. They are silent for a while and, when Clara finally speaks, Francis is brought round to the impracticality of his mission. She persuades him to come home.

The two share a rickshaw back to 183 Wu Hu Street. The driver has to get off his bicycle to push the weight of his passengers up the hills.

Ng Yuk has been waiting anxiously and is relieved when Francis walks past her, without acknowledgement, as she sits smoking in the kitchen. They never speak of what happened, and she never hits him again.

PLANES AND PAPARAZZI

Candidates must be between twenty-one and twenty-seven years old, well proportioned and pleasant to the eye. Vision must not be impaired. Conversational in English. Hold a British passport. No coloured nail varnish to be worn to the interview. Hair must be natural colour. Extreme fashion should be avoided. It is regretted that no reason can be given for rejecting an application.

Theresa finishes reading aloud the glossy three-colour leaflet, then grins and waves it excitedly at her sisters. She is twenty-one, only just able to apply. 'Clara, Mary! This is our chance, sisters. This is our opportunity to really go places. If I can get in, when you're old enough I can help you do it too!'

In the golden age of flying, air hostesses have one of the most glamorous jobs in the world, in the same league as actresses and models – and the prestigious international airline British Overseas Airways Corporation, known as BOAC, is in town for its first Hong Kong recruitment drive. Hundreds of excited young women in the colony are busily getting ready as Theresa unfurls rollers from her hair. She sprays the curls in place and pins an unruly clump behind her ear.

Ng Yuk scolds her as she leaves. 'Western clothes, no good. If you wish to be respected, you should wear your cheongsam.'

Theresa gives her mother a wistful smile; she is not going to let Ng Yuk get her down today.

When she arrives, the queue seems endless. Young ladies of Chinese and British descent are waiting mostly in shift dresses or tailored suits, though some do wear traditional attire. Most will be scrutinised, interrogated and turned away, with only a lucky few to be corralled into a second waiting area, asked to fill in additional forms and come back in a couple of days for the next round. Theresa joins the line stretching around the block.

Although she holds herself with a confidence and poise beyond her years, today Theresa is anxious. This could be her big break, and she doesn't want to blow it. She has prepared written references from a few friends in high places, the professor for one. Oh, how she wishes she had practised her Rs more. What will the panel think of her speech?

The queue moves as one by one candidates reach a registration desk, handing over their applications to an officious and immaculate woman in a BOAC uniform. She is wearing glasses – so she mustn't be an air hostess, thinks Theresa, as the pamphlet stipulates 'perfect vision'.

Nervous girls file into the first room to wait for their names to be called. There aren't enough chairs for everyone, so most of the hopefuls stand, speaking in low voices, trying to pass the time and muster their courage. Everyone weighs up the competition. A couple of older blonde candidates snicker under their breath at the other contenders. 'Just look at her nose. She'll never get in.' They are striking and overly confident they'll take home the prize. It is very much like being behind the scenes of a beauty pageant: an intimidating environment for the uninitiated.

'Theresa Kwa.' A uniformed woman emerges with a clipboard. 'Theresa Kwa,' she repeats, looking around at the assembled women.

Soon Theresa is standing at the centre of a carpeted room before three adjudicators seated in gilt armchairs behind a long table. It's like an audition but no singing or dancing is required. The two men and one woman are in their forties. They are not in uniform, instead elegantly suited, their expressions giving little away. They assess Theresa's every move and take notes as she answers their questions. She has no idea how she is going.

'A very impressive list of references, Miss Kwa,' one panellist says.

'Yes, I love meeting new people. I find it easy to make conversation with strangers. We have an expression in Chinese: *Chen mo shi jin*. It's a bit like your own King James Bible expression: "a fool's voice is known by a multitude of words". Meaning that it is better to be a good listener than a good talker.' Theresa pauses. 'Although I'm also a good talker,' she quickly adds. *Keep smiling, keep smiling*, she thinks.

The panellists smile back.

Theresa runs in through the front door. A maid is cooking rice on the stove, Ng Yuk is reading a Chinese newspaper, and Francis is studying at the dining table.

'They want to see me again! Mary, Clara, come, come.' The girls come out to greet their elder sister, their eyes wide with excitement.

Ng Yuk goes back to her paper, pretending to read. 'What will they pay you?' It's the first sign of interest she's shown for the idea.

'Mama! It will pay to support you and the family. It is more than enough. We need to pray they will choose me. They have selected forty of us to go back again, but they will only choose six from that group.'

The family gets out the joss sticks and gives them a workout. Kwa ancestors and gods look up from their mahjong games, listening intently.

The BOAC board agrees unanimously on hiring Theresa. She will be the world's first Chinese BOAC hostess. Having been born in a British colony, she has the same advantage of a homeland passport as the other five successful candidates, all from English expat families. The new recruits look forward to becoming firm friends while they crew long-haul flights together for the rich, powerful and famous. 'It's not all glamour, you know,' they are informed. 'There will be British boarding-school students returning home between terms, as well as household servants following their employers.' But to the inductees, those things are hardly a downside. There is no downside! They are going to be air hostesses, which is more than most mid-twentieth-century girls could ever dare to dream.

There are endless safety and security drills to learn, along with ranks and titles, and what one may and may not say or suggest. Finally, the day arrives for the most important training component of all: hair and make-up! The women cheer. It's time for Elizabeth Arden. A crack team of professionals give step-by-step instructions on how to achieve an approved list of styles – well, not just achieve them, *own* them. The young women savour every moment. When Theresa has her first high-end haircut, she's on cloud nine and may never come down.

Not long into the job, Theresa becomes BOAC's Hong Kong pin-up girl. She poses holding a basket of fruit, looking like a movie star on billboards and buses. She feels like one.

It's the era of aviation glamour and sophistication, and Theresa Kwa is at the centre of it. She struts through airports in capitals around the world, she and her gang of crew members walking behind their captain. People stare at the immaculate group as Theresa holds her head high, her smile dazzling, broad and deeply satisfied. The world is her oyster, and she is bringing home more money than she could ever have hoped for. It covers her siblings' schooling and her mother's cigarettes.

It pays for the maids. Theresa buys a car and adds a driver, and Ng Yuk stops selling off her jewellery.

Theresa crews flights of fifteen passengers at full capacity, bringing them drinks and engaging in polite conversation. During the many hours spent confined with them, she befriends some of the world's most powerful and interesting people.

Her sincerity wins over even the most austere guests. Across miles and miles, Theresa smiles and smiles. Her travellers cannot help but be intrigued by her beauty and gentle, familiar manner that puts everyone at ease. She is both diplomat and counsellor to her frequent flyers: lords and ladies, prime ministers and their wives. Queen Elizabeth II invites Theresa to a garden party at Buckingham Palace.

One passenger, Hilton, is a blue-blooded aristocrat and the first of Theresa's many suitors. He falls for her at first sight, mesmerised by her casual charm and impressed with her worldly knowledge. He wants to make her his bride. They attend fabulous events in London, and she meets his family, who immediately disapprove of him courting a foreign 'chink'. They not-so-secretly hope it will come to nothing and that Hilton will meet a local – white, blue-blooded – girl. He ignores them and continues to write to Theresa when they are apart, hanging on to the happy memories they have created. He is chivalrous and wouldn't dream of overstepping the mark with his oriental sweetheart, but he is growing impatient, hoping that she might reciprocate his love with the same level of intensity.

Theresa, on the other hand, is relishing her unprecedented access to the world and enjoying her global citizenship. Moreover, she is acutely aware of BOAC's requirement that its air hostesses remain unmarried: to wed would be to give up her coveted position with the carrier, and she is not about to do that. She has seen death and destruction firsthand – freedom and family are her number one priorities.

My dear Hilton, she writes. *If only our worlds aligned. I am deeply sorry, I am not ready for a life of marriage. Besides, there are far more worthy contenders than me for your hand. With much love, Theresa xxx*

Hilton is the first in a string of broken-hearted eligible bachelors who vie for Theresa's affections. By now she has moved from Hung Hom to the Island side of Hong Kong, purchasing her own apartment at Peace Mansion on Tai Hang Road, just above Causeway Bay.

One day a German magnate pays a visit, accompanied by his security detail in a convoy of vehicles winding its way up Theresa's narrow street. Her cook just about has a heart attack when she pulls the curtain aside to see the visitors. Paparazzi follow the train of cars up the hill. Once the cook realises they are not *all* coming in for tea, she heaves a sigh of relief.

The German gentleman, Jacobsmuhlen, is good company, and Theresa is flattered by his attention and fond of him. A photo of them together on his yacht appears in newspapers around the world, as he is a well-known eligible bachelor. 'Who is that girl?' the press wonder, but they don't get another opportunity to find out. Theresa is not interested in living through a European winter. Her answer to Jacobsmuhlen is a tactful no.

Theresa throws everything into her career, graciously declining multiple proposals of marriage. Clara has been in a courtship with a British police chief in Hong Kong ever since Theresa introduced them. Mary has no interest in having a boyfriend just yet and longs to follow in Theresa's footsteps in the air one day.

When Theresa is home in Hong Kong, she keeps a watchful eye on Francis. She is as invested in his future as she is in her sisters', and scolds him if he fails an exam. Despite her misgivings, she will keep paying for his education. She will never give up on him, for he is Kwa.

SHIP AND SHOES

THERESA HUMS THE DORIS DAY SONG 'QUE SERA, SERA' TO Francis as she drives him in stifling heat to the dock amid Hong Kong's famous sensory assault of crowds, signage, buses, trams and beggars. The usual peacetime streetscape scene, with its tapestry of activity, is a welcome sight. Bleak years are far behind them, and an optimistic hustle and bustle has replaced hunched shoulders and emaciated faces. How far the Kwas have come.

Theresa has squirrelled away enough money to send Francis abroad to study. There are Kwa half-siblings and cousins in Germany, Canada and England now, some even earning their doctorates. This would be enough to make a Chinese tiger mother proud, although that is not Theresa's style: she is only keen for Francis to improve his chances, since he has graduated from high school, thanks to even more intervention from First Brother. His college prospects are, thankfully, good – Canada was a little expensive, but Australia affordable enough, particularly outside its capital cities, and its proximity to Hong Kong means Theresa can keep an eye on her little brother. He will have room to spread his wings and establish some independence, while she watches over him from afar.

'Make sure you *always* use your manners and *always* speak English,' Theresa emphasises, speaking in Cantonese.

At the dock she pulls over and winds down her window before saying something charming to a bewildered parking attendant, who opens the manual boom gate and lets her through. She winks at her brother and does her signature double-click *tut-tut* sound with a shoulder wiggle to go with it – a little 'aren't I the cat's pyjamas?' performance. She grins and Francis grins back. He is twenty-one, excited and nervous about the voyage ahead.

There couldn't be a more perfect degree waiting for Francis in Australia: he is off to study Mechanical Engineering. He has not only had a keen interest in this subject since he could crawl, but he has also witnessed Hong Kong's structural resurrection. His fascination with tools has only grown since he worked at the blacksmith shop and cleaned weapons for the Japanese; he seizes any opportunity to examine and pull things apart – from cars, bicycles, and mowers to clocks, calculators and kerosene lamps – to see what makes them tick.

When Theresa and Francis get out of the car, they are distracted by a commotion near the boom gate. Vehicles are banking up as they try to enter the carpark set aside for officials, dignitaries and, evidently, Theresa. A driver is arguing loudly with the parking attendant, insisting he be allowed to bring his important passenger closer to the vessel.

'Such very bad behaviour,' Theresa says in Cantonese, shaking her head. Then she winks and does her cat's pyjamas routine again. 'Smooth, smooth,' she says in English. 'Never lose your temper. Always stay smooth.'

Theresa makes light of the farewell with her brother, hiding her deep concern for him. Francis doesn't notice; he is not at all sentimental. As he gives his sister a stiff hug, his mind is already south of the Pacific. He is off to teach Australia a thing or two. He knows he could also teach his sisters a thing or two but is wise to keep that to himself.

Theresa has worked hard for Francis's fare and two years' tuition. He is not travelling first class, as she deemed this unnecessarily expensive, but she has also given him a thousand pounds in cash to last him the twenty-four months to the end of his course. He has this excessive sum in a pouch around his waist, and he boards the vessel with only that, a small case and the clothes on his back. He waves to Theresa, then walks up the gangway and steps out of Hong Kong. He is leaving home for the first time.

Aboard the ship, Francis's friendly disposition and adaptable traits work well for him. What he considers to be a healthy amount of civil disobedience – his rebellious streak, which Theresa has tried hard to quell – is lauded here among these passengers. Nevertheless, word that he's not really 'one of them' circulates.

'He isn't on the Australian government scholarship migration scheme.'

'Well, if he isn't on the program like the rest of us, he must be rich.'

Four weeks later, on Boxing Day 1954, the great ship docks in Brisbane, and one crew member, who has been watching Francis with particular interest, follows him down the gangway.

Water has been in short supply, rationed for drinking and cooking, so onboard showers are a luxury reserved only for those in first class. Francis and a group of his fellow passengers head straight for a YMCA for their first shower in over a month. Relishing the water flowing over his skin, he neglects to notice a hand reaching above the curtain and sliding his money pouch off the rail. The rushing of water and happy chatter mask the sound of a thief running out.

Francis had diligently kept the pouch on him at all times, day and night, around his waist or strapped to his hand under his pillow as he slept; he fiercely protected the cash intended to feed and clothe him for two entire years. So as he steps out of the shower and finds the precious money gone, panic sets in.

He looks left and right in a fractured blur. *This cannot be happening*, he thinks. Other men in the change room seem oblivious, while Francis feels as though his whole life is crumbling around him. He flings aside a row of shower curtains, screaming in Cantonese, 'Where is it?' Then, in English, 'Bag? Bag?' He pushes people, overturning and rummaging through belongings, before collapsing on the tiles, screaming. A man slaps him across the face, returning him to his senses, and he discovers his shoes are also missing.

He pulls on his clothes and returns to the vessel, barefoot. They set sail for Melbourne, and Francis notices a white Australian crew member wearing his shoes; they are unmistakably his – light-brown stitched leather, an expensively custom-made gift from Theresa. Francis rants in Cantonese and raves in English, embarrassing the sailor into returning the footwear before his captain hears the commotion. This is one small consolation for Francis, but the money is never forthcoming and the culprit never identified. He spends the rest of the trip eyeing everyone on board with suspicion, keeping to himself and falling asleep with his hand under his pillow where the pouch used to be.

This incident nags at Francis. Perhaps it always will. Coming into that sort of cash would be life-changing. Losing it is too. Everything changed for Francis that day.

Life has buffeted him every inch of the way to this point, but there has always been a Kwa to bring him in from the storm. Not now.

On the surface, he displays the resilience of the little boy in Hong Kong who bore witness to war crimes and their aftermath. He had been full of optimism for his new life abroad, only to be humiliated before it had a chance to begin. When Ng Yuk would bring a cane down on his open palm for the hundredth time, Francis would make sure it was his last humiliation at his mother's hand.

He vows that the theft of his life savings – or, more accurately, Theresa's – is the last time he'll be shamed by anyone.

As the ship docks in Melbourne, Francis has shoes on his feet but empty pockets. He's a different person to the young man he left in Hong Kong. There has been a coming of age, and walking down the gangway Francis has determination in his eyes. He sets his sights on survival – not for the first time – as he steps onto land and enters a different kind of war.

SPIT AND LAUNDRY

THE COLLEGE FRANCIS IS TO ATTEND, THE GORDON INSTITUTE, is about two hours from Melbourne by road, in the portside town of Geelong. He can't buy a train or bus fare, and there are no rickshaws here; he may need to resort to hitchhiking. Although he's never done such a thing before, he has seen it in the movies. How he misses Hong Kong, where he could simply run after a moving tram, grab the rail, fling himself inside and travel for free. Melbourne is already beginning to feel inhospitable.

Francis makes his way to an information booth. Fortunately, Australia is less foreign to him than it would be to a mainland Chinese person, given that for most of his upbringing Hong Kong has been part of the British Empire. In both places, cars drive on the left, police have batons not guns, street signs are in English and civic order appears intact. But Melbourne seems awfully quiet, less bustling than Hong Kong, with a lack of urgency and purpose.

The woman at the information desk is chatting to a scruffy dustman or other menial worker, or so it seems to Francis. He puffs out his chest – still, he receives no attention. The woman keeps chatting, and Francis looks down at the information sign on the front of the booth. It's on its last screw, so he bends to examine it. He looks behind and around it, assessing the situation, then takes a toothpick from his pocket. He considers the thin wire that he used to fix his suitcase handle when it became loose on the ship, and unwinds some of it, bending it back and forth until it snaps. He twists the wire around the toothpick, coiling it tightly, and lines up the newly fashioned screw with the hole in the sign and the hole in the booth. He twists, and the thread of the wire-toothpick-screw grips perfectly. Voila! (A term he has heard Theresa use.) The sign sits straight again.

Francis is pleased and stands up. 'Your sign.'

'YES, DEAR?' the information woman shouts. Does she think he is deaf? 'DO YOU KNOW ENGLISH? LITTLE BITTY THE ENGLISH.'

'Gee-long,' he says, more as a statement than a question. He hasn't mastered English, despite Theresa's insistence.

'GEE-LONG,' the woman mimics at triple the decibels. 'BUS NUMBER FORTY-SIX. OVER THERE.' She points to a bus stand. 'That takes you to the city and then you need BUS NUMBER NINETY. They go twice a day. You've missed the early ninety-nine so you'll have a TWO-HOUR wait in the city. TWO-HOUR WAITY. OKAY?'

Francis doesn't understand a thing she is saying. 'Map,' he says. 'Please,' he adds, remembering his sister's instruction to be polite.

'OKAY. A MAP OF MELBOURNE OR A MAP OF VICTORIA, DEAR?'

'Gee-long.'

'OKAY. HERE YOU ARE. I'LL GIVE YOU BOTH.' She hands him a parcel of folded green paper and turns back to her conversation with the dishevelled dustbin man. 'Those Chinese,' she says, rolling her eyes, 'don't any of them have a word of English? They all come here to take our jobs, and they don't even know where Geelong is.'

The White Australia Policy laws are slowly being chipped away. Until recently, migrants other than Europeans have been mostly barred from coming into the country in order to eliminate the threat of 'cheap Chinese labour'. Francis doesn't yet know what an oddity he is.

He gently tugs at the sign to test his handiwork before walking towards the number forty-six bus stop.

'Sorry, matey, no money, no ticket. No ticket, no comey on the bussy, see.' A conductor speaks to Francis in a slightly quieter tone than the information lady.

'Money, stolen, thief,' Francis offers, pulling his pockets inside out to illustrate.

The conductor steps into the bus and speaks to the driver, who looks down from behind the wheel at Francis. He shakes his head. 'Sorry, mate,' says the conductor, a little less condescendingly this time. 'We're not a charity, mate, and we can't just let people on without paying even if they have no money.' Then, in a dramatically ironic statement, 'There's a phone booth over there. Go and call someone to pick you up.'

Francis watches the bus pull away.

Hitchhiking isn't all that bad. It's free and adventurous. Francis deciphers the map – which is easy for him to do, being such a visual person – and works out a direct route to Geelong. Cars speed past, and people lean out windows with advice like 'Go home, chink.'

Eventually a middle-aged couple approach in their Ford. They can tell from the man's clothes and the awkward way he stands by the road – arm rigid and thumb out in a Hollywood imitation of hitchhiking – that he is probably educated and definitely harmless. They slow down to rest beside him and ask where he is headed. The couple are well travelled, one a lecturer in antipodean history and the other a schoolteacher. It's Francis's lucky day.

Three hitched rides and five hours later, Francis arrives in Geelong. He steps down from a truck cab, his 'thank you, sir' barely audible over the engine's roar. He swings shut the door, using all his might, and watches the truck pull away from the kerb. It's late and all the shops are shut. Alone in the centre of Geelong, Francis surveys the deserted country town.

Francis completed a semester at Hong Kong Technical College before he left, and summer holiday bridging classes will commence at the Gordon Institute in a week, so he has little time to find suitable accommodation, let alone settle into the 'Australian way of life'. Acclimatising to this environment is an overwhelming proposition – language and cultural differences will surely take years to manage – but Francis is practical. As he stands in the middle of sleepy Geelong, he prioritises his basic needs just as he once did under the Japanese: food and shelter.

He wanders the quiet streets looking for a sign. Not a sign to mend, by the way, although if one was broken, no doubt he'd fix it. He examines the buildings he passes, muttering to himself that they would be far more structurally sound had he project-managed their creation. Years of watching Hong Kong rebuild have given him a high degree of confidence in his limited skill set. He runs a palm along walls and up posts, tapping and examining, exploring the town's constitutional integrity like a doctor listening to a pulse.

Geelong's population is in the tens of thousands compared to Hong Kong's two and a half million. However, Theresa thought Francis might feel at home in Geelong because they are both textile and manufacturing hubs by the sea. The Australian town, just like Hong Kong, has experienced a depression-driven economic slowdown followed by strong post-war growth. But Francis finds it hard to believe he has arrived at a prosperous time – to him, there is no hint of it. Unlike in Hong Kong, where everything stays open until late into the night, in Geelong almost everything is shut by six.

Francis imagines a tumbleweed blowing along the centre of the street like in the American Western movies he enjoys so much.

Distant talking and laughing grows louder as Francis turns a corner to see a neat row of restaurants and a cinema: exciting signs of life. One dining venue is called a 'Chinese' restaurant, which is perfect because he is hungry. He expects he can wash dishes in return for dinner, like in the movies. Perhaps the owners even speak Cantonese.

Half a dozen men and women walk past. 'Go back to your own country,' one man says, spitting on the ground.

'Bloody chink,' says another, and they disappear around a corner.

Francis swings the restaurant door open, letting the warmth and appetising scents envelop him. A laughing-eyed Chinese woman greets him in Cantonese and introduces herself as Mrs Chew, the restaurant owner. The kindly woman takes him in and feeds him on this first night. The spicy noodles are hot and delicious. Careful not to spill anything on the white tablecloth, he watches the steam from his bowl rise up against a red wallpaper backdrop patterned with roses.

It turns out that as well as a restaurant, Mrs Chew owns a Chinese laundromat. He can start there in the morning.

'Why should we pay for you to go to school? Go back where you came from, bloody chogie.'

It is a daily obstacle course of torment. Francis must circumnavigate ignorance, outrun resentment, skirt spite, hurdle hatred, shot-put cynicism, scale scourge, bounce belligerence. He likes to think of it in these terms taken from the English dictionary he studies every night – a word Olympics. Somehow the sport references make him feel as though he's 'going for gold'. Each time he gets over the finish line unscathed, unbruised and unaffected, he can chalk up one more day of survival in this foreign promised land.

Kwa tenacity and resilience help keep his spirits high. And he hasn't forgotten his vow not to be taken advantage of again, which makes some Geelong attitudes all the more challenging.

Mahjong-playing ancestors and gods watch over Francis, pleased that things are beginning to work out for him. He increases his workload to a double degree, with Mechanical and Electrical Engineering the perfect streams for his interests. Over the next two years he studies hard, and he supports himself by working at Mrs Chew's laundry; he delivers clean, pressed linen and towels on a pushbike to local hotels and elite private houses.

He still can't admit to Theresa that he lost her money in a YMCA shower and writes to her irregularly, omitting key facts. He never mentions supporting himself or the racist remarks directed at him whenever he leaves his dormitory – he writes only of study and scenery.

Francis has had a string of girlfriends and, to the fury of the local white men, they have all been young local white women. He has assimilated by behaving like a white man courting their own, and the girls appreciate his handsome face and charming, funny demeanour. They like the way he shrugs off cynical and racist remarks by retaliating with self-deprecating humour, and that he is never afraid to dance. He's a refreshing alternative to the macho jocks, but his popularity with the ladies comes at a cost: the white men are out for blood.

'You slope heads come and take our jobs and steal our women, you bastard Chinaman.'

Francis is escorting his girlfriend Anne towards the Geelong Town Hall for a biannual dance. He ignores the angry man shouting at him.

'I said, you bloody chinks come in and take our jobs and our girls. Go back to where you came from, bastard.' Angry Man is with two other men who don't look quite so sure, but they jeer their support anyway.

'Now, now,' says Francis. 'Look, I do not come to take your job or your women.' He straightens his posture to prepare for his next comment. 'If you're not smart enough to keep your job or your women, then that's your problem.'

Angry Man runs up the steps and pushes Francis against the stone wall.

Francis can tell the man has been drinking alcohol. 'Mate, mate, mate.' Francis uses his best Australian English.

But it's too late — Angry Man is punching him in the stomach. Anne screams.

Other couples on their way into the dance appear reluctant to intervene, until finally a few men step in and break up the one-sided brawl. As they pull the aggressor away, Francis brushes himself down and straightens his bow tie, taking Anne's hand to lead her up the remainder of the stairs.

Angry Man stands with his companions and glares up at the couple. Francis shakes with humiliation and rage. Adrenalin courses through his body. He raises his fist and wags a finger violently at the men. 'And don't you come back,' he manages to say before disappearing inside with Anne on his arm.

Francis and Anne are smitten with one another. *Anne is*, Francis writes to Theresa, *my first true love.*

Anne leaves Geelong to further her studies in Melbourne, and Francis follows her to find a job as an apprentice electrical engineer. He joins a choir in the gentrified, leafy south-eastern suburb of Malvern, where he rents a house with a student and a young architect. 'Only one number away from Toorak,' he says, referring to the postcode being a digit off the most sought-after suburb in the state.

With her airline career in full swing, Theresa is looking for a permanent helper. Although most domestic help hails from the mainland, following the advice of a friend, she takes on a girl called Brigit to be her maid. Brigit is fifteen and — like many tens of thousands of Filipina girls who will eventually walk a similar path – is in desperate need of work. She has three sisters, two brothers and a mother back home to support, and, ahead of her time, she is farmed out by an agency that hawks human labour between countries, and will, decades later, lead the Filipino Labor Code charge to place girls from the Philippines with wealthy Chinese families in Hong Kong and across South-East Asia. Filipina maids go to the Middle East as well, but nowhere will the throng of them be so obvious than in this British colony.

Every Sunday the square outside St Joseph's Cathedral in Central heaves with domestic helpers. Maids live with their employers and are expected to be of service twenty-four hours a day. One day, the Hong Kong government will rule that domestic workers must be given twelve consecutive hours off per week, which will mean that on Sundays the maids of Hong Kong are entitled to just be girls, women and friends – free for a little while, to giggle over idle gossip, compare lives, show off trinkets, and talk about how their masters treat and pay them. With all their money going home to loved ones, they cannot afford to visit the pictures or restaurants, so whenever they can they congregate to feel less alone and have fun together. They exchange romance novels, play cards and laugh. They cannot afford picnic blankets or even straw mats, so they lay out old newspapers to sit on.

These young women are used to a basic existence and are often forced to sleep in corridors, kitchens and broom cupboards. The lucky ones, like Brigit, have their own room with a television. Brigit considers herself incredibly privileged to have found herself a job in the house of Theresa Kwa.

From the beginning, Theresa takes on Brigit like a guardian would her charge; Brigit is almost like a dutiful daughter to Theresa – a loyal, enduring servant. At its core their relationship is transactional; in many ways Brigit is part of the family but she is acutely aware of her place. Theresa grooms her as an invaluable asset. In this era in Hong Kong, a successful maid never questions and doesn't argue, but a Filipina usually has a ripe sense of humour and a likeable personality beneath her obsequious exterior. Brigit has both, and she's smart too, able to master the boundaries and perfectly understand the extent to which she can question or tease Theresa in a well-meaning way.

In her spare time, Theresa is an avid painter. Illustrious artists offer her tuition, and she works hard to hone her talent and compose an impressive series of Chinese brush paintings. She is trained by the pre-eminent master Qi Baishi, and international newspapers report on her first overseas exhibition:

Jul. 1959 – Chinese Air Hostess Holds Exhibition Of Her Painting In London. An exhibition of paintings by B.O.A.C. air hostess Miss Theresa Wai Ching Kwa from Hong Kong opened this morning at the Commonwealth Institute, South Kensington.

Theresa takes her work to Leningrad, Vienna, Lisbon, Paris and Rome, the proceeds of sales going directly into her dream to educate the children of House of Kwa.

Mary is still single and finally of an age perfect for BOAC recruitment, so Theresa helps her find a position with the airline.

In airports around the world, the sisters exchange knowing glances as they pass one other with their respective crews. When the two stunning women travel the same leg, they are a sight to behold. Their way with people is enchanting. Passengers are enraptured, especially Tony, a judge, who falls head over heels for Mary. Her laughter lights up a room. She and Tony are an item but don't marry, as she doesn't want to lose her job, flying the BOAC flag for House of Kwa alongside her sister. Mary makes headlines herself, exhibiting her paintings at David Jones World Fair in Sydney, Australia. She wins hearts as she's photographed smiling broadly despite *discovering the shattered glass on her framed pictures upon unpacking them*, as the papers report.

Four years later, Francis steps out onto his own stage at twenty-eight, making his solo singing debut at the Malvern Town Hall. He is accompanied by the Melbourne Symphony Orchestra. The piano comes in, introducing violins, with brass and woodwind instruments soon to follow. He sings 'Moon River' along with 'Autumn Leaves' and a few other favourites, which he records onto a vinyl LP with a photo of a serious and debonair Francis on its sleeve. He sings his heart out, relishing the privilege and honour. It is his heyday.

But his love affair with Anne peters out, and his musical aspirations give way to a travel bug. He plans to see more of Australia, and sets out in an old Ford.

Francis discovers a more vast landscape than he could ever have imagined – infinitely bigger than Hong Kong and immeasurably sparser.

Francis takes his fascination with mechanics, structures and architecture on his bushwalks, marvelling at lofty gum trees and stooping in awe at wildflowers. He admires the cantilever of branches and the mathematical precision of a sprig of yellow bloom. God must have created with rulers and angles on a drawing board. Francis wonders how koalas calculate what weight a bough will take, and as he watches ants build their hills, he imagines Egyptian slaves constructing the pyramids. At the Great Australian Bight, he estimates the voltage of lightning strikes as they hit the horizon. Whenever he can, he thinks of the mathematics behind natural phenomena. This is how Francis Kwa makes sense of the world, and how he feels in control.

The tyres on Francis's Ford turn over the dirt road, leaving clouds of dust in their wake that will settle until the next car passes over the Nullarbor Plain. He visits the Blowholes of Albany and dines in a roadhouse full of rough-looking men. When they call out, 'Go home, ya chink,' he realises he should have gone to dinner with the two friendlier fellows he met at the hostel. The bartender tells the patrons to leave Francis alone; it's more of a well-humoured suggestion than an order, but they shut up and drink their beer. Francis gratefully leaves once he has finished his meal, then runs all the way back to his hostel.

After a few weeks, he arrives in Perth.

NEW KWA

外柔内刚

Mouse on the outside, tiger within
– Chinese idiom

BUSH AND SWAMP

MELA BRYCE IS NINETEEN AND PREGNANT. SHE IS WELL educated with an honours degree, but she 'hears voices' and is sometimes paralysed with paranoia. She is an undiagnosed chronic and severe schizophrenic. I sit in her womb, growing cell upon cell, unaware of anything to come or why I chose her.

My parents met bushwalking. This is the official story: Mela and Francis are walking separately under a blue sky interrupted only by a canopy of eucalyptus leaves. As Francis marvels at cockatoos and kookaburras, he trips over a log. Mela is also in wonder at nature's creation when she sees that a man has stumbled. *Oh dear,* she thinks, *that poor fellow is scrambling under the weight of his backpack.* She helps him up.

The bush rescue leads to a six-week courtship. In the beginning Mela's parents, Thelma and Roger Bryce, are civil to Francis, distantly polite. But then, all too quickly, Mela becomes determined to marry this young Chinese man. It turns out he is thirty-eight – not so young after all.

He drives Thelma and Roger through the suburbs of Perth, showing off his properties to emphasise his eligibility. Technically they aren't really Francis's properties – Theresa has made investments in Perth to 'assist' Francis's independence and to give her an excuse to fly in and check on her younger brother: a block of flats, an apartment here and there. She has also bought a catamaran that is docked on the Swan River. Of all the places in the world she could have made these investments, she chose Perth – a beautiful, rough backwater – because family is family and Kwa is Kwa.

'Look, look.' He gestures excitedly, with one hand on the steering wheel. 'Look, I'm a very rich man!' He breaks into laughter and waves his hand again in the direction of Theresa's block of flats.

Mela sits silently in the back seat, Thelma next to her, and Roger is in the front.

Thelma and Roger feel sick with worry. Mela has broken the news she is pregnant to this man they've just met, a man almost twenty years her senior, and that she plans to marry him. Her parents are heartbroken. She attended an exclusive girls' school and is enrolled at university. This is not the life Thelma and Roger imagined for their daughter. And there is something else: they don't know what to tell Francis about his fiancée's mental state. They themselves don't understand it, and doctors are uncertain about Mela's symptoms and behaviour. For the past four years, Roger and Thelma have simply hoped for the best.

In the car, Thelma looks at her eldest daughter, who is about to wed and have a baby when she seems like only a baby herself, still at university and barely an adult. Mela looks straight ahead, and Francis turns up the radio to fill the awkward silence.

Next on the Kwa portfolio tour is a property by the beach, in Scarborough's Snake Pit, which in the 1950s was a gathering ground for bodgies and widgies to meet over rock 'n' roll. Now, in the 1970s, it is a place for hoons and bikies to meet over burnouts and hard liquor. Roger and Thelma appear alarmed by this location.

Francis pulls over to the kerb, and Mela, Roger and Thelma follow him onto a vast vacant lot of land overgrown with weeds. There's a large fenced-off council swamp with a stormwater drain jutting out into algae-covered water, with a couple of ducks, who seem to have lost their way, paddling on top. Apart from these signs of life, it is a barren wasteland.

'This,' says Francis triumphantly, 'is where we will live.'

Francis and Mela tie the knot. The wedding ceremony takes place at Mela's parents' home in the affluent riverside suburb of Bicton. Despite Roger and Thelma's devastation at their daughter's decision to marry this stranger, they grit their teeth, and they invite only their closest of friends for moral support. They will never fully accept Francis into their family, but they are certainly not about to allow their first grandchild to enter the world illegitimately.

Awkward photos take place against timber-panelled walls, in a home reception atmosphere that is forced and tense, perfectly befitting the shotgun nuptials. Thelma and Roger pose alongside the bride and groom. It is unfashionable to smile, and they don't feel like it anyway.

A photographer ushers the group onto a balcony, where Thelma casts her eyes out at the boats on the Swan River, rocking gently on glass-like water. She glances at her nineteen-year-old daughter then back down to the beach where Mela used to play for hours with her brother, Roger, and sister, Zora. A typical Perth girl living an atypical privileged life. Mela would dress up and roller-skate up and down Blackwall Reach Parade at a time of little traffic and unlocked flyscreen doors. Girls' annuals populated her bookshelves, and theatre and ballet attendances punctuated her calendar. But then puberty struck, and day by day the voices became louder, persistent.

Now Mela is studying for her Diploma of Education – post honours – and is pregnant and married.

Tears well in Thelma's eyes. *Maybe the baby will save her*, she thinks.

Having travelled Western Australia extensively while staying in backpacker accommodation and YMCAs, Francis dreams of owning a travellers' retreat. He decides that his arid Scarborough property is the perfect place for one.

After the wedding he and Mela move in together, and he begins building his compound for travellers, right next to the swamp. Inside my mother, my cells form and assemble like construction blocks, while Francis lays the first bricks of his empire. Very quickly his buildings begin to sprawl: one house then another attached, creating a duplex that he can rent out immediately; a huge brick barbecue area – perfect for frog and snail racing when I get there; a shed with a ladder to a roof that connects to a tree, leading down to the swamp – excellent tadpole breeding grounds; another house, this time of weatherboard and asbestos; another shed with a mezzanine floor to double its storage capacity; a flat roof on the original house where he can later build a shed.

'You can never have too much storage.' Francis surveys his growing kingdom. 'It's good metal. It's good wood. It's good things. You never know when we will need it.'

Mela has never lived away from her parents until now. Each night she continues to seek solace with Thelma, if not in person then over the phone. Mela's 'voices' inhabit teachers, fellow students, people in the street. 'Everyone is out to get me, Mama,' she cries. 'They want to kill me!'

Since she was fifteen, Mela has gone through significant mental 'episodes'. Thelma's lack of vitamin D during gestation in bleak London is one reason doctors give for these symptoms.

At sixteen, Mela was diagnosed with manic depression. When she was seventeen, doctors prescribed an electric-shock treatment called ECT: electroconvulsive therapy.

The doctors at Perth's Graylands Psychiatric Hospital insisted Mela must be separated from her parents while she underwent the 'necessary' treatment. She struggled against the grip of two large orderlies, trying to follow her parents out, but the orderlies were strong, and Thelma and Roger left them to it, reassuring each other that this was the right thing to do. Being strapped to a hospital bed then having her brain charged with four hundred volts for six seconds was a terrifying and immobilising experience for Mela. She was still just a girl, and ECT – normally prescribed for depression and schizophrenia – seemed an extreme approach to manic depression. She suffered side effects including nausea, memory loss, headaches, jaw pain and muscle aches.

Two weeks later when the Bryces collected their daughter, they were met by a broken child, worse than when she'd arrived, frightened and desperate. In low and measured tones, doctors spoke of improvements, but her parents saw none and promised never to return Mela to this type of medical care. From now on, they decided, her condition, still undiagnosed, would be contained and managed at home, brushed beneath the carpet.

They don't tell Francis how bad it can get; he will find out in his own time.

I don't want to come out of my mother. Perhaps I know what I'm about to land in.

Mela walks the length of Scarborough Beach, all the way to the Trigg rocks and back, pushing her bare feet into the sand. The autumn breeze skims off the ocean, cooling her face. It's a mild day, but Mela is beginning to sweat. I am a week late. My mother cannot stand it anymore and tries to run, a heavy-footed plod through the coarse granules, her enormous belly rising and falling.

Finally Mela is induced, and at 1 am on 23 May 1974 at King Edward Memorial Hospital, Subiaco, Western Australia, a new Kwa is born.

MOUNTAINS AND VOICES

THERESA HADN'T MADE IT TO MY PARENTS' WEDDING; SHE wasn't told about it until afterwards. Her brother may have forgotten to tell her, but it's more likely he wanted to prevent her from trying to talk him out of it.

The minute she found out, she booked a flight to Perth. When she arrived and saw Mela's very apparent pregnancy – which Francis had neglected to mention – the rushed ceremony suddenly made sense. Theresa then met Thelma and Roger, with whom she had far more in common than the girl her brother had just wed – Mela being twenty-five years Theresa's junior, after all, and the Bryces much closer to her own generation. For her brother's sake, though, Theresa made a concerted effort to bond with his wife.

Theresa no longer works for BOAC. She resigned after falling in love with a man called Tony, who coincidentally shares the same first name as Mary's boyfriend. Tony had opened the Mandarin Oriental Hotel on Hong Kong Island, and Theresa took over the registration of the old family business name, which had closed in 1964, to open her own shop – Swatow Lace – in Tony's hotel. She also designed the bridal suites near the top floor, but she never had the opportunity to use one.

Tony died before they could make things official – for all the many marriage proposals she had attracted over the years, Tony's was the only one she would ever accept. Clara is single too now, she and her husband Donald having divorced, but she is staying in England for their children Josephine, Steven and David's education. And yet not a week goes by without the three Kwa sisters staying in touch.

Now I've arrived, Theresa visits Perth every now and then, always keeping at a respectful distance and staying with friends rather than the newlyweds. Respecting our privacy is a convenient excuse because she'd really prefer not to be woken by a crying baby in the night. Even in Perth, she has her own social circles and stays in the west wing of a sprawling house in one of the city's richest suburbs, Dalkeith. The owners are usually at their beach house in Margaret River, and they give her full run of their place. Private drivers and cooks aren't common in Perth, but Theresa's friends have one of each, so a chauffeur ferries her between our place in delinquent Scarborough and her ritzy riverside accommodation.

Francis decides to take his wife and baby daughter on a trip to Hong Kong to visit his sister. This will be Mela's first time travelling into Asia. I am almost twelve months old, and Francis is overjoyed that I am still eligible for complimentary travel: 'Free-free-free, she travels free!'

The past eighteen months have been a baptism of fire for Francis. When his wife, studying and pregnant, wasn't throwing up in the bathroom from morning sickness, she could be found sobbing in her room for no apparent reason. When he asked her what was wrong, she said the neighbours had been awful to her again. Then the new baby came and the throwing up was replaced by leaking breasts, but the sobbing didn't stop.

Francis wants to introduce us to the place he grew up, and he's keen for us to experience Theresa's hospitality. He talks at great length about his sister, who is very 'upper class' and has 'a driver' and 'a maid'. He proudly shares these facts with lots of people in Perth, anticipating their high regard. But Mela is sceptical about her sister-in-law's conduct – having drivers and maids at your beck and call smacks of an inequality she struggles to abide. 'It sounds like Theresa doesn't lift a finger,' she says.

Although my mother is privileged too, she harbours some basic socialist views. Her cocooned private school education at St Hilda's on the banks of the Swan River, and her upbringing of roast dinners, carpeted bathrooms, opera and ballet recitals, plus her innately sympathetic and compassionate nature, are not adequate preparation for this trip.

She's also never had to parent away from home and is unsure how she will ever get through this. Usually Thelma would be by her side or on the phone to advise on nappy-pin, burping and settling techniques, but Thelma is not accompanying us. To make matters worse, Mela is anxious about the flight; voices in her head say they will steal her baby, that she is a terrible mother and they will kill her.

Francis's idea of a getaway to Hong Kong is as much about giving his wife a holiday and saving their relationship as it is about reconnecting with his roots. Theresa will be so pleased to see him.

I still cannot get used to the new BOAC branding, Theresa thinks as she stands at the arrivals gate waiting for Francis, Mela and me.

BOAC merged with other companies to become British Airways, or BA, two months before I was born. It will always be easy for Theresa to remember my age because it's the same as BA's.

'Welcome. Come, come, come.' Theresa ushers her brother, his bride and baby away from the crowded arrivals area. Mela is holding me on her hip and juggling a hard plastic sippy cup with her free hand. Theresa makes a funny sound with her mouth, 'Oh, bloblobobloh,' and winks at me as if we share a delicious secret. Then she hides behind her hands and plays peekaboo; I pull her hand away from her face. 'See, see,' she says. 'Mimi, very clever girl. Oh, bloblobobloh.' She scrunches up her face at me, and I squeal with delight. 'Let me take her.' Theresa claps her hands and holds out her arms. I cry because she is a stranger to me, but she is not taking no for an answer. 'Oh, come on, come on.' She jiggles me up and down. She is wearing jeans and a red polo shirt with a Yves Saint Laurent scarf tied elegantly around her throat. As we move through Kai Tak Airport, she points at the mountains beyond the vast terminal windows. 'Look, look, monkey out there.' She laughs as I look for the monkey.

Mela tries to close her seatbelt in Theresa's Volvo but her blouse gets caught, so Francis helps her to free the fabric and fastens the clasp. She holds me on her lap. I watch the Kowloon Mountains and highrises give way to a lower-lying landscape as we travel the ten-minute drive from the Kowloon side to the Island. 'Wow, wow, wow,' Theresa says, noticing her brother ogle the concrete entrance to the Cross-Harbour Tunnel. 'See, we're very modern here in Hong Kong, brother.'

It's an engineer's dream: the underwater tunnel connects one side of the harbour city to the other, allowing residents to cross without a ferry.

'Holy Moses, this is better than looking at the picture in the newspaper.' Francis knows no photo can do justice to an engineering masterpiece like this one, with its sweeping curves and defiant cantilevers. He wishes he could run his hands over the concrete fascia and examine the structure.

We emerge onto what is known as 'Hong Kong side', and Theresa takes Hennessy Road to turn right onto her street: Tai Hang. She is driving today because her chauffeur only works certain days; she shares him with a friend – or borrows him, to be accurate.

She notices she has been doing most of the talking, pointing out this and that for Mela's benefit, and the young woman hasn't responded once. Since she got off the plane she has been silent as she hangs on to me and stares straight ahead.

The voices have had a field day on the plane and at the airport. Mela doesn't do well in crowded spaces; they are confusing and frightening. 'Why don't you just die?' To think that strangers are out to harm her and her child is terrifying. 'We're coming to kill you.' No matter where Mela goes, she needs to be on constant high alert for our safety. 'I'm going to murder you.'

She is exhausted and closes her eyes. Whenever she has told Francis or her parents about the horrible things people say to her — on the street, in a supermarket queue, at work, university or home — no one believes her. When they say, 'But I was right next to you and I didn't hear them,' she has any number of replies: 'You were distracted.' 'They whispered it to me.' 'It was when you went up to order.' 'You just want me to think I'm crazy.'

Theresa swings her Volvo up a steep concrete driveway. A guard nods, manually lifting the boom gate.

After we get out of the car she greets her neighbour, an imposing tall figure of a white man in his mid-forties. 'Ah, Mr Columbo, how do you do?' He is wearing as close to a safari suit as someone can get away with when they aren't actually on safari — well, he has been on one recently.

'Just polishing up the old Rolls, Theresa.'

Another man, a local Chinese, looks up from rubbing the bonnet with a cloth. 'Miss Kwa.' He smiles and bows his head.

She nods back.

'Theresa,' says Mr Columbo, 'would you like me to get Freddie here to give your car a bit of a polish as well?'

She beams at him. 'Lovely. That would be wonderful, thank you, thank you.'

Francis paces up and down the length of the Rolls. 'You know I can tell you how to make this run even better, if you let me look under bonnet,' he tells Mr Columbo. 'I'm a mechanical engineer, you know.'

Theresa frowns. Mela stands in the heat, holding me.

'Come, come,' says Theresa. 'Brigit will have cool drinks and food for us.' We take a small lift up to her apartment. 'Mr Columbo has so many titles, you know. So many. And that was his Tuesday car – he has several others, all Rolls-Royce. He just loves Rolls-Royce.'

The elevator opens and Brigit is there, like magic, having seen us arrive through the window. She bows to Francis, who loves that sort of thing, then to Mela, who does not. Theresa claps her hands at me and extends her arms to take me from Mela again. I go willingly this time. Her energy is free as a bird's, and I like her holding me. 'Brigit, Brigit, bring the bags, please, and then we are staaaarving.'

As this is my first trip to Hong Kong, it is also my introduction to humidity, and my eczema clears up immediately. Lush green foliage wends its way up the mountain side, and intense smells escape Brigit's wok-centred kitchen. I crawl across Aunty Theresa's fastidiously spotless parquetry floors. When we go out, strangers tip their hats and bow, and I smile when they talk to me in local dialect. I sit in baby swings in playgrounds where children speak Cantonese and their nannies speak Tagalog. In Hong Kong I am dressed up like a life-sized baby doll and given lots of toys and attention.

Mela doesn't have as easy a time there as I do. When we leave two weeks later, she is no more rested than when she arrived. She did find some respite from her voices, though, as most people around her did not have a command of English, the only language the voices speak. She mentioned nothing sinister about anyone in Hong Kong to Francis, which was a welcome break for him too. She had to be on guard the whole time, however, for conspiratorial Westerners – this is why she's so tired.

I pull at Theresa's scarf as she hands me over to Mela at the airport. We say goodbye, and Theresa waves us off. For me, she opens and closes her hands and tilts her head from side to side, blowing her cheeks out, pinching them, then exhaling as though she's popped a balloon. 'Don't forget to look for the monkey.' She points to the mountains beyond the windows. 'See you later, alligator,' she calls after me, and we disappear through the gate.

Theresa walks back to her car, where she has a driver waiting today. She smiles and waves at familiar airport staff, already mentally planning her next trip to see us. She has the lifelong privilege of drastically reduced fares on BA and affiliated airlines, awarded for her years of service at BOAC. She also has plenty of friends to catch up with in Australia, such as Lady McMahon whom she met as long ago as 1965 – ten years, they've been friends now. Sonia McMahon is elegant and savvy, and Theresa took an instant liking to her. They exchanged numbers on a long-haul flight Theresa was crewing, and they've stayed in touch ever since.

When in Hong Kong, Lady McMahon would send Theresa notes to meet for dinner or a party, and they'd flit about town. No door was closed to them. Theresa, ever the gracious hostess, had the key to local customs, and Sonia, ever the diplomat, A-list access to expat events. They made a fun team. 'Don't forget to call when you're next Sydney-side,' Sonia sang out with a wink as they parted ways after a soiree at the Peninsula Hotel.

When Theresa did next arrive Sydney-side, of course she called her friend, and Sonia immediately invited her over for dinner. 'It really is high time my husband met you,' she said.

At dinner, after chitchat about her flight and the weather, Theresa leant in and asked Sonia's husband, William, 'What is your line of work?'

After a long pause, Sonia and her husband smiled broadly at each other.

'I'm the prime minister,' he replied.

Theresa smiled too and, without skipping a beat, returned, 'Oh. And what is that like?'

Theresa loves to squeeze the cheeks of the three McMahon children, particularly the boy, Julian. She thinks of my chubby cheeks now and sees no need to delay; the BA office is only a slight detour to her car. She has trips to Paris, London and Amsterdam coming up soon, followed by Saint Petersburg then Cairo. She puts in a request for another flight to Sydney, in three months or so, and plans to book a connection to Perth once it's approved.

ANTIDEPRESSANTS AND GLASS

HAVING A BABY HURRIES LIFE ALONG FOR FRANCIS AND Mela. The Scarborough Beach property continues to take on a life of its own. As more buildings, sheds, gazebos and barbecues spring up, Mela and Francis's marriage is constantly on the rocks. Mela moves back home to her parents intermittently, always taking me with her. But each time she returns to Francis after a few days. They are caught in a pain cycle. He calls daily. He threatens, reasons, apologises, promises things will be better and pleads with her to come back. She cannot bear to be at either home because the voices follow no matter where she goes – it's impossible for her to escape the torment by packing up and moving. But, of course, she doesn't know that. She scoops me up, and we return to Francis.

Mela's symptoms worsen, leading to more frequent marital separations, lasting longer and longer each time she and I move away. Francis tries to get her help but her illness remains undiagnosed.

* * *

I am three now, and my dad has taken me to visit Hong Kong once a year. Mum went with us the second time, but the third time she backed out at the last minute, and Dad carried me onto the aeroplane anyway. There is no time difference between Hong Kong and Perth, so Mum telephoned every day, trying not to sound distressed.

Dad was often out, 'meeting important people', so Aunty Theresa kept me entertained with all kinds of funny games. She showed me her abacus and we counted the beads together, over and over. While I sat on her lap, she showed me albums filled with photos of people I have never met. Aunty Mary spent a lot of time with me too; I was at the centre of their universe.

'Brigit, Brigit, bring some more watermelon. She loves the watermelon.' Aunty Theresa would gleefully summon Brigit, who was always already standing in the doorway, holding a silver tray of peeled and chopped tropical fruits: watermelon, mango, dragon fruit, papaya and banana.

But now I am home in Perth, three years old and far too experienced at packing my things so I'm ready to go to my grandparents' place at short notice.

'We're going to see Paw Paw.' Mum forces a smile. 'I think we'll stay the night.' Paw Paw is what I call Thelma. It is Cantonese for 'maternal grandmother', and even though Thelma is an auburn-haired white Englishwoman, she is tickled pink to have a Chinese title.

Three days – and many phones calls from Dad – later, Mum and I are doing the dishes back in our Scarborough kitchen. I love kneeling on the stool as I push my pudgy arms into mountains of suds. I'm wearing an apron sewn by Paw Paw, the fussy flower pattern and embroidered edges contrasting vividly with our minimalist kitchen of burgundy tiles. Woks and turners dangle from a hanging rack above the island bench, and we look out onto a garden of dry, patchy lawn. We also have a view of Dad's shed where he is hammering something on an iron anvil mounted on a jarrah plinth. He lowers a mask over his face and lifts a cutting torch from a trolley. Sparks hit the front of the mask, sending a thrill up my small spine; it's my own little fireworks display with orange lasers shooting in every direction, a giant sparkler. The lines of light lose intensity at the edges, and a few tiny balls of fire break free to disappear on the brick paving. Mum and I sing the 'Johnny Works With One Hammer' song the whole way through, twice, with the actions and all the merriment a normal mother and daughter might enjoy. The family home is complete, and we are happy for a moment.

A couple of days later Mum swallows glass in an attempt to kill herself. She does it alone in her ensuite while I am in the lounge room watching *Play School*. I hear a sound like groaning, choking and throwing up all at once. Mum is lying on the bathroom floor, spluttering blood and barely breathing.

I am screaming. 'Mummy. Mummy? Wake up, Mummy.'

Dad has prepared me for this, so I have memorised the speed-dial button to reach him at work. I run to his study – there are so many speed-dial buttons, but I know the right one and press it. 'Daddy, Mummy is bleeding. She is sleeping on the floor.'

Dad calls an ambulance that arrives before he does. I can't reach the doorhandle to let in the paramedics, so they gesture I should move away from the window. More broken glass.

This is one of my earliest memories that will stick.

Mum is treated at the scene, then lifted onto a stretcher and taken by ambulance to an emergency department. In what becomes a routine, I am whisked off to my grandparents' place to be cared for by Paw Paw and Granddad. In times of trouble, Francis seeks help from his in-laws. But when it becomes clear that the marriage cannot be saved, Francis's relationship with my grandparents sours. When he turns to the only extended 'family' he has here, it turns away from him.

* * *

Mela loves me unconditionally. She would die for me. She protects me from the wolves and the voices. They want to kill us, so we must be armed with the skills to fight both the war that only she can see and the real war raging in the 1970s for girls' and women's rights.

Mela wants her daughter to walk in her shoes, a pair of very feminist flat ones, so she coaches me in Germaine Greer and teaches me to be wary of men from a very young age. She gets a crew cut, starts to wear dungarees and joins a women's soccer team, so I wear dungarees too and cheer her on from the sidelines. I am her number one supporter and enjoy going to matches, but then her voices inhabit the soccer team. The other players say nasty, unspeakable, violent things, and they may kill us, so we don't go back.

Mela hides in her motherhood of me. She gets her teaching qualification, and when other toddlers are toddling, I am in private tuition with my mum. I am three years old reading words like 'fire engine', 'letterbox' and 'wonder woman'. Mum paints the words in white on grey cardboard strips cut from Cornflakes packets.

I'm soon reading fluently and am also fluent in protecting my mother: looking out for her, speaking on her behalf and living in anticipation of what she may be hearing and what she might do. She shares her paranoid thoughts with me. There is no question they are real, although I cannot hear them – I must not have been listening, or it was said quietly because I am a child and they did not want to involve me. I'm on the lookout to catch people running up to our house as they hurl abuse or throw stones. I'm on high alert for snide comments at the supermarket, the park, in the bank queue.

The time I found Mum bleeding on the ensuite floor, with glass spilling from her mouth, has made me very afraid of the monsters who are out to get her, and it has deeply ingrained my fear of losing her.

PUNCH AND MEDALS

IT'S MY FIRST DAY OF SCHOOL, AND I AM THE ONLY CHILD here who is even vaguely Chinese. I already stand out, but Dad wants me to make an even bigger impact, to be top of my year and have lots of friends. 'Everybody likes me,' he says. 'You need to be like me and get everybody to like you.' That's quite a lot of pressure for a five-year-old.

But thanks to late nights watching whatever I want on Dad's TV, I'm mature for my age, and thanks to Mum, I'm two years ahead with schoolwork, so it might be possible for me to live up to Dad's requirements. He constantly tells people how brilliant I am. 'My daughter is very, very advance,' he says, leaving off the 'd'. 'Everyone else is dumb,' he says to me. When I make mistakes, though, I'm 'an idiot and stupid' and 'should have been a boy', and when I do well I 'could do better' or 'Have you seen how smart that person's son is? He's going to be a lawyer.'

Although my grandparents offer to pay for me to attend a private school, Dad insists I go to Deanmore, the local public school. How can I get 'everyone' to like me, as ordered by Dad? The best way I can think of to stand out is to dress differently – a departure from the school uniform on my first day should get everyone's attention. After we settle into our Grade One classroom, our teacher, Mrs Bailey, asks us to go around the room and introduce ourselves; when it's my turn I unzip my school sweater to reveal a red boob tube. The other kids snigger and laugh, and Mrs Bailey looks surprised and at a loss for words. I am the first five-year-old in the history of Deanmore Primary to do lunchtime detention.

Apart from misguided misdemeanours like that one, I'm a good student and read anything I can get my hands on: books, comics, cereal packets, instruction manuals – if there are words, I'll read them. I'm devoted to learning but have to remind myself that I am also on Dad's mission to be popular and still have no clue how to achieve this.

One recess I start eating a banana with the peel on. I'm sitting on the wooden bench that runs along the concrete corridor outside our classrooms. 'Yes, it's true, I always eat the peel,' I say casually to the group amassing around me.

'No way,' says one girl.

'That's disgusting. Pft.' An older boy spits on the ground.

Mouthful after laborious mouthful I chew and swallow the entire banana. 'That's how monkeys eat bananas, and we're evolved from monkeys so we should eat the peel too. If you think about the Darwinian approach ...'

Their eyes glaze over, and I quickly lose my audience to handstands, downball and foursquare. Ugh, why do I always spoil things with a history lesson?

At five years old, I'm regularly tossed, tugged, pulled and manipulated between my two homes, Bicton and Scarborough. Back and forth, back and forth. Mum is living with her parents permanently now. I get to see her three and a half days a week, but even with this agreement in place Dad finds reasons for conflict. One day, he and Granddad lock horns – not for the first time, but for me it's the most memorable.

Standing just outside the front door, Dad demands that I come back with him early and claims that this is within his joint custodial rights. He shouts at Granddad as I curl up beside the broad glass balcony doors overlooking the Swan River. I'm crying while I watch the two men in my life gesticulate aggressively at one another, and I know that Dad's angry visits only ever mean one thing: I'm about to be ripped from my mother's arms again.

Mum storms out to join in the argument on the landing, and Paw Paw wraps an arm around me, pulling me in to her warm bosom.

Granddad's protective instinct is peaking, but he maintains his composure. Mum's shoulders slump, and Dad's shouts rise. Granddad can't stand it any longer – he strides towards the front door that opens into a glass atrium entrance on the balcony. 'Mela, get inside,' he orders his daughter. Dad keeps ranting as she hurries indoors. I watch Granddad assume a wide armed and legged stance in the doorframe, like a human X. His fists are clenched against the jambs.

'Give me my daughter!' Dad screams. 'Or … or … I'll hit you.' He shakes with rage.

'Go on, Francis. Hit me.' Granddad stares him down, and I bury my face in Paw Paw's arms. She is on her knees embracing both me and my mother now; she has that much love and that big a hug, she can accommodate us both.

I turn to see Dad's fists connect with Granddad's lean frame, again and again.

Granddad doesn't flinch. He is motionless and solid, a stone wall. 'Go home, Francis. Get off my property.'

Dad nurses his wrists and drives away.

Granddad is like a second father to me. He sits me on his knee and tells me stories. He has a jar of cashews beside his armchair, along with a menagerie of wooden African animals: a hippo, a giraffe, an antelope and a small herd of elephants. There's also a tiger – I was born in the Year of the Wood Tiger, Dad is always quick to remind me, so I relate to this ornament the most.

Granddad tells me the most incredible stories about his war-hero rescues; he is the original James Bond. 'And then I climbed into the attic and got the British pilot out.' I gaze at this great man in awe. He was a paratrooper and an MI5 spy, he helped to liberate Auschwitz, and now he has countless stories to share with me.

Granddad and I walk Whisky, our cocker spaniel, and he lets me hold the lead. 'When we built our house, all this was sand.' He gestures to the mixture of bungalows and mansions along the river now. 'We were the first ones here.' The two of us stand together, looking out over the water. 'That's where your mother and her brother and sister would row across to Mosman Park on the other side, all the way to that boatshed.' He nods towards a green box on the opposite bank. 'Do you see it?' I nod. We walk further, into the Point Walter bushland reserve. 'Mimi, sometimes your mother behaves differently to everyone else, but she will always love you. She will do anything for you.' Whisky tugs on the lead. I run ahead for a bit. When Granddad has caught up, I say, 'Tell me again about your secret mission in Brussels.'

One day I walk past Granddad's bedroom on the way to mine. He is sitting on the bed, looking down at a small case open on his lap. 'Come here, young'un.' I sit beside him, mesmerised by the glow of metal, the intricate patterns and the ribbons against the felt. 'These ones are for bravery. If you are brave, it helps you to get through difficult things.' He places a medal in my palm. It's heavier than I expected. I stroke the ribbon. 'And this one, young'un, is for honour. If you stand by what you believe in, you will have honour.' I run my fingers over Granddad's engraved name. 'And these ones are stars for different places where I fought. The same places I brought back the Zulu shield and wooden tiger from. In one of those places, a prince gave me that statue of Buddha in our hall. That place was Thailand.'

We sit in silence for a while, staring at the medals.

He returns them to the box and closes it. 'But, young'un, these mean nothing.' He stands up and walks over to his open wardrobe. 'The greatest reward in life is survival. Keeping your health and staying alive are worth more than all the medals in the world.' He places the case of memories on the top shelf and slides it to the back, out of sight.

Surviving five has had its moments, and as I'm turning six soon, things are bound to get better.

A week before my birthday, I wonder why Dad is at my school gate handing out flyers. 'Hi, Dad, what are you doing?' He hands me a flyer of a hand-drawn girl with petals around her face. It's an invitation to a birthday party – my birthday party. He has given one to every kid at school as part of his scheme to fast-track my popularity.

A week later, more than sixty people turn up to our place in Scarborough for free food and cake, mostly school families trying to make an effort with the new 'Chinese family' who clearly don't understand party etiquette.

With a bowl-cut bob Dad gave me and a floor-length velvet dress, I welcome strangers into my home. We play Mr Wolf – I am the wolf, and the other children step cautiously behind me – then we eat cake and red jelly cups served on a ping-pong table on the back patio.

Children and parents, unfamiliar to me, sing 'Happy Birthday', and I hear Dad's distinctive kookaburra laugh rise up over the third and final 'hip-hip hooray'. He looks pleased with himself and starts handing out business cards.

That night I dream that all the children behind me in the Mr Wolf game are chasing me, but suddenly I'm able to lift off the ground, I am a tiger cub leaping up through the sky as high as the clouds, to escape. The air is thick, though, and getting away is a real struggle, like swimming against a syrupy tide; I watch my front paws as they run towards the night and jump from star to star, sending golden sparks of dust into the darkness at each one. I don't dare to look back at my tail behind me, I must get away, I can't afford to slow down.

The next phase of Dad's popularity strategy involves an even more spectacular public performance. He persuades my school principal, Mr Green, to let me play at assembly. Deanmore Primary has a piano but Dad insists our Yamaha is better, so he loads it onto a trailer connected to the back of his Ford Fairmont station wagon. Once he arrives at the school, he tows the trailer through the gates and onto the quadrangle, then the entire school watches as he wheels the piano off the trailer onto an outdoor concrete stage. We are introduced, and Dad begins to sing. I hope no one will notice I am his accompaniment. Mr Green and a row of teachers applaud, but all I notice are the kids sniggering and whispering behind their hands.

GUCCI AND GECKO

BEFORE DAD GETS ANY MORE WILD IDEAS, IT'S SCHOOL holidays, which almost always means a trip to Hong Kong. I don't know what to pack as I have hardly any clothes that fit me at Dad's, so I roll up my school uniform and push it into my suitcase. We'll be stopping in Singapore to visit an aunt and uncle whom I've never met, and Dad says I must call them Uncle Number Eight and Aunty Number Ten. I'm not entirely sure about the system, but I know Uncle Number Eleven in Hong Kong so I have some experience with relatives as numbers.

'He is my brother from Second Mother,' Dad says. We're in a taxi between Changi Airport and the home of Uncle Eight and Aunty Ten.

'So what number are you, Dad?' A row of palm trees sprints across my window.

'So many baby die. It depend if you count all the baby or just the living one.'

It's humid here, like in Hong Kong, but the built landscape looks modern in comparison, clean and new with none of the grubbiness that clings to Hong Kong's old signs, shopfronts and residential highrises.

'First Mother, she had five but then it depends if you count First Adopted Son, so she really only had four.'

The cab pulls over in front of a dress shop, a pink, sequinned, taffeta dress, made for a child, in a front window. In another window there are five less gaudy dresses on hangers, all designed for a more casual occasion; the fussy floral prints and frills on the sleeves and skirts still worry me, though.

'But another two sons die, you see. And then Second Mother. She had more girls and only three son but three more die.'

I hope Dad's not going to make me wear a dress to meet these relatives. I prefer to stick to my dungarees, the ones I'm wearing now, with a large embroidered apple on the bib. These or my school uniform, which looks like a netball outfit, are my clothes of choice. Everything else I have is second hand or handmade by Mum or Paw Paw – all items that other people want to see me in.

'My elder brother from Third Mother die. But he was already grown up so he keeps his number.' Dad reaches into a coin purse strapped to his middle and shuffles through different currencies: Australian, Hong Kong – 'Ah!' He pulls out Singaporean dollars, hands the driver a note and waits for change, but the driver places his hands on the steering wheel.

'Okee, lah.' Singlish makes English singsong-y.

'Hey, hey, hey.' Dad is not standing for this. 'You Singaporeans are supposed to be well behave. Where's my change?'

I open my door to get out.

'Mister, the tax, see?' The driver points to a sign above his mileage machine, explaining that taxing tolls are added to the final fare.

Dad does a calculation in his head. 'You still owe me ten cents.'

We stand outside the dress shop after the driver has handed Dad the change.

'Always trying to ripping you off. Buddy taxi driver.' Dad unzips his pouch, puts in the ten cents and zips it back up.

'Maybe you can bow when you meet Uncle and Aunty. And then I get you to tell them your school mark.'

He opens the door of the shop which, it turns out, belongs to Uncle Eight and Aunty Ten. It would have been easier if each *child* had a number rather than numbering boys and girls separately, I think; that way the new aunt or uncle by marriage could just assume the same number as their spouse. Being Chinese is so complicated.

'Mimi!' Dad shoves my arm – I've been daydreaming and forgotten to bow. They are not royalty, mind you, they are dressmakers, and I'm not sure where Dad picked up the idea I should bow to them. 'They are senior. You must bow.'

Instead, as a joke, I pull on the sides of my dungarees and curtsy. The couple clap and laugh and look happy to meet me, although because I don't speak Chinese I cannot communicate with them very well. Their Singlish is limited too.

Dad speaks to them in Cantonese, but when they don't understand – either they speak Mandarin or Dad's Cantonese is too poor these days – he reverts to English. He asks them if they're acquainted with the engineers responsible for the new Changi Airport terminal; he would like to meet them because he has some things to say about the structure. 'I am an engineer,' he says in a tone that suggests they might be deaf. 'I'm very big engineer in Australia.' He puts his hand above him to suggest he is indicating the height of someone taller than himself. 'Very big.' They don't seem to personally know the engineers behind the airport renovation, but they do know a good noodle place for dinner.

'They're not very clever,' Dad says afterwards, folding a suit bag over his arm. He convinced them to give me a dress that I will never wear, and he didn't offer to pay. 'They owe me, you see. I am the baby brother. Youngest brother of thirty-two!' (Technically he's the last boy if you count brothers by numbers according to their mother number.)

We're walking towards the noodle restaurant, but Dad decides on something from a street-food vendor instead.

'I am very important, your father. Everybody like to give thing to me.'

The smells wafting into my nose are exciting and delicious. The bustle of people at Newton Circus, the traffic sounds and exotic voices of people ordering food, speaking up to be heard over sizzling woks and rotating skewers, the humid night air – it's all wonderful. Naked bulbs are strung between metal posts, tables and benches cemented to the ground.

Dad butts in. 'Waste of time to come here. They don't introduce me to anyone important.' He hands me a few coins, and I skip off to buy fried banana on a stick.

The next day we're on a plane to Hong Kong, and the comforting familiarity of a routine I look forward to every time: Aunty Theresa at the gate with a big embrace, squeezing my cheeks, always with something kind to say. 'Oh my, so beautiful. Haven't you grown.'

If she is appalled by my bowl cut and shabby clothes, she never tells me. But she shakes her head as I show her the dress our Singapore relatives gave me. 'Tut-tut. Not your style. Not your style at all.' She zips up the suit bag so I never need to see the bejewelled taffeta and frills again. 'I know just the girl I can send this to. She will love it. And you, my girl, are old enough now – you are six years old. I will take you to do … The Shopping!' She says this as though it's some wondrous and powerful rite of passage to conquer; as though she should be putting her closed hand to her chest and pointing her chin valiantly skywards. 'Your choice. You want shorts. You have shorts. T-shirt. Jacket. Whatever you want.' She smacks her knee with her hand and brings it up into a bent elbow and fist, like a running arm. 'Shall we go?'

We're sitting on her bed, angled towards each other with the suit bag in between. In the corner of her room is my favourite piece of furniture in the whole world.

'Yes, Aunty, I would love that, thank you.' I smile broadly. I can never quite believe that I am here; it just makes me so happy. 'But first, Aunty, may I please use your massage chair?'

She stands up and wraps a Gucci scarf theatrically around her neck, bends to inspect herself in her dresser mirror and whisks round to face me. 'Of course, madam, please be my guest. Be my guest. It's the first electric massage chair in the world, you know?' She says this snootily, for fun. 'The baron's company was trying them out, and he gave me one. I use it every day.' She wiggles her hips as if to say the chair is responsible for her good figure. I giggle and pull myself onto the seat, leaning back on the rollers. 'The control, madam. You know what to do.'

'Yes, thank you, madam. I did visit this establishment not long ago, and I did so enjoy this chair.'

We laugh, and she hands me the plastic control on a cord. My favourite piece of furniture in the world! The rollers travel up my spine with reassuring pressure.

Aunty goes to tell Brigit what we'll have for dinner and to call a driver to fetch us for 'The Shopping!'

'Today we go to Lantau to see Aunty Mary. Tomorrow Mama for mahjong.' Aunty ties a red YSL scarf to the strap of her alligator-skin handbag. She's wearing all white: long pants with a T-shirt tucked into an elastic waistband. I have on denim shorts and a red T-shirt. We tie up our canvas sneakers before heading out the door.

'Ma'am, ma'am!' Brigit calls frantically – it sounds like an emergency. She appears from the stairwell as Aunty and I step out of the elevator. Brigit puffs and wipes sweat from her forehead with a handkerchief she takes from a yellow pocket on her pale-blue apron. She holds out a lunchbox. 'Snacks,

Mimi. Snacks.' She squeezes my left cheek. 'Ma'am, I must scold you. She is a growing girl!' Aunty does a little stomping tantrum impersonation of Brigit, who just smiles and takes the lift back up.

Aunty has borrowed a driver from a friend in her building, just to take us down to the pier in Central. It's opposite the Mandarin Oriental Hotel, where her shop is; we stop in there on our way. Two familiar turbaned Sikh men bow and greet us as they swing open two heavy glass doors. 'Miss Kwa.' Aunty beams at them and nods. 'And little Miss Kwa.' I smile and nod too. It's like a scene from *Annie*.

We pass under a ceiling of sparkling chandeliers arranged in square sections boxed in gold, then visit Aunty's shop, Swatow Lace, to check on her workers, Christina and Amy. I am greeted by the familiar smell of wood polish and wall to wall pigeon holes stuffed with silk garments in crisp plastic sleeves and two glass display cases with a village of carved stone and ivory characters trapped inside: fishermen, Buddhas and celestial gods, as well as the most fascinating of all to my young eyes – the erotic figures.

'Hungry Jack today?' the shop girls tease me in broken English, because our routine is going for a burger and vanilla milkshake when I'm left with them in Aunty's store.

They're a bit like older cousins: Amy entertains me with a game of noughts and crosses on a scrap of paper, while Aunty instructs Christina about a big potential sale with a hotel guest. 'Room 329. Veeeery large lady. I suggest the man robe with the blue flower. I do not tell her it's the man robe but the lady robe is too small.'

Aunty clacks away at a slim wooden abacus on the glass counter. 'Second thought, steer her to the scarves instead. And this is the discount if she goes ahead with the jade man who holds the fishing rod.' She slips into Cantonese to wrap up the conversation and slides the abacus towards Christina.

The girls wave us off. 'Have fun in Lantau, Miss Kwas!'

We catch a ferry from pier six. 'Slow or fast?' Aunty asks me. The slow ferry is more scenic and cheaper, but the fast ferry gets there in half the time.

'Fast!' I do a running move with my arms. 'I can't wait to see Benji.' I love Aunty Mary and Uncle Tony's dog. 'And Aunty, of course,' I add with a grin.

I don't really know Uncle Tony that well. When Aunty Mary has visited me in Perth, it's been because she's flown over on Qantas after requesting a long-haul shift to Sydney – she has taken time off to do this at least twice – and I only ever see Tony in Hong Kong. He's still working as a judge, so he's very busy and doesn't always make it to family gatherings when my dad and I are here. But I remember going to Tony's office once; he let me climb onto a cabinet to look at the leather spines of all his law books, then he let me wear his wig and cloak. He and Mary aren't married, and Dad has told me it's so she can keep her job at the airline. I can see how much they adore each other – I have never seen that in my parents.

Aunty Theresa and I get onto the ferry and go up to the top deck. I open the snack box as we watch the view of Hong Kong Island disappear. Brigit has packed me some fruit and, in a separate compartment, a cheese sandwich with Bovril, the closest thing she can find to Vegemite for me.

I am living in a different world when I come here. Tomorrow I'll be visiting Mama, Ng Yuk, in her musty North Point apartment that Aunty Theresa pays for along with two maids. I'll sit holding her hand and we'll be like a chicken speaking to a duck. She'll shuffle around the flat pulling me along, opening drawers and telling me in Cantonese about the treasures within them. Then she'll squeeze my fingers with hers and utter in English, 'Good boy.' She'll give me a sniff kiss, which is when she breathes in hard through her nose against my cheek, inhaling me, and then she'll say, 'Daddy, bad boy.' She is sad that he left her I suppose. Theresa makes up for her sibling's absence by visiting frequently and paying people to let Mama win at mahjong. Whenever I say goodbye to Mama she sends me off with a soft toy from an old collection she keeps behind a glass cabinet.

As our vessel approaches land, Aunty faces the wind. She's wearing enormous Chanel sunglasses, and her YSL scarf flaps behind her. Aunty has a way of making even the most ordinary transportation look glamorous.

We catch a blue taxi from the edge of the island and take it inland to Cheung Sha, where Aunty Mary will meet us. She comes careering down a concrete slope in a white golf buggy – most local expats get about in them here – a resort-style blue-and-white canopy shading her from the scorching sun. Benji is under her arm. Her smile is so big it could swallow the sky. Her sunglasses are big too. The sisters resemble strange, beautiful insects in their oversized accessories.

I hug Aunty Mary tight and dash out onto the beach with Benji. My two beloved aunties are already immersed in chat. As I get close to the water, I remember I have my bathers on under my clothes, so I race up the sand to strip down then sprint back to the invitingly cool sea. Benji shakes water from his coat, spraying smiling passers-by.

At Aunty Mary's place the floors are tiled, giving it a much more beachy feel than Aunty Theresa's formal home. I rinse the sand off my feet before we get into the lift, and there's a stone bowl of water outside the front door, just to be sure. A maid brings us freshly squeezed orange juice on ice, and I sit on a balcony in front of a fan, drinking through a bendy plastic straw. Benji is on my lap. We look out over the tropical scene, palm trees giving way to dense jungle on one side, and on the other an endless stretch of sand and sea.

'Can you see my giant gecko?' Aunty Mary asks, coming out to join me. She is wearing shorts and a bather top, standard

Lantau uniform. It's so casual here, yet infinitely more refined than Scarborough Beach. 'Look, look,' she squeals. A long, fat lizard is plodding its way through the garden. A butterfly flutters onto Aunty Mary's shoulder. It's as if I'm living in a dream.

NUNS AND LEGO

I AM SIX AND ENJOYING TIME WITH MY GRANDPARENTS. IT'S much less complicated at their place than at Dad's – but just as I settle in again, Mum decides to give her marriage another go, and we're back on the road to Scarborough.

Dad greets us enthusiastically, and we put our clothes back in drawers and toothbrushes in cups by sinks in the house that he designed and built himself, brick by brick. There is always a concrete mixer in the yard, along with a trailer, a welding machine, a ladder and an axe; Dad always has a building project on the go.

On top of building and design, Dad now has a new hobby. He's become interested in the law, and after attending lectures at the uni on an unofficial basis he has embarked on several court cases, suing various people and even businesses. He runs his own cases and represents himself. Like building, it's time-consuming, but it keeps him busy.

This only adds to the difficulties between Mum and Dad, and before long, the struggles resurface.

It's four in the afternoon and, as usual, I am the last kid to be picked up from my primary school. I wait on the lawn out front, cross-legged, pulling at blades of grass. I look up at a soaring gum tree and down an adjacent road where groups of kids walk home together, kidding around and having fun, carefree. I eye them with envy.

Mum chugs up in our white VW Beetle. Clothes and bags press at the windows, and I realise the small car is so full it might burst. There are sleeping-bags, pillows, blankets, suitcases and crockery – along with almost every type of belonging I can imagine – crammed into the back seat. Our black cat, Susie, is burrowed into a pile of clothes.

I can hardly fit, the passenger seat is as far forward as it can go, but I get in, squeezing my schoolbag under my feet in front. Susie leaps onto my lap. 'Mum, what's going on? Why is all our stuff in here?'

She doesn't speak, so I'm not sure if she is 'having an episode'. She starts the engine and drives us down Deanmore Road. Right turn. Left turn.

'MUM! Where are we going?'

'We are leaving your father,' she says eventually. She is looking straight ahead. 'We are going to live with some very nice women.' She pauses. 'They are nuns.' I'm trying hard to process what she's saying. 'We'll stay with the nice nuns while I work out what to do next.'

'Why don't we just go home to Paw Paw and Granddad? How long will we be gone? What about school?'

Mela keeps looking straight ahead. Doesn't say another word.

We end up in Leederville, a suburb about a fifteen-minute drive from Scarborough, at a women's refuge for domestic violence victims. Two nuns ceremoniously open enormous oak convent doors and usher us into a courtyard. There's a sandpit, so I run over to it and get busy sifting and building; I sit on a little metal seat and dig with the yellow steam shovel.

We stay there for a few days, until one morning there's a loud bang on the door. It's Dad. He shouts something about legal action and threatens to shut down the refuge for harbouring me against his will.

Schizophrenic delusions and hallucinations have made Mela a challenging guest for the nuns, so when Francis shouts something about his wife needing medical attention, they gladly turn us over. I ride with Dad, and Mum follows us in the Beetle, her tear-streaked face staring straight ahead again, expressionless. I'm crying as I gaze at her through the rear window of Dad's car, but she looks through me as if I'm not here.

I'll miss the old man next door to the refuge. He made me a wooden train on a string that I loved to pull behind me up and down the driveway, between the houses either side.

Dad is taking me to Hong Kong again. 'While your mum gets sorted out,' he says at the airport as he checks in our empty suitcases. He likes to take them empty so we can fill them with tools and trinkets to bring back – mainly tools, usually sharp instruments like drill bits and circular saws that get us stuck at customs for what can feel like hours. The airport staff always ask me to sit on a chair outside a room with a glass window, while Dad goes inside to explain why he is within his legal rights to bring these objects in. There are bags of food as well: dried mushrooms and beans with special medicinal properties, vials of donkey this and tiger that, but mainly royal jelly because, he tells me, 'It's so cheap in Hong Kong.'

Although Dad pushes the boundaries, he knows the law better than the 'buddy security' who don't know what they're 'buddy doing'. He will tell me this, as he always does, on our way home to Scarborough with our overfilled cases shoved on the back seat of a taxi.

That is our arriving-from-Hong Kong routine, but right now we're in the middle of our going routine, with empty cases and mandatory duty-free browsing. 'Mr Francis Kwa, Mr Francis Kwa, please make your way to Departure Gate 2.'

We're the last passengers on board while everyone stares at us after they finish sarcastically applauding us for holding up the flight – standard going-routine stuff.

'Doesn't matter.' Dad takes triple the number of complimentary peanuts we need, thanks the hostess and leans over to me. 'They always wait for Francis Kwa. And I don't even have to look at the time – they always call me on the speaker.' His laugh fills the cabin.

If you happen to be a passenger who isn't taking full advantage of the complimentary peanuts and orange juice, don't worry, Francis makes sure he gets value for everyone's ticket. 'Yes, Mr Kwa,' a hostess says as she switches the call light off above his head. 'Two more orange juices and three peanuts coming right up.' She smiles graciously and nods. Her elegant red-and-white Cathay Pacific uniform fits her perfectly, and her hair and make-up are immaculate. *Aunty Theresa must have looked glamorous like that in her air hostess outfit*, I think as I scribble with a pencil from the children's airline pack.

Outside the airport Dad and I catch a taxi to Tai Hang Road, on our own this time. When we arrive, a guard telephones Brigit to say we're here. Aunty Theresa appears and I throw myself into her arms. She likes a hug but not too much effusiveness in public now that I've started school. I almost cry but, as if she senses it, Aunty steps back and holds my shoulders, her grin broad. 'Now let me look at you. So *beautiful*. You have grown again.' She casts a glance of dismay at our tatty suitcases and nods at the doorman to bring them up to her apartment.

Brigit blushes with embarrassment as I fling my arms around her too. 'Oh, Mimi. Oh, stop it.' She holds me out from her as well. 'Look at you, Mimi, you need to eat.' Her jolly chuckle makes her bosom shake. 'Miss Kwa,' she addresses Aunty, 'may I peel some grape for the Madam Mimi?'

* * *

On this trip, as usual, Dad and Aunty Theresa argue in Cantonese frequently when he isn't out haggling for cheap tools for his workshop. 'It's as if you're re-creating the blacksmith shop,' she says in English during one such exchange.

I'm relieved Dad is out so often on his 'important business', as it gives me uninterrupted time with Aunty. But she has to go out today on business of her own, and she doesn't want me to watch TV or pester Brigit in the kitchen. 'Today,' she announces, 'I introduce you to my neighbour's child!' She says this a bit like 'The Shopping!' Aunty leans towards her dresser mirror and winds up an Elizabeth Arden lipstick. 'He is home from boarding school for the holidays.' The red pigment glides onto her plump bottom lip. 'His father is an Arab banker.' She rubs her lips together to spread the colour, using her pinky finger to remove an undetectable smudge in the crease at the top of her pout. 'His mother is often out of the house, and he could do with company.' She replaces the lid and turns to face me. 'I like him. He has chubby cheeks. I can squeeze them.' She squeezes my cheek. 'Just like this.' I smile.

As if by magic, the doorbell rings. 'Ma'am, ma'aaaaam, he's here,' Brigit sings.

'Ahhh, come, come.' Aunty ushers me towards the door. 'He has very good parents.'

It's like an arranged marriage: all of a sudden I'm standing face to face with a boy, almost identical in height to me, with no idea what to say. He's wearing trousers and a collared shirt and tie, while I'm in shorts and a T-shirt. His maid is standing a few feet behind him. We are both wearing slippers.

The matchmaking introduction continues. 'Rukin, this is my niece, Mimi.'

'Lukin, ma'am,' Brigit corrects Aunty and sweeps my hair behind my shoulder.

'Yes, yes, RRRRukin.'

The boy extends his arm formally, and I shake his hand. 'How do you do, Lukin?' This is awkward but far more interesting than being bored on my own.

'Do you like Lego?' he asks with a smile.

'Yes.' I smile back.

Lukin and I play Lego and talk and listen to music. He never asks me to speak about my parents if I don't bring it up. They have finally divorced after being separated for so long, but Lukin doesn't treat me differently for coming from a broken home like some of my classmates do. We alternate between his place and Aunty's, and sometimes Brigit or his maid takes us for ice-cream. When this happens, we sit in a minibus side by side as it wends down mountainous Tai Hang Road. On one side, a vertical jungle pushes its way through gaps in concrete retaining walls; on the other, there's a steep drop. But for the most part, it's a smooth ride.

'I will write to you after I go back to Australia tomorrow,' I tell Lukin.

Brigit is seated two rows behind us, pretending not to know us while never taking her eyes off us.

'Okay,' he says. He places his hand over mine, resting in my lap, and gives it a quick awkward squeeze. 'But you had better send your letter to my boarding house or I won't get it until I'm back here at Christmas.' He pulls his hand away, and we sit in silence the rest of the way to Jardine's Bazaar, the market at the bottom of Tai Hang Road.

Aunty teases me playfully about my friendship with Lukin, and I can't help but cry when we say goodbye the next day. I think he wants to cry too, but stops himself. It has been so enjoyable spending time with this new friend who is smart and funny, with no peer-group pressure or expectations, bullying or sudden snide remarks. We've looked an odd pair playing around Peace Mansion's grounds, Lukin in his shirt and trousers and tie – sometimes even a bow tie – and me in my scruffy shorts and well-worn T-shirts, or my favourite dungarees. He doesn't mind that I can be a bit of a tomboy, and I don't mind that he dresses and behaves like a Middle Eastern prince. His manners are almost incomprehensible compared to those of the rough kids at my school.

Before we part, Lukin hands me a box. 'A gift to open on the plane.'

Aunty has something for me too: she takes a bright graphic print scarf from around her neck and loops it over mine, arranging it in her signature ascot knot. 'This is pure silk. It is delicate and strong at the same time. It is also mine.' She smiles and wiggles her hips. 'Which means ...'

Dad is trying to force the boot of our taxi closed. And even though it's overflowing with his suitcases, he's commandeered most of the room in my case.

Aunty tries to ignore his complaints about the size of the taxi. 'You must come back to visit me again soon.' She gives me a warm embrace and squeezes my cheeks. 'Next time, Mimi.' Then she glances at Dad and whispers out of his earshot, 'Next time we put him in a hotel. What do you think?'

It's time for the going-home routine: haggling over the excess luggage allowance Dad hasn't paid for while he lets everyone know he is an engineer, visiting the duty-free store, then being paged through the loudspeaker system. 'Calling Mr Francis Kwa. Please make your way urgently to Gate 50.' Dad hands a $20,000 watch – which he was never going to buy – back to a very disappointed duty-free saleswoman. 'See, see,' Dad says as we move towards the gate. 'See, they like my diamond earring. They see that and they think I'm rich.'

A golf buggy driven by a desperate-looking flight steward approaches us.

'No, Dad,' I say, 'it's because you *tell* everybody you're rich.' I'm at an age where I am starting to speak up about these things.

The steward talks into a microphone, its black cord bouncing with the energetic movement of his arm. 'Mr Francis Kwa. Paging Mr Francis Kwa.'

I grab Dad's hand and pull him onto the buggy. We show our tickets to the steward, who shoots us a stern look as he swerves to avoid throngs of meandering people in transit. He swipes a card next to a pair of reinforced metals doors labelled 'Staff Access Only'.

We speed along concrete corridors. We've been this way before: past baggage handlers heaving suitcases onto long trailers, past crew lounges, past mechanics covered in grease, lying on trolleys as they check the mysterious workings of catering lifts. This is behind the scenes of Theresa and Mary's world, the hustle and bustle of an international airport, the excitement of travel and glamour of flying.

A light on top of the golf buggy spins and flashes, and our attendant waves and nods purposefully at the cabs of other vehicles on the tarmac, who stop or move out of our way. Four men are pulling a staircase from a Boeing 747 so it can begin taxiing for take-off.

'*Dang! Dang!*' our man shouts in Cantonese over his megaphone. 'Wait! Wait!'

My heart races. Dad and I run up the stairs, and the other passengers applaud.

Six packets of peanuts and two tomato juices later, Dad has wrapped himself in pillows and made a bed for himself in the aisle. Finally, I can open the box from Lukin.

I gently prise away the three neat strips of sticky tape holding the wrapping in place, careful to preserve the handmade paper. I run my fingers over a mass of blue and green fibres, bumpy but not rough; the paper is beautiful in its imperfection. I roll it up and use a hair elastic from my wrist to keep it secure. Beneath the wrapping is a Brand X Huaraches shoebox. *Funny that he should buy me sandals*, I think. But when I lift the cardboard lid there's another box, this one made of Lego – red with yellow hinges. I open it and read the note inside. Lukin's handwriting is neater than anyone's in my class.

I don't know when I will see you again because sometimes Father and Mother come to visit me on my school break. Dad's snoring travels down the aisle, filling the cabin; I have to concentrate. *But next time I'm coming back to Hong Kong, your Aunty Theresa said she will try to arrange for you to visit too. This is for you to store something special in until then. Your friend, Rukin.* He has drawn a smiley face above the R.

I fold the note and put it back in the Lego box. I slip Aunty's scarf from around my neck and try to perform the triangulated fold I have watched her do a hundred times. 'It's a Japanese way,' Aunty told me. 'Very neat, very calm, very polite people.' I place my scarf ball over Lukin's letter and smooth it on top, the way Aunty would do.

GRAVEL AND SAUSAGE

MELA'S WHITE VW BEETLE COMES TO A CORNER AT THE crest of a steep hill in Bicton, less than five hundred metres from the riverside home she shares with her parents. She applies the brake at a stop sign, but the car goes straight through. At any other moment, on any other day, this would be of no consequence on the quiet suburban street – any other day, Mela would coast through, doing a gradual handbrake stop at the bottom of the hill. But not today.

An eighteen-wheeled truck comes down the hill at the precise moment Mela turns the corner, the bigger vehicle far too heavy and fast to stop in time. When they collide, Mela hears the splintering sound of her head smashing through the driver's side window. Her face is embedded with glass. The car rolls. Her ribs crack, and her nose and right eye socket break, as chunks of gravel collect in her open wounds.

My grandparents say that my father is a scrooge for providing Mela with the battered old car that led to her accident. They have forever been offering her financial help, but she has forever refused to take it and insists on relying on Francis for a car. Mum and Dad have been to the Family Court, and Dad has to provide the transport for me between households, which most likely means he should drive me. But Dad's interpretation is that he is to 'provide the vehicle', and Mela must do the driving. When he donated the beaten-up car to Mum, she accepted it against her parents' better judgement.

Giving over the car was better than giving over his time to ferry me back and forth – besides, he has four VWs, so he can afford to spare one. He tinkers with them in his front yard, exchanging parts for other parts, then stands back and observes his work, beaming with pleasure as engines roar and fanbelts spin.

Paw Paw holds my six-year-old hand reassuringly as we walk down the wide, long hospital corridor into the light. Mum has been released from intensive care. I'm desperate to see her every day, although I find her appearance very frightening: the right side of her face is deformed with fifty coarse black stitches, knotted at the end of each wound, poking from her swollen red cheeks. The other side of her face still looks like Mum, so I position myself carefully on her left, and she now knows not to turn her head.

When I first saw her after the accident, I ran screaming and crying from the room. So from then on, every time she's read to me in the hospital from my favourite Golden Books, I've tried not to look at her. Of course I can read them myself by now, but it's nicer to be read to, and it gives us a chance to act as though nothing has happened. Our family is really good at that: pretending. It's easier than facing the truth, after all, so Mum and I behave as though it's normal to sit together like this on a hospital bed, reading. She can't put an arm around me, though; her broken ribs make that too painful.

Today's long walk down the corridor happens in slow motion. At first I don't know it's her up ahead. She is running, hurtling herself forward – barefoot, racing out of the light towards me and Paw Paw, terror on her face. She seems possessed and looks right past me, almost through me, the stitches that frighten me so much making her appear even more crazed. Her hospital gown flies behind her.

'Mummy!' I scream. 'Muuuuuuummy!'

Paw Paw and I turn to see Mela run out through the hospital's glass entrance.

I watch as my mother throws herself in front of a moving car. The driver slams on the brakes, but it's too late. Mum rolls across the bonnet, her body hitting the windscreen in a tangle of arms and legs.

Paw Paw screams and pushes my face into the front of her dress. I wriggle free enough to peer out and watch hospital staff run to save the injured woman on the car.

Slow motion ends, sound comes back and real time resumes. I sob into Paw Paw's soft, warm body, and she is crying too.

Paw Paw protects me as best she can from the reality of not only her daughter's illness, but also the harsh truths of living between two homes and never really belonging in either.

Everywhere I go, I am different, even at home – especially at home. There are rules at my grandparents' house like 'Keep your shoes on,' and 'You must eat three big meals a day,' and 'Don't leave any food on your plate,' but at Dad's the rules are the complete opposite: 'Take off your shoes at the door.' 'Eat when you feel like it.' 'Put leftovers in a stew.'

At one end I'm mollycoddled and at the other it's 'fend for yourself'. At Bicton I'm tucked in at night and told stories like a proper little girl, with lights out at seven-thirty. At Dad's I go to bed when I like and will stay up watching a tiny black-and-white TV in the corner of my room until the test pattern comes on.

Paw Paw tells me stories about the Flat People, who live in a big apartment block. There's a 'cleany-clean tribe' and a 'smelly foot tribe'. I'm not sure whether it's a coincidence or she's having a go at Dad, but the cleany-clean tribe sound an awful lot like my Bicton family and the smelly foots a lot like him.

'Sausage, I love you.' Paw Paw gives me a bearhug and tucks me in.

'Where's Mum?' I ask as she turns on my nightlight.

'She's okay. You'll see her tomorrow.'

I lie in bed listening to Mum's screams. The sliding door down the corridor, separating my wing from hers, is closed. Low voices, now. Then nothing. I keep listening, afraid something terrible will happen if I go to sleep.

'Come and watch me,' I call out to Paw Paw the next day. I am up to my sixty-seventh jump on my pogo stick; my record is a hundred and seventeen.

Paw Paw comes out through the laundry to the back step, wiping her hands on a red apron. 'Do you want to do some baking? I have a surprise for you if you do.' She ties up my apron, then, 'Ta-da!' On my head she places a chef's hat that she has sewn for me in secret.

I love it. I wrap my arms around her. She smells like jam toast and hairspray.

'You know, when your mother was your age she loved to bake too. And sew. Just like you.' She squeezes me a little tighter. 'You know your mother would die for you, don't you?'

I look up from my rolling pin, my face and sleeves covered in flour that's somehow missed my apron. *Yes*, I think, *of course I know that, you tell me all the time*, but I don't say anything.

Paw Paw gazes wistfully out the window at boats rocking gently on the water. She has tears in her eyes. 'Well then.' She forces a smile then brings out an array of sugar baubles and cake toppings. 'What are we going to use as decoration? Let's really jazz it up this time.'

PICNIC AND PONYTAIL

I MUST SPEND HALF THE WEEK WITH DAD AND THE OTHER half with Mum – but only under my grandparents' strict supervision; Dad is very specific about that. Another of Dad's rules is that I have to attend Sunday school on Mum's time, so technically I have only three days a week with her.

Switching houses twice a week has its perks: I have two of everything. And its challenges: 'This is an English custom.' 'This is a Chinese custom.' I try to see the bright side – I'm the only child I know from a broken home, let alone a multicultural one. What a trailblazer. Things are now complicated by the fact that Dad has a new girlfriend. Twenty-six years younger than Dad, Angela is a nurse from New Zealand who is now part of the eccentric life of Francis Kwa.

Mum's bones have healed since her car accident a year ago but she has terrible scarring on her face. She refuses additional plastic surgery and instead religiously massages vitamin E cream into her right cheek, chin and forehead twice a day in an attempt to reduce the unsightliness. Today Mum brings me to Dad's place at the usual time, right after compulsory Sunday school. She has packed a picnic of white bread, cheese and Vegemite sandwiches, and she lays out a rug in Dad's backyard on the dry patchy grass between the kitchen and his shed. It was her backyard not so long ago, and although this is a deviation from Dad's rule to leave me at the front door, it seems like a harmless idea. I'm pleased to spend an extra half-hour with Mum.

Then Dad's girlfriend, Angela, flings open the back flyscreen door, and Mum and I look up from our sandwiches. Angela is furious. 'Get lost!' Angela yells.

Mum suddenly seems terrified and hurriedly gathers up her picnic blanket and sandwich container. She opens her car door and flings her things onto the passenger seat. She has that look again where she sees right through me, and drives off without saying goodbye.

After that, Mela refuses to come onto the property – into the house designed and built for her – ever again. Instead, every Sunday she drops me at the top of the driveway. Sometimes Dad and Angela are home, sometimes not.

One day after Mum has dropped me off, I'm mucking around on an old skateboard that Dad picked up from roadside rubbish, trying hard to balance – I'm getting better the more I practise – when I'm shoved in the back. The skateboard shoots out from under me and I fly, headfirst, into the brick wall near our front door. My scalp starts bleeding. It hurts, and I can hear kids laughing as they run away. 'Smackhead,' one shouts and he's not referring to heroin – the inference is that my Asian features make me look as though I have been smacked in the head. 'Hahaha. Dishpan!' Apparently, with a dishpan. These are common racist insults in Scarborough. Towards me at least. I didn't think anyone was home – no one answered when I called out earlier – but now Angela appears and wraps an arm around me. I sob while she bandages my head, enjoying this rare tenderness from her. I often feel like a ghost in my own home so I soak up the attention.

* * *

One Sunday when Mum drops me home, I find wedding photos strewn across the kitchen table. They are Dad and Angela's. I examine them one by one in puzzlement and disbelief, recognising many of the guests, and noticing most of all that I wasn't there and – missing out on every little girl's dream – wasn't asked to be a flower girl. I didn't even know they were engaged, and suddenly I have a stepmother.

By the time I am eight I have been to Hong Kong every year of my life, sometimes twice. I used to go with my dad and mum, then for a while it was just Dad and me, but the last couple of times it's been Dad and Angela, and me.

This trip we're catching up with an 'old friend' of Dad's at our hotel. Her name is Evelyn, and she instantly beguiles me with a dazzling smile. From beneath a plush fur coat, she reveals a hand shimmering with diamonds and holding a large plastic doll with blonde pigtails, dressed in a white skirt, collared shirt and classic Mary-Janes. 'For you, Miss Mimi.'

The doll is just what I've been wishing for, and wishing to be. 'Thank you, Evelyn.'

She grins wider and pats me on the head. 'Oh, darling, please call me *Aunty* Evelyn.'

We all go to yum cha – Evelyn, Dad and Angela, and me. Afterwards, at Evelyn's insistence, I browse shops alone with her while Dad and Angela go back to the hotel.

'I want to marry your father,' Evelyn tells me in a matter-of-fact way, as if this is the most normal conversation to have with an eight-year-old. 'And you can help me.'

Once Evelyn releases me from her clutches, I return to the hotel, loyally keen to alert Dad and Angela to her plan. 'Evelyn says she wants to marry Dad,' I blurt.

'You're lying,' Angela says. My stepmother glares at me then looks to Dad for a response.

I remind myself again that it's safer to keep to myself: quiet on the outside, a tiger's roar within.

'Charm and disarm,' Aunty Theresa coaches me a few days later in her apartment. 'Just smile sweetly!'

I'm still incensed. 'But, Aunty, she is so, so, sooooooo mean to me.'

Aunty thinks for a moment. 'Well then, don't let her bother you. If she does not know how to behave, you can show her how to behave. If someone has bad manners, you do not have to have bad manners too.' We're sitting side by side on Aunty's chaise longue, facing the view from her sunroom windows. 'Now, sit properly.' She illustrates this by straightening her posture. 'Lift your head up, Mimi.' She raises her chin slightly. 'You are Kwa.'

A number of Hong Kong visits go by, all with similar amounts of family drama and a heavy dose of Aunty Theresa's patience and calm, until one trip coincides with a visit from Aunty Clara, who is still living in England, and my grown-up cousins Steven and David. They are all often here – sometimes with Clara's daughter Josephine as well – but our time rarely overlaps. Theresa insists Clara and I must both stay with her, that way my cousins can have a hotel room to themselves. We can share her room, and she will sleep on the fold-out bed in her study. Dad and Angela are at a hotel, the usual routine since the Evelyn incident.

Aunty Theresa is like a maypole at the centre of us all. We are connected by ribbons that we weave in and out.

'Clara is divorced,' Theresa tells me quietly, 'and she's still a "little" upset about it.'

Apart from Clara's charming disposition, the first thing I notice is that she pinches Brigit hard on the arm as soon as Theresa turns her back. Clara obviously thinks that her sister and I aren't looking. I blink to check my eyesight is okay, but

I'm sure I saw it. Brigit just leaves the room, and I don't go after her.

Later we all go to the mall, and without provocation or warning Clara tugs sharply on Brigit's ponytail. Her head is yanked backwards. There it is again – so I'm not crazy. The assault is over quickly, and Brigit keeps walking with her head bowed just a little lower than usual, otherwise acting as though nothing has happened.

Clara realises I've noticed and tries to distract me from Brigit's distress. 'Look, look, Niece Mimi, wouldn't that coat in the shop window look lovely on me?'

Brigit gestures for me to follow Clara, and I catch her wiping away tears as my aunt and I disappear into the store.

'Brigit,' I whisper later on, 'you mustn't let her do that to you. I'm going to tell Aunty Theresa.'

Brigit puts on her best confused look. 'Do what, Mimi? Oh, Mimiiiii. You must not do the worrying, Mimi. I will be in the very big trouble if you are doing the worrying.'

That night, Aunty Clara keeps me awake with a scary story. It's about a man who feels guilty because he stole from his brother, so he spends hours hitting his stomach against the edge of a desk until he dies. Clara does the actions against Theresa's desk to illustrate the brutal suicide. 'And there, that is the lesson,' she says triumphantly.

I'm not quite sure what the lesson is, other than to never share a room with Aunty Clara again.

I lie awake all night staring at the ceiling. *Is that how her father died?* I wonder. *My grandfather.* Maybe it wasn't poison after all – maybe Grandfather stole from his brother during the Japanese occupation, then couldn't live with the guilt. I have no idea.

The next day Clara's two adult sons visit Theresa's apartment. David and Steven are twenty-three and nineteen. They tower over me, so I have to stand on a chair to be in a photo with them.

'Hold still,' chirps Theresa as she takes the Polaroid. She claps her hands joyfully, happy we're all there with her, together.

'Mother,' says David, turning to Clara, 'what time is convenient for *you* for me and Steven to meet friends for dinner?'

Clara swings around with the frightening precision of a martial artist and, to my great surprise, slaps him hard across the cheek. 'You must ALWAYS call me MUMMY.'

A red mark appears on David's face, made worse as he turns crimson with embarrassment. 'Yes, Mummy,' he says, bowing his head.

Brigit, who is standing in the doorway to the kitchen, lowers her eyes too.

'Come, come now,' says Theresa, putting an arm around David, 'none of this. Clara, I have a necklace for you. Come to my dressing-room.'

The four of us can hear the sisters shouting at each other, and we awkwardly make small talk. Theresa emerges composed and calm, but Clara looks angry. She cuffs David around the ear and ushers her sons to the door, then turns to hold my ten-year-old face in her hands. 'Pretty, so pretty. *Ho lang, ho lang.* You must be careful and smart too. You are so pretty.' She pauses. 'And little bit fat. So be careful your waistline too. Ooooh, so chubby fat. Fat. Fat. Fat.' She squeezes my cheeks and laughs at her own joke, moving towards the door again before stopping with an expression that suggests she's forgotten something important. 'Ah, but Brigit, you are the one who is the fattest. Must be the happiest then, huh?' She looks at Brigit, who is in the corner, clearly trying hard not to meet her eye. 'Jolly and fat, haha.'

Brigit rushes over and gives Clara's black patent leather Chanel loafers a quick polish with the shoe kit kept religiously at the door for just such an occasion, before bending over to help Clara put them on.

'Goodbye, Mrs Bryan, thank you for coming to visit us,' she says earnestly, honouring Clara's decision to retain her married name since her divorce fourteen years ago.

'Ugh.' Clara treads on the sleeve of Brigit's cardigan and holds her foot there just a fraction too long for it to be accidental, then walks out the door.

David and Steven pull Brigit to her feet. Each young man gives her a warm, apologetic hug as they leave. Clara, halfway to the elevator, doesn't see David shoot me a wink – my favourite cousin is telling me not to worry, it's all okay.

I can tell that Aunty Theresa is flabbergasted by Aunty Clara's visit. Still, she speaks no ill to me of her badly behaved sister. Perhaps to Theresa, what she and all her siblings have been through is more than enough reason for a little madness.

That night, Aunty sings to me as Brigit tucks me in. I've reclaimed the sofa bed in Aunty's mahogany study, where, surrounded by ivory and jade statuettes, I lie on plush, tasselled velvet cushions, snuggled under a featherdown covered in embroidered silk.

Brigit's small, plain room with her small, plain bed is just on the other side of the wall.

Aunty sings the Doris Day song 'Que Sera, Sera' as I drift off to sleep. She loves singing me this carefree song about letting go of trying to control everything in your life. When she sings it my worries disappear. We can't control or predict the future – we can only resist or surrender and, either way, what will happen will just happen.

There's a sense of calm tonight in Peace Mansion. This is the only world I need, and I wish I could live in it forever.

Back at Mandarin Gardens, I receive a letter from Aunty Theresa every few weeks. But one day when I check the letter box, I see her handwriting on a letter addressed to Dad, so I take it to him.

It is so terrible, she writes. Patrick and Elaine need to get out. They have two daughters. You can help them. I will pay for you to go. I think you can get them out.

When Kwa blood calls, there is no refusing it. Dad announces he is going to 'rescue' some Chinese relatives from the Communist party in China and he will bring them back to Perth. He prepares sponsorship documents to bring his half-brother's family to Australia, then flies to Beijing to meet the Kwa family of four – Elaine and Patrick and their two daughters, Gar Ping and Gar Hong. The girls' Western names are Karen and Cathy. Patrick is eleventh brother and son of Grandfather Ying Kam's wife number two. In other words, Patrick is Dad's half-brother.

During the Cultural Revolution in China, art and artefacts were defaced and destroyed because they represented the 'old way of thinking'. Patrick and Elaine and their neighbours hid Chinese art under the floorboards and behind false walls, but the Red Army unearthed most of it and set it alight. Patrick and Elaine have only a few pieces left.

Francis arrives in China carrying an almost empty suitcase with a false bottom.

He and Patrick meet for the first time since they were boys. Francis meets his past; Patrick meets his future. Francis asks for the art, and stuffs the 'priceless' paintings into the false bottom of his suitcase, covering them over and praying they won't be detected. Not much escapes the Cultural Revolution, and the penalty would be long-term imprisonment, even death, a far greater cost than the paintings are worth. Francis takes the risk anyway, and returns home with the artworks, having lodged the migration documents with the Australian authorities.

Very soon, the family's visas come through and, as promised, they move to Australia, staying in our Scarborough house for a time while they try to adjust to the new language and culture. Patrick and Elaine are so grateful they cry tears of relief.

WOMBLES AND GOOSEDOWN

I HAVE A FEW FRIENDS AT SCHOOL — I'VE WORKED HARD TO make them — but I'm not often allowed to have them over. Meanwhile, Dad has been renting out our next-door duplex to a string of temporary tenants, and he says their kids 'have to' play with me because I am the 'landlord's daughter', so I share my swing set and trampoline with these children passing through. Sometimes they seem to like me, sometimes the opposite, and I try not to get attached either way because they always leave me.

More reliable, I find, are characters in books and on TV shows. They are always there for me. I'm particularly fond of a grey-haired bunch of chilled-out mole-like creatures who walk on their hind legs and forage through rubbish, having wonderful adventures wherever they go. *The Wombles* is my favourite show; I have the picture books too. They are a happy part of my life — the opening soundtrack has me running to the television every time.

I was born into a kind of Womble family, with pathological hoarders on both sides. Yes, pathological, I'm talking TV documentary level. Hoarding will one day be recognised as a psychological disorder, but in the 1980s we call this extreme behaviour 'eccentric'.

The local council's hard rubbish day is a special event for Dad. Anything kerbside is fair game – bad luck if you rested something against your front fence while you went inside for a moment, because it won't be there when you come back if Francis Kwa was driving down your street.

I help Dad hook up a trailer to our station wagon, and off we go, bobbing up and down on the vinyl seats, on the lookout for stuff, any stuff. You just never know what will come in handy when you're a Womble. 'Keep your eyes peel,' Dad says. His favourite cautionary tale is that if we don't keep our eyes peeled, who knows what precious junk – I mean gems – we will miss.

Scraps of metal, broken microwaves and kettles, toys and bikes beyond repair, and building materials – especially building materials – all get loaded onto our trailer. Dad has a meticulous mad-scientist sort of way to classify nuts, bolts, nails, pipes, poles and planks, so he can keep them forever, 'just in case'. He also collects old furniture: couches, dressers, drawers, even skanky mattresses. 'You never know,' he says when I protest about having to haul items three times my size onto the trailer, 'we may need them one day.'

Our property is about four and a half thousand square metres, amply sized for excessive storage.

I help him haul steel pipes and splintered wood in from the trailer as I wonder if this is a metaphor for some major void in my father, a hole in his heart, perhaps a result of the years lacking love from his parents or of the childhood he had, what he saw and what he lost. A chasm in a dragon, so hungry that no pile of loot can ever be enough. He's the dragon in *Lord of the Rings* lying atop a mountain of treasure, guarding it with his life.

Dad commits to memory a blueprint of what sits on every shelf, what's stacked in every corner, what's wedged into every crevice of every shed, mezzanine and rooftop. When I air my concerns over the ever-growing junk mounds cluttering up our lives, he snaps tersely, 'Iiiiiiiii neeeeeeeeed it.' Then he gathers his patience, explaining slowly and deliberately that I'm 'just a kid' and 'don't understand'.

Sunflowers cover a quarter acre of our land. They're taller than me, their beautiful faces turned towards the sun, their stems thick skinned and strong, hardy armour in scorching heat and torrential rain. Even as a child I have no delusions these friends – as I've grown to regard them – will stay either, as it won't be long before Dad concretes over them with his dreams. The flowers stand in rows, stoic warriors. They shield me from the dragon as I hide among them; their rough leaves make it far too uncomfortable to stay all afternoon in the cool shade, but I have peace for a while. I am a tiger cub. I curl up and close my eyes.

Later on, Dad and I shoot tin cans off the rail of a fence between our garden and the sunflower patch, the petalled warriors unmoved by the danger.

Dad shows me how to load his rifle, then he aims and fires, missing the cans. A bullet sails into the yellow distance. 'I'm going to build a hotel there,' he tells me as he reloads. 'I'm going to build a hotel, and we will be rich.'

He hands me the rifle. I aim and fire at the cans and miss too, making a hole in the fence, the force flinging me onto my back on the ground.

'Buddy hopeless,' Dad says, laughing as he picks up the rifle, reloads, aims and fires again. Metal hits metal, making a sharp *ping* that gives me a fright.

'I don't really want to do this anymore, Dad,' I say as I dust myself off and stand beside him. 'What if we hurt someone?'

'Ahahaha, always worry. Buddy hell. Worry like a woman. When I was your age, I was looking after the guns for the whole Japanese Army.'

Dad takes his gun back to the Wombled school locker next to our Wombled ping-pong table. Once he has placed the rifle upright inside, he locks the door with a rusty padlock. He returns the key to a large metal ring of twenty other keys, enough to make a prison warden green with envy. Dad has attached it to a length of elastic that retracts back to the belt loop on his jeans, so the cacophony of keys casually hangs from his waist next to his brown leather coin pouch, in which there are washers and thumbtacks as well as coins.

Francis Kwa continues to build his dream: Mandarin Gardens, the biggest youth hostel and backpackers in the Southern Hemisphere. Past the firing-range fence and over the sunflower field, he lays slab after slab of the foundation for his hotel, along with more sheds.

My favourite addition is a 25-metre swimming pool, half the length of an Olympic-sized pool. Ours is actually only twenty-three metres, but Dad says no one will ever check. I roller-skate in its concrete shell, pretending to be the figure-skater Torvill with her Olympic partner, Dean – until I fall over, grazing my knees on the rough surface.

Then a concrete and Besser-block monster rises up from the ground. Its thirteen apartments are like Rubik's Cubes that can be converted into various configurations to accommodate various needs: two bunks and a double, two singles and a queen, a room for a large family with a partition that swings across for two smaller families to fit. Dad has thought of everything. At Angela's behest he even buys a Volvo like Aunty's, only it's a station wagon not a sedan. He puts custom KWA numberplates on it, so everyone will know who we are.

Scarborough is as magnetic to vagrants and transients as ever, and in local slang it now has the nickname Scabs. On the Mandarin Gardens flyer, the services we provide are beyond anything a Scabs hotel has ever offered. Dad lists our amenities and services at every opportunity: on our signage, our flyers and his business cards, as well as in most conversations.

MANDARIN GARDENS AMENITIES AND
SERVICES
(in no particular order)
- Resident gas fitter (Dad)
- Resident structural engineer (Dad)
- Resident electrical engineer (Dad)
- Legal advice (Dad)
- Arbitration advice (Dad)
- In-house babysitter (Me)
- Room service (Me)
- In-house video (pirated) (Me)
- Kitchen facilities
- Laundry facilities
- Printing and office services (Me)
- Proofreading (Me)
- Marriage celebrant (Dad)
- BBQ facilities
- Trampoline
- Table tennis
- Playground
- Telephone booth
- Carparking
- 25-metre pool

Mandarin Gardens achieves a 4.5-star 'Hotel' rating under the governing Royal Automobile Club's independent 200 criteria system. Unfortunately, we fall short of the half star for not having a restaurant. Undeterred, Francis comes up with a number of ideas to obtain this. They include assigning me to be the full-time chef, then ruling me out not because I have school to attend but because I'm not confident cooking with a wok yet, or catering for eighty people. The fact that I am only ten years old doesn't enter into the equation. Next, in another attempt at the elusive missing half star, Francis approaches the RAC with the idea that a barbecue could qualify as a restaurant because there's seating nearby, but his proposal is rejected.

My dad establishes a ramshackle system where backpackers provide cleaning services in return for free accommodation or reduced rent, and I have to pick up what they don't do or don't do well. 'Pay peanuts, get monkeys,' Dad says. He loves that expression.

Angela leaves me to-do lists, and they're often long:

MIMI: TO DO
- *Empty and count coins from gold phone*
- *Empty and count coins from washing machine and dryer*
- *Change linen U4*
- *Clean U8 for guests arriving 2 pm*
- *Engrave new toaster and cutlery U13*
- *Scrub pool tiles*
- *Wash Volvo*
- *Collect rent – Bunkhouse tenants Rm4 not paid*
- *Man check-in counter (take cordless phone and intercom when doing jobs so tenants can contact you)*

Once I'm done I am allowed to see my friends, but my list of chores is usually long, so most days I can't.

One day, after I've emptied the gold phone, someone yanks it off the bench in the phone box under the stairs and tries to make a dash. Dad chases them and they throw the heavy

My grandfather Ying Kam, who was born in 1868, with my grandmother – his third wife, Ng Yuk – and his second wife. I had always been told that Ying Kam had died of a broken heart, but recently Dad said his father had died because he refused to give up his business to the Japanese, suggesting he was killed during the occupation.

A Kwa wedding. Ying Kam stands in the middle behind his daughters, the two brides. My dad, Tak Lau, is in the front row, fourth from the right.

The four children – Clara, Francis, Mary and Theresa – with Ng Yuk (centre)

Dad in Australia. He thinks this was taken in Victoria.

Aunty Theresa's BOAC days

Aunty Theresa at her shop in the Mandarin Oriental Hotel

Mum and Dad on their wedding day, with my mum's sister, Zora, brother, Roger, and parents (my paw paw and granddad)

Mum and me

The only photo of Mum, Dad and me together

Watching over me. Aunty Mary, left, Aunty Clara and Aunty Theresa
with her hand on my shoulder

On holiday in Hong Kong. Me in my school uniform, next to Ng Yuk,
then from left to right, Clara, Steven, Mary, David, Theresa, Dad and Angela

Dad and me in the sunflower patch, where I would play and hide,
and where we shot his rifle

Mandarin Gardens. Our pool and all those balconies

Me, John, our kids and my mum

Jerome, me, Dad and Adrian – House of Kwa

telephone at Dad, damaging his hand. One of his fingers is never the same after that. Crooked forever.

With dozens of travellers to organise, Mandarin Gardens becomes too unwieldy for Dad, Angela and me to manage on our own, so Dad hires the first in a long line of managers. They get free accommodation and loose change for food in return for on-call attendance, twenty-four seven.

For a time, I'm best friends with the daughter of a couple who oversee our resort, Jill and Dale. Everyone calls her Monkey because she likes climbing trees and is a tomboy. She's a year older than me, wears dungarees and has unruly curls and equally unruly freckles. I like her right away. We play endlessly, keeping walkie-talkies permanently on us so we can stay in touch even when we're in bed.

One day, Monkey accidentally jumps on a rusty nail and leaps off it just as quick. Tears well in her eyes, but she doesn't cry or complain. She is the bravest girl I know.

Jill is a truck driver. Dale isn't really Monkey's dad, but she pretends he is. She says her dad didn't want her so she prefers to live as if he never existed. One day Monkey takes a big run-up and pushes Angela into the pool. She is still the bravest girl I know.

After that I'm banned from seeing her. Luckily, it's hard to separate us: she lives next door, and our bedrooms share a balcony with only a partition in between. We sit back to back either side of the swinging wall, talking and telling stories.

No one can keep us apart, until Angela fires Jill and Dale. They leave, taking Monkey with them.

SOAP OPERA AND PHILOSOPHY

'WHAT, YOU'RE GOING TO HONG KONG AGAIN?!' MY classmates always ask in disbelief. Most of them have never been further south than Esperance or north than Bali. 'Back to see all the Ching-Chong-Chogies,' someone will sneer. Then the group will chant, 'Ching-Chong-Chogie, Ching-Chong-Chogie,' and I'll laugh as though I'm in on the joke, not the butt of it.

The next time I visit Hong Kong, the second time this year, Lukin isn't there. It's already 1986 and we've caught up four times since our first awkward meeting, usually playing Lego and video games or digging in and around the Peace Mansion gardens. We kept writing in between, but that's become less frequent because his father has been transferred back home to Dubai. Lukin now flies there from his British boarding school during semester breaks, and I doubt we'll ever see each other again. The year before, it got a bit weird when he kissed me – we were only ten. It was an innocent kiss on the cheek and would have been sweet if it hadn't happened while I was admiring my effort to build a taller Lego tower than his. One minute he was reading an Astro Boy comic book, the next his lips were on my cheek. It kind of spoiled our friendship, but I still miss him a little.

'I know!' says Aunty, doing a hip wiggle. 'Let's go to the beauty parlour.' She always thinks getting my hair and nails done will cheer me up. 'Rukin is such sweet boy. You can stay in touch, you know. One day you could be a diplomat and he could be a diplomat and you may meet again.'

Every year I am Aunty Theresa's little protege for a month or so – two visits, roughly a fortnight each, sometimes more. I am like a daughter to her. Aunty really wants me to be a diplomat, but I don't quite understand what that is. 'You hold your head high,' she explains. 'You talk to people. You travel. You are like royalty. You meet royalty. I met many, many diplomats on my flights. They really do have the life. Parties and socialising. Wearing nice clothes. I was like a diplomat once. I did some translating for some important men. I was very young, my English was terrible. I don't know what they ask me, or what they are saying at all, but I'm good at pretend.' She laughs, and I giggle. 'Did I tell you about the elocution lessons I had with stones in my mouth?'

We sit side by side having our nails done. I choose a lurid fluorescent pink for my fingers, while Aunty just wants her toes done – in red.

'I always leave my fingernails natural. On the airline it was forbidden to have a colour. And I swim so much these days, they'd get ruined now anyway.'

I drink in the way the salon staff defer to Aunty as if she is some kind of aristocrat, and then how quickly she puts them at ease. In no time they're treating her like an old friend.

'You know' – she winks, and a young apprentice places a milkshake in front of me – 'you must know how to treat people.'

I draw the delicious vanilla-flavoured milk into my mouth through a straw.

'If you smile ...' Aunty pauses for me to finish her sentence.

'The whole world smiles with you,' I complete the phrase, wiping a drop of milkshake from my chin.

She grins as I fan out my fingers and blow on my wet nails.

'Everyone loves you, Aunty.'

She raises her chin and looks down her nose at me. 'Well' – she smiles again – 'maybe it's because I am interested in everybody and I do not judge them or what they tell me. Rich or poor. Important or not important. Complaining or happy. I simply say, "Is that so?"' She laughs. 'If the news sounds good, I smile. If it is so-so or not so good, I keep a face like this.' She straightens up her face. 'Serlious. Velly serlious.'

I adjust my expression to match hers.

'Many people likes to complain very much,' she continues. 'So I do like this.' She nods slowly with a serious expression. 'And I say ...' she pauses, and we finish the sentence together: 'Is that so?'

'Never frown,' she tells her little shadow. She reads me Lao Tzu philosophy. 'Never boast. Boastful people do not know how to behave.' She teaches me Tai Chi. 'Let the light from within you shine. Never let them know if you are upset.' And she paints with me. 'There are so many ways to express yourself.'

At night while Brigit irons, I hear the maid's laughter and dismay – 'Oh no, Ferdinand!' – over her favourite Filipino soap opera on Hong Kong free-to-air. It flickers on a small black-and-white TV on the chest of drawers in the corner of her tiny room.

I sit beside Aunty in her palatial study as she writes letters to ladies and baronesses, and an occasional Kwa. When she writes to a Kwa, it's usually in delicate staccato pen-stroked Chinese characters down a page, often finished off with a marble chop of her name character. She dips it in red paste from a green stone bowl with a carved dragon on its lid, gently wiping any excess on a spare sheet of clean paper before bringing the pillar-shaped stone chop down firmly to stamp the denouement of her prose. After just a second, she lifts the chop back up and cleans the chiselled stone with a soft leather navy-blue rag.

Aunty writes a cheque and slips it into an envelope addressed to a Kwa. She does this a lot – sends thousands of dollars to help educate half nieces and nephews, distant cousins and their spouses. 'If we can help, we should.' She turns over the monogrammed envelope and dabs her finger into a small round carved wooden dish containing a wet circular sponge. 'You know, your third cousin, Nin Hua, in Guangdong, is a doctor now.' To moisten the glue, she runs her finger along one side of the triangular flap then the other. 'And Seventh Brother from Second Grandfather has a daughter in Montreal studying law.' She seals the envelope. 'I helped them both.' In her desk drawer, she finds a stamp. 'This is for your niece in Hainan province.' Aunty wets the stamp on the round sponge and presses it down with her forefinger. 'She wants to be a chef and work in a big hotel one day.'

The more I visit Hong Kong, the closer I become to Brigit. I enjoy being in Aunty's Swatow Lace shop with Christina and Amy, but I love my time with Brigit more. To me, she is an in-house beautician, nail technician, chef and counsellor. She is like a sister. She has watched me grow up.

I've started trying to mirror my life of independence in Scarborough by setting out on my own between Peace Mansion and Causeway Bay, so Theresa enlists Brigit as her clandestine spy. There are legitimate fears I could be kidnapped – children of wealthy Chinese tycoons often are. 'Aunty, the kidnappers will get a shock once they learn Dad has no money,' I joke, but she is still protective. So, instead of us going out together like we usually would, Brigit follows me clumsily through Hong Kong's streets. She stops at newsstands, leafing through magazines and pretending to read like the spies in the corny dramas she watches while she's ironing. People stare at me because of my Eurasian looks and my height, making Brigit more nervous on my tail. I give her a few scares for fun but never really try to lose her.

On my way home, she boards the same bus as me and sits at the back.

I turn around and smile at her. 'Come sit with me, Brigit.'

'Oooooh, Mimi, I didn't see you there.'

It's the perfect charade. No one ever arrives back at the apartment unhappy, and Aunty scolds us both, in jest, for being late. 'Brigit, I'm soooo hungry. Eat-eat-eat, fat-fat-fat. Where is my dinner, Brigit?' Aunty laughs and rubs her belly, and Brigit serves a five-course meal.

While she cooks, I often flit in and out of the tiny kitchen, the output of which is like that of a Michelin star restaurant. 'Teach me, teach me, Brigit,' I beg. She shoos me away, but I sneak back in and skirt around her, my head bobbing up either side of her round frame, trying to catch a glimpse over her shoulder or under her arm. 'C'mon. Teach me, Brigit.'

But she never does. She seems embarrassed that she might know anything worth teaching. 'Oh, Mimi, you are so funny. Why would you ever need to cook?' Brigit knows I am born of privilege and cannot comprehend that where I'm from we don't all have maids and cooks and drivers. 'How do you eat, Mimi?' 'How do you have clean clothes?' 'How do you survive?' 'Oh, Mimi, I am so sorry for you.'

I wander into Brigit's room where she is watching another overacted soap opera, ironing and folding to the soundtrack of her life. I stand next to her and fold too. TV is her escape – it must be a nice break from her life of servitude and more plausible theatrics, and the very real act of survival. Brigit was born with a script in her hands and knows the role she must play: Theresa is master and Brigit servant, with no deviation from birthright.

'Go. Go, Mimi.' Brigit snatches the laundry from me. 'Aunty will be cross if she catch you here.'

I find it hard to make sense of the inequality. Brigit stands while we eat and serves us with a lowered gaze. She follows behind Aunty, forever folding, dusting, replacing and rearranging, sweeping away dirt and disorder in our wake. Wiping, polishing, straightening, placing a stray necklace neatly in a golden dish. Everything is perfect, though not without significant effort. Brigit retires to her tiny room, exhausted from making our lives decadently comfortable. I sleep on layers of sheepskin under woollen blankets and duvets of goose down. Brigit is up before dawn, cooking and scrubbing, and whenever I offer a hand, 'No, noooo, Mimi. Off you go.'

She heads to the market, knowing the optimal days and times for the best produce and catch. I tail *her* this time, following from a distance, watching attentively as she navigates Hong Kong as if it's her home. I watch her compete against other maids, haggling over prize broccoli and rare mushrooms. She is one of them – one of Hong Kong's hundreds of thousands of maids. She turns and sees me, then quickly pretends she doesn't.

She sends every cent she earns to her parents and siblings back home, an hour south of Manila, visiting once a year at least when Theresa is travelling.

When no one is looking, I laugh with Brigit at silly things. I ask her questions about her life and family that no one else in House of Kwa has ever bothered to ask. She longs to go home. I hug her and cry. But I know Aunty needs her, and I tell her how valued she is and how Miss Kwa could never manage without her, adding to the guilt that keeps her here.

I am part of the problem. Aunty has taught me carefully and deliberately; she is kind and wise, but also at pains to keep some distance between mistress and servant. She and Dad grew up with maids, and until Dad moved to Australia he'd never known a life without one.

Aunty's friends and acquaintances frequently offer advice on how 'one must keep "the help" in their place'. One day she tells me, 'Do not tip too much. Because next time they will expect more and then they will tell their friends. And then they will tell their friends. And then everyone will expect more, and prices will go up everywhere.' I feel heavy with the weight of responsibility not to start a global economic crisis. I'm not allowed to tip Brigit, so with the money Aunty sometimes gives me I buy clothes for her to send to her siblings and nieces and nephews.

Another goodbye. I hug Aunty. I hug Brigit.

Dad scolds me on the way to the airport. 'You don't go spending your money to give her anything. That's why your aunty employ her. She is lucky enough already. You're too much like your mother – she give away everything to the beggar in the street.'

STICKYTAPE AND BELLS

I'M ELEVEN, AND MUM IS MOVING OUT OF HER CHILDHOOD room at Bicton into the basement. She can't take the constant shouting of the man next door any longer. The light he shines through her bedroom window keeps her awake all night, even though she pulls her heavy curtains tightly closed. His nasty threats torment her despite the earplugs and earmuffs and beanies she layers on. It's particularly upsetting that he rings bells just to annoy her; they make a horrible din, despite the classical music she plays louder and louder each day, turning the volume up so high that Paw Paw, Granddad and I have to keep the solid wooden sliding door along the corridor to her bedroom permanently shut.

In the night I hear her cry out and moan in pain. Occasionally, she stomps past my room on a mission. Paw Paw always tries to stop her. 'Mela, go back to bed. It's late. Let's talk about it in the morning.' Usually, Mum pays no attention and flies through the kitchen and out the back door. One night, before anyone can get their dressing-gowns on, she strides up the neighbouring Moss family's driveway. She takes their front doorknocker in her fist and slams it down forcefully, again and again. It's 1 am. 'Leave me alone!' Mum screams at Mr Moss, who has opened the door dazed and confused in his pyjamas. 'Just leave me alone!'

Paw Paw tucks me into bed again. 'Mrs Moss drowned in their pool,' my grandmother whispers. 'There's a touch of it in their family too. They understand. Granddad is over there now to smooth things over. Don't you worry. You get some sleep now.'

Moments later, Granddad brings Mum home. She's screaming, 'Let go of me! He is trying to kill me! Don't you understand? He will kill me. I hate you! Let me go.' The sliding door closes, and I bury my head in my pillow.

We all hope the relocation to the room downstairs will be a positive change, but instead Mum's behaviour intensifies and her self-isolation increases, creating a hermit in a hoarder's den.

'Hi, Mum, can I come in?' I ask. Then I wince, overcome by the unbearable stench. 'Mum?' I look around, horrified.

It wasn't this bad last time I was down here; now it seems there's nowhere to sit. I wade through the bathroom and kitchenette, past boxes filled with clothes and toys.

It is a generous-sized house, but Mum prefers this small corner. She feels safer here. There's a lot of storage space in the house as well, but she prefers to keep everything with her, 'just in case'. She and Dad have hoarding in common, at least. Hoarding to answer voices. Hoarding to answer loss.

Frantic lists occupy every vertical space not already intruded upon by stacks of books and engorged rubbish bags. Mum has used Blu Tack to attach them to walls and cupboard doors, the wallpaper groaning with notes and reminders, and stickytape holds up line after line of words: random words, sequential words, shopping lists, notes to self, notes to others, plans, strategies, labels. It's dizzying. And the room smells of fear, which makes me afraid too, though of what I'm not sure. There is nothing on any of Mum's lists that offers me any hints.

I look around again for a place to sit, but everything is covered in newspapers. There's nothing to say, anyway. Mum only talks about Mr Moss, who rings a bell at her door all day and all night, in his pyjamas.

'But Mr Moss wouldn't do that,' I say.

'No, it's definitely him.' Mum goes on to tell me I don't understand and I'm just a child. 'Oh, Mimi.' She looks at me with burdensome pity. 'One day, you will see.' She shakes her head. Then she tells me Mr Moss only goes away when I visit and will continue shouting at her after I leave.

I am afraid to stay. I am afraid to go. My mother's fear seeps in through my every pore, filling me up until I can't breathe.

CINDERELLA AND CIGARETTES

THE YEAR MY MUM MOVES DOWNSTAIRS, I BECOME BEST friends with Michelle in Grade Six. We are close and highly competitive, developing a sadistic way of showing our mutual adoration by jabbing each other in the thigh with freshly sharpened pencils. It hurts and we bleed, but we keep playing the stupid game during class, determined to see who will give in first. We're fascinated with self-harm, sometimes turning the pencil on our own legs to condition ourselves against the pain. She calls me 'chog' and I call her 'wog'. It helps us both be in on the joke of racist remarks we receive.

Kids at my primary school with older siblings at Scarborough High, the tough public school down the road, are a source of the worst ideas. Michelle's fifteen-year-old sister, Sherrie, goes there.

'Get a rubber,' Michelle says to me. We giggle because even though she means 'get an eraser', 'rubber' is slang for 'condom'. 'Get a rubber and rub it like this on your arm so it burns the skin, and then you'll end up with a scar like you've cut your wrists.'

Among local teenagers, suicide attempts are a sick badge of honour. 'Life sucks and then you die,' is the quote that circulates. The rubber trick is meant to give you a scar as if you've at least tried, although anyone who cares knows you've used a rubber, so really there's no point other than desensitising you against pain.

Even so, I rub with an eraser day and night until the red turns raw, and the red raw becomes an open wound. I hope it will scab and scar nicely, but instead it festers, becoming so infected Mum takes me to a doctor, where I make up a story. 'I slid my arm across my school desk in a sudden movement. The desk was splintering, so it caught my skin and cut my wrist.' No one comments. I'm put on a strong dose of antibiotics and end up with a scar shaped like the underside of a slug.

My other best friend is Narelle, a year younger than me. Her wild brown hair is a lion mane; she is a lion, and I'm a tiger. We find each other in the schoolyard jungle. Youngsters lost in family sadness finding refuge in empathetic friendships, getting so close we inhabit a life together. We don't belong anywhere, so we band together. We fear, and we fight, getting tougher and stronger.

Narelle's dad hung himself when she was small. No matter how many seances we conduct in the middle of the night, I'm never convinced that her older sister isn't pushing the pointer to frighten us, and it does frighten us. Lying head to toe, we share a mattress and a blanket. We smoke a packet of cigarettes between us and resort to scrounging butts from an overflowing ashtray. Our dinner is white bread Smith's Lites crisps and cheese Twisties sandwiches with butter and tomato sauce. Of course, we use either the crisps or the Twisties – you wouldn't mix both in the same sandwich, that would be ridiculous.

Narelle's mum, Carol, does the best she can with two daughters. She's so young herself, sitting quietly reading Mills & Boon novels, smoke swirling around her. A motley crew of her daughters' friends come and go. It's like a halfway house, but Carol prefers it that way because at least she knows where her daughters are. She figures that's better than the alternative: to have them 'God knows where on the back of motorbikes at parties with older men', sometimes old men. She does the best she can.

I ride the bus with Carol and Narelle to collect food with pension stamps from a warehouse far away. A volunteer hands over toilet paper and bags of cornflakes, tomato sauce, Lites, Samboy chips and Spam: non-perishables to get Carol and her kids by, along with dozens of freeloaders. I'm one of the latter, so I make myself useful by providing an extra pair of hands to take home additional provisions. Carol has saved up her vouchers to make the long trip worthwhile.

'You're rich,' Narelle tells me one day.

'No, I'm not,' I reply, but I know my life is luxurious compared to hers.

Friends like Narelle and another girl, Liesle, come over to my place to enjoy the middle-class life for a change. A high life. They live on Stanley Street, a few hundred metres from one another, and I live a street away – a world away – on Wheatcroft.

Liesle lives with her father, a huge heavy-set German man who sits in an armchair all day in an apartment too small for him. You can turn one way and touch the kitchen table, then the other and you're standing in the bathroom.

'But you're rich,' Liesle says one day when I complain about a long list of chores I've been given.

She's right, I realise. I should stop moaning. But although I have so much, I feel terribly lonely, sometimes even when I'm surrounded by friends. They cocoon me, and I call them family, the family I choose. They are my people and they see me – or at least I think they do. We're all running so fast from our own lives, perhaps we don't see at all.

Narelle and I discover shoplifting, smoking cigarettes and pot, drinking Southern Comfort, and snowdropping (stealing clothing from washing lines). Adults buy alcohol for us. We befriend a group of men who are more than happy to assist, and I tell Dad I'm staying at a friend's.

I tell myself our motley crew is all that matters, and my eleven-year-old life gradually becomes about booze and boys, so by twelve I'm pretty good at pulling off a double existence.

'Goodnight, Dad.'

'Goodnight,' he replies.

I close my bedroom door, pull on a coat, slide open the balcony window on the third storey and climb onto a railing, gripping the narrow surface with my bare feet. It's a dizzying height, and I cling to the gutter as I try not to look down at the concrete staircase and brick driveway. 'Okay.' I expel a breath. 'You can do this.'

I must be a sight: a twelve-year-old girl in a long black trenchcoat, barefoot and shimmying along the side of a three-storey building. I've got my shoes in my coat pockets. I have to stretch to manoeuvre around the partitions dividing the flats, a silhouette against the night sky, not looking down. I sidestep along the edge of units eight, nine, ten, eleven, twelve. No one sees me, but I can see tenants watching TV, having dinner and drinks.

I can't go any further so I jump down onto unit thirteen's balcony. The door is open, and the backpackers inside get a big fright. 'Jesus Christ! Aren't you the owner's daughter? What are you doing?'

I explain I'm sneaking out and use their front door to escape into the darkness, a tiger running alone in the night.

How I'm not raped and killed on these adventures, I don't know. I'm lucky to have survived the balcony let alone the streets of this rough suburb. I feel invincible, though, and free.

Whether I'm singing at the top of my lungs with Narelle as we traipse the footpaths, or I'm walking in the shadows on my own, I don't feel vulnerable. I'm entitled to own the darkness, and I am whoever I choose to be among strangers of the night, on the beach, by a bonfire, or rolling in sand dunes. At home, I am powerless; outside, I take control.

Carol always knows where Narelle is, because Narelle never lies to her mum. My parents have no idea.

One day Narelle and I wag school. That's another thing I learned from my friends, or maybe we learned it from each other. I master both parents' signatures, bringing in notes to explain my absences. I'm asthmatic, and forging also helps me to avoid sport.

Today Narelle and I play truant from school to sit in a toilet block at Abbett Park. You can do a lot of graffiti when you have all day. I'm on a scholarship at St Mary's and am in my uniform, while Narelle is in her public school uniform. We draw anarchy and peace signs on the walls, smoking Alpine cigarettes and talking about our fears. We are misfits.

We've missed school so often lately that the toilet block has become boring and by noon we head to the beach, where men in their twenties and thirties skateboard and lie around, spending their dole money on arcade games – *Galaga*, *Wonder Boy*, *1942*. They're notorious for supplying cigarettes and alcohol to underage kids.

Narelle and I give them our saved lunch money, and they produce a bottle of Southern Comfort and a cask of Fruity Lexia wine, known as goon juice.

We're joined by Louis Johnson, a teenager who is wagging school too. When he gets drunk, he inflates a cask-wine bladder like a pillow and pretends to sleep on it. A man shoves straws up Louis's nose, and everyone laughs.

Louis is the child of a Luritja and Arrernte family, stolen from his mother in Alice Springs when he was three months old and adopted by a white family in Perth. He is bullied at school and drifts in and out of various social orbits; you never know when he'll turn up. He is called 'nigger'. I am still called 'smackhead' and 'dishpan'. The name callers are people we know and people we don't. They're people we call friends and people we don't. Usually no harm is meant – it's just the way it is, just an ignorant way to make sense of difference. No one, not even me, comprehends the damage being inflicted.

Louis drifts away again, and Narelle and I take the hard liquor and goon juice from the men and start making our way to the sand dunes. The men call us back. One of them has a house nearby. We can go there.

It's a derelict place with no furniture. Narelle and I sit cross-legged on the stained carpet, the men sitting beside us or leaning against a wall. An ashtray is passed around, and we smoke and drink. Someone rolls a joint.

I'm almost thirteen, and Narelle has just turned twelve. I'm a Gemini and she's a Taurus; we love to talk about star signs and read *Dolly* magazine predictions.

I've smoked pot before, just not this strong. One of the men pulls me into a bedroom and takes off my clothes. I'm saying, 'No, no. Stop. Please no,' and I feel weightless as he lifts and pushes me, then I feel like lead as I try desperately to move away. He is too strong for me, though, and I lose my virginity to a man at least ten years older than me.

I sober up and straighten out, struggling to put my school uniform back on. I stagger to the bathroom and vomit. I am bruised and violated and have barely hit puberty.

Mum picks me up from school. It's the first time I have seen her since the rape. I am self-absorbed, having spent the past two days curled up crying and grieving my loss of innocence. As usual, Mum says nothing, her eyes fixed on the road.

'Aren't you going to ask how my week has been?' I ask.

'How has your week been?'

Then I say the worst, most horrible thing a daughter could ever say to her mother, because I want to punish her for my pain, for not being there for me, for not even being here right now. 'I was raped! Okay. That's how my week has been.'

Mum doesn't speak.

I scream the news at her again, but she must be 'having an episode' and battling 'the voices'. I scream at her a third time, 'I've been raped. Can you hear me?'

Silence.

I jump out of the moving car. I roll onto the verge and run and run, to bushland along the West Coast Highway where I crouch down and hide.

Mum comes looking for me. She screams my name. 'I'm sorry, Mimi. Please come back. I'm sorry.'

I sit in the bushes, silently sobbing. She searches for me for a few more minutes, then drives off.

That night, Granddad knocks on the door of Narelle's house, the only place I would go. He stood outside the window for at least ten minutes before he made his presence known, watching his beloved granddaughter on the other side smoking and listening to death metal music, huddled with tattooed, pierced, dangerous-looking characters – friends of Narelle's older sister.

Granddad pounds on the door. 'Let my granddaughter go, or I shall call the police!'

He walks to his car down a long driveway snaking between two rows of units, hoping to avoid a confrontation. He has no weapon and just wants me to come home and be safe.

I follow him a few minutes later, not wanting trouble for Narelle and knowing I have to go back to my other life eventually. Mum has been crying in her own mother's arms, and I'm filled with guilt for what I told her. I go home with Granddad, and no one says anything. My twelve-year-old shame is handled much like Mum's mental illness: we pretend it isn't there.

A few of my friends are bulimic, but when I stick my fingers down my throat to gag and throw up, I realise it's not me, and I wonder how else I can escape this horror I've had.

'How could you do this, Dad? Why didn't you tell me?' I slam my bedroom door without waiting for an answer, then fling myself onto the bed, burying my tear-streaked face in the duvet.

Later I sit in the bookshelf nook just outside my room, leafing through old photos. I trace Aunty Mary's face with my fingers. She is beaming a contagious smile. Her hair is high from the large hot rollers she put in that morning, and she's wearing a T-shirt and white shorts. I'm standing next to her on Uncle Tony's work desk, next to his judge's wig on its stand, against a backdrop of legal journals. We are so happy together.

Now she is dead.

Dad crouches beside me, and tears pour down my cheeks again. 'Mi,' he says gently, 'I didn't know she was going to die when I flew to Hong Kong. I thought she was just sick. She died in my arms. There are no cars on Lantau. She died in my arms.'

First Uncle Tony died in his sleep, then Benji died, now Aunty Mary's gone too.

I can only look at Dad with disbelief. 'You didn't even tell me she had cancer. You must have known you would be seeing her for the last time. I was close to her too. I should've been there.'

He straightens himself up. 'Mi. It is not children's business. I didn't know, alright. Anyway, you should be happy. She left you a lot of money.'

I don't feel happy at all.

'Buddy hell. I can't change it, okay! She's gone.' He storms off to his office.

There's a photo of Aunty Mary with five-year-old me at my grandparents' house in Bicton. Despite their estrangement from my father, Paw Paw and Granddad welcomed Mary and Theresa into the family. Both Kwa aunties would bring gifts and sunshine to Bicton when they visited, and I loved my two worlds meeting in such a normal, amicable way, without shouting, violence or tension.

In the photo Aunty Mary is lying on a Persian rug in the living room. She is Cinderella in a glass coffin in the forest, waiting for me, the prince, to wake her. Although I have my fairytales confused, Aunty Mary plays along. I lean down in my dungarees and kiss her lightly on the cheek. 'Arise, Cinderella. Arise.'

Cinderella opens her eyes and looks around. 'Oh, Prince Charming,' she says, delighted. 'Thank you. Thank you.'

The memory is vivid as I run my fingers over a faded corner of the photo. If only I could awaken my Aunty Mary Cinderella again.

SOUTHERN COMFORT AND HAIRSPRAY

BY THE AGE OF THIRTEEN, HIGH SCHOOL IS A HYBRID OF HIGH marks and experimentation: study on the weekdays, alcohol and drugs on the weekends. All the bad behaviour happens at my place, the only house my friends can come for sleepovers then sneak out to beach bonfires.

It's a chilly Saturday night, but I'm wearing a short skirt and singlet top with kitten heels and hoop earrings. I cover up with my trusty long black trenchcoat, bringing it in at the waist with a belt. I grab a duffle bag and head out. 'Bye, Dad, I'm going to the ice-cream parlour. Then I'm staying at Zarn's house.'

Dad hands me twenty dollars.

Down at the roundhouse on Scarborough Beach, bottles of Southern Comfort and tequila are already being passed around when I join the circle. We splinter off, collecting sticks as firewood. Sand moulds to our backsides and beers, and a boy called Josh runs into the ocean. We lose sight of him and run screaming his name down to the shoreline. Our feet are wet, and Josh emerges soaking and exhilarated, running circles along the tide's edge with his arms outstretched. 'Woo-hoo!'

he cries. We laugh, and the night wears on into drunken deep and meaningfuls that turn into awkward pashes. The days that follow are always a map of teenage heartache for me and my schoolfriends to pore over in the library and at lunch.

Friends are my life rafts. When I'm not with them, I write a diary. It begins as a bit of fun, decorating pages with doodles and poems, but eventually it turns into full-scale typical teenage angst. Then something else altogether, something dark. On some pages I'm brutally candid, and on others I outright lie, even to myself. If I die tomorrow, I want to impress the reader with a normal, perhaps even enviable teenage life, so I write about crushes and parties to keep things light. But then all of a sudden my real feelings break through.

One afternoon, I come home from school, throw my backpack on my neatly made bed, and then I see it: my diary is wide open on a page describing an intimate moment, and on the opposite page I've scrawled, *I hate Angela.* My stepmother has found my book of innermost thoughts, the pages where I rewrite and try to make sense of my life in order to save it. There's a cigarette and matches on top of the open diary – Angela is letting me know she found those too.

I call my best friend, Fee, looping the spiral cord of my pink phone around my hand. After a minute or two we both hear a click, indicating that whoever has been listening in as usual has hung up. We lower our voices. I had intended to have a whinge about my stepmother, but Fee is crying. She's hiding under a desk. This happens sometimes – Fee's dad on a rampage. She's frightened and I try to comfort her but then he storms in and rips the phone away and all I hear is 'Please, Dad' before the line goes dead. Fee hides her bruises and the police are never called, no matter how heavy handed he is with them all. Whenever I suggest that I will call them, Fee is horrified. When I hug her inside the school gates, we have a knowing between us that no galaxy of words can begin to express.

When I complain to Dad that Angela has been going through my things, he says it doesn't matter, 'she can do what she likes'. And with that, whatever little corner of the universe I felt was mine, instantly isn't.

Then one day Dad catches me smoking and strikes me so hard across the face I fall backwards down the stairs, just managing to catch myself on the rail. So I run away to Paw Paw and Granddad's place, just like Mum always did, and stand in front of the mirror, hitting myself in the face with the hairspray can in the hope the bruising will be so deep I won't ever be sent back. As I stare at my reflection in the bathroom mirror I wonder when it'll be my turn, when the Kwa madness will strike or, worse still, whatever illness my mum has. The girl in the looking-glass gazes back at me with tears in her eyes.

When things get tough I head to the beach. Louis Johnson and I spend hours locked in philosophical discussions while we sit on a wall overlooking the surf. We aren't remarkably close, but we are friends.

One night, years later, Louis is bashed by four people on his birthday. He's heading home from a party on a train when they lay into him with fists and boots, dragging him onto a road where one of them runs him over with a car. A passing cyclist calls triple zero, and an ambulance officer takes Louis home to 'sleep it off'. But Louis is dead by morning. The killers are caught, one telling police he *only* wanted to break Louis's legs and that he drove into Louis 'because he was black'. The ambulance officer tells police he thought Louis was 'drunk and high from glue or petrol sniffing'. His death will become a significant case, and one day there will be scholarships in Louis Johnson's name.

But for now, in the moment, life is simple: Louis and I just sit and talk and look out at the sea.

SWORDS AND FLANNELETTE

THE HEADMISTRESS, AUDREY JACKSON, IS HAVING A QUIET word to my teacher at the front of our Year Nine classroom before asking me to accompany her outside. I'm frequently in trouble, but I sense this is different and follow my headmistress to her office in silence. She doesn't know what to say, and I'm not sure what to ask.

As soon as they see me enter, Paw Paw and Granddad jump up from their seats, stilted and awkward as they nod their thanks to my headmistress. In the car, they give the impression I am about to see my mother for the last time, to say goodbye.

'What happened to her?' I scream. 'What's going on?'

My grandparents maintain their composure and say nothing more, even though I shout at them all the way to Fremantle Hospital.

At home, Granddad has half a dozen swords on display alongside muskets, shotguns, sabres, arrows and shields – war memorabilia and artefacts, reminders of time served. Mela took a sword down from the wall and drew it from its sheath. She carried it to her old upstairs room. Standing to face the neighbour's house, she sliced her wrists then stabbed herself through the chest and stomach seven times. 'She would never hurt a fly,' Paw Paw always says, 'but there is no stopping her from hurting herself.'

Mela's sister, Zora, found her lying in a pool of blood while it rushed from her veins and soaked into the carpet. Zora, who once worked as a nurse's aid, knew how to stem her sister's haemorrhaging. When Zora screamed, Granddad ran down the hall. He immediately recalled his military first-aid drills and kept his daughter alive long enough for paramedics to arrive.

Mum is in the operating theatre for ten hours. When I'm finally allowed to see her, she's on life support, her chest rising and falling to the rhythm of machines. Doctors tell us the marathon surgery went well, so Mela's desire to leave life has been thwarted again. Again I've been sitting in a hospital, wondering if my mother will pull through.

Now Mum lies in a coma. I visit her each day. When I travel to see her, I like to be alone. When I'm with her, I like to be alone as well. I refuse my grandparents' offers to drive me: I'm not up for company, and especially not for being around anyone I love.

They never answer my questions about Mum's state of mind. If anyone knows what's wrong they're not telling me. It's excruciating to be ignored and to live in this vacuum of pretending everything is fine. I find it much easier to isolate myself. I discover the truth on hospital clipboards and in folders, anyway – more information than any adult ever gives me.

Two weeks into Mum's hospital stay, I again catch a bus in to see her. I cut across the carpark on the hospital's east side; this way I can bypass the rigmarole of reception, front desks, lifts and corridors. I think I'm clever to have found this route.

There's a small alcove to pass through before I enter a side stairwell, but today a bearded man in a flannelette shirt seems to be following me across the carpark. I look at him, behind me. I must be imagining it. He's bound to stop or go another way. I walk faster. The man walks faster. He casts a long shadow in the afternoon sunlight, catching up to me just as I enter the dark alcove.

I panic. 'What do you want?' My trembling voice betrays me. I am yelling but my screams are inaudible. I am mute and this is a horrible nightmare.

The man moves towards my frozen body, groping me and forcing me up against the wall under the staircase.

Finally, my scream breaks through the glass, and he panics. I keep screaming. I've found my voice, and the man runs.

He's caught by police an hour and a half later, humping on top of a nine-year-old girl in the middle of a school crosswalk. I give a statement at Fremantle Police Station. In movies, line-ups take place behind one-way mirrors; real life is a girl hiding behind a filing cabinet as a policeman holds an accused man by the neck, parading him up and down until I say, 'Yes, that's him.' The man can't move his head, of course, but he moves his eyes and looks right at me. Me, in my school uniform, crouched by a doorway as police type details into computers.

Finally I'm allowed to go home. The police have my details and will be in touch.

Weeks later, they call to tell me I'm not required to appear as a witness. The man has pleaded guilty to multiple counts of molestation and rape.

The police don't consult my parents or grandparents, and I am not offered counselling. I don't talk to Paw Paw and Granddad about it, and I don't tell Mum. She's in a stable condition, but I know this news would do her no good. So I stay quiet and wonder if the police ever spoke to my grandparents; if they did, Paw Paw and Granddad never mention it.

I can't sleep at night. I still feel the tightening of my throat, the panic, when I tried to scream and nothing came out.

After Mum pulls through, we enter a new cycle of schizophrenic episodes and worry. I can barely keep up the facades of my friendships, let alone relationships at home. I decide to follow my mum's example and try to die. I don't want any pain, so I resort to pills and rifle through the drawers in Mum's bathroom. It's a fancy bathroom, beautifully decorated and designed by Paw Paw; the pink shellac finish is cutting edge, along with shag-pile bathmats and quintessential Ponds soap garnish.

I bolt the door and window, then swallow pill upon pill – I don't care what they are, the more colourful their exterior and the less decipherable their ingredients the better – and, in a stupor, fall to the floor. I can vaguely hear the desperate banging of my grandparents on the glass door, but I certainly cannot respond.

Granddad smashes the bathroom window and climbs though. Ambulance officers lift me onto a stretcher, and the next thing I know, I'm waking up in Emergency. The demeanour of the doctors and nurses is condescending, as if I'm some rich, attention-seeking kid who doesn't deserve the bed.

For three weeks, I cannot speak properly. I have spasms, my mouth opening wide, my tongue connipting, my face contorting. None of it is within my control, nothing ever has been, but all of this is my doing. I'm terrified I will be permanently disabled, but luckily the only permanent damage is memory loss – unfortunately not the memories I'd like to lose, just things like what I had for breakfast.

My suicide attempt meant Granddad got to use his first-aid skills again. Daughter and granddaughter, lucky him.

BEGGAR AND PRINCE

However overambitious Francis's hotel ideas are, he succeeds at making Mandarin Gardens an international budget destination of choice: the number one choice in Australia. Travellers, backpackers, sports teams, rock bands, performers, adventure seekers, couples and families of every kind are our guests. But there are also drug dealers, thieves and lowlifes.

What I love most is that everyone has a story. They wear them on their faces and their clothes, and very often sit down and tell me their whole tale. I'm a good listener, so this is a perfect storm for a lonely, curious girl.

With amazing things from far-off lands to ponder, and constant dramas to deal with and conundrums to solve, I become worldly in my own backyard. Fire dancers and Olympic athletes parade across my days, and I sit on our lawn watching them rehearse and train. I meet people from every walk of life, and it inspires me – to do what, I don't know yet.

In summer especially, Mandarin Gardens is a hive of activity. Youthful travellers are everywhere, tanned, fit and up for a good time. Surf, beach, lying by the pool – who doesn't want a holiday like that? But beneath this wholesome picture is an underbelly of older men, attracted to the life of the young, who also stay at Mandarin Gardens. They're free of the responsibilities and rigours of work and family, and I sense something not quite right. To me, these guys are ancient, probably forty, maybe fifty, overtly preying on youth as their anti-aging elixir. I listen to them use their wiles under pretence of wisdom to talk twenty-somethings into bed. *Perverts*, I think, when they make eyes at me and my teenage friends. As the owner's daughter I'm off limits, but not immune to their leers and comments.

Fortunately, almost all our guests are nice to me. It helps that I hold the key to rent-deadline extensions and dorm-room allocations. Mandarin Gardens is my giant dollhouse to rearrange with new characters every day.

The entrance to the compound is flanked with white rendered walls, one side emblazoned with the name in brass lettering. Apart from our monstrous backpacker accommodation, our street is suburban, populated by duplexes and units. On the other side of the swamp, next door to us, is a video shop, and next to that is a YMCA. Then a Chinese restaurant, pawnshop, hairdresser, pizza bar, fish and chippery, and – my favourite – the corner shop.

I regularly push Dad's wheelbarrow full of one-litre glass soft-drink bottles down to the corner shop, and they pay me ten cents a bottle. Backpackers go through a lot of Fanta, Coke, Sprite and Red Creaming Soda, so I do a good trade.

At Mandarin Gardens, Dad has welded together a designated bottle recycling shelf. My job is to take the bottles to the corner shop and collect the pay, the deal being that Dad and I split the profit eighty–twenty. He's the eighty, and I usually spend my twenty, on the spot, on one- and two-cent lollies – as many as I can fit into a small white paper bag.

The change I take home for Dad always goes in his coin jar, and he reaches into this jar when a beggar comes to call one day. She's in her fifties, grey haired and dishevelled, wearing a faded purple skirt with an elastic waist and a pale-brown cotton blouse, the kind that has two collar strings with tassels.

She stands at the top of our red-brick driveway for a moment, surveying Mandarin Gardens, before she commences an elaborate performance. The bell sleeves of her blouse billow, her dramatic sweeping motions and pleas for help attracting a curious audience. 'Ooohhhh, come to save me. Save me and my baby. My baybeee neeeds milk. I cannot feed her. Please give me money. Please heeeelp me. Pleeease don't let a baaaby starve.'

Backpackers reach into their pockets and toss her a few coins. Dad hears the commotion and comes downstairs. He's wearing a white singlet coupled with a brown Balinese batik sarong tied round his waist and brought up through his legs to be tied again – like a nappy. 'Oh, oh, oh, I'll be back,' he says excitedly, dashing upstairs to grab coins from his money jar.

The beggar smiles in anticipation as Dad emerges, rattling the coins in his hands as though he's about to roll dice. 'So you come to my kingdom to beg for money, is it?' he asks, facing the woman.

Her eyes widen. 'Is this your place?'

'Yes, yes, yes, and you are trespassing, but that is okay. Ahahahahhhhah.'

The woman begins her theatrical routine again. 'Ooohhhh, come to save me.'

'How old are you, old woman? You are grey and cannot have a baby, isn't it?'

She's startled; clearly no one has ever pulled her up on her story before.

'If you need milk, I buy you milk. Let's walk to the corner store together.' A cold expression falls over her face. She wasn't prepared for Francis Kwa.

As if reading her mind, he says with a smile and a gleam in his eye, 'How much money have you begged today with your impossible story?' He looks pleased with the gathering crowd. 'I will tell you my story. I am a poor old Chinaman. My child needs medicine. See, I only have one leg.' He pulls his foot up behind his backside and holds it there to look like an amputee. 'Give me money, give me money. Ahhahahah.'

Her eyes bore into him, and I can see her anger grow as his performance continues.

'How much money have you got? Let's see who's richer.' Dad squats down in front of the woman and begins counting out his coins. There's scattered applause from the small assembly of backpackers.

The woman can't take it anymore and reaches into her pocket, throwing a handful of coins at Dad's feet. Ten- and twenty-cent pieces roll into cracks between the red driveway bricks. 'You are cursed,' she screams at him. 'I cuuuurse you.' She does an elaborate witchy movement with her arms, which ends with her gazing towards the sky, a grave look on her face. 'You are cursed!' she shrieks and storms off.

'Ahahahahah.' Dad picks up the coins. 'Look at me! I got money from the beggar. I turn three dollars into ten.' He laughs again and shows the group of backpackers the coins, doing a triumphant little jig.

I shake my head, but our guests are smiling broadly. Mandarin Gardens is entertaining, I must admit. Dad could add 'in-house drama' to our list of amenities, with a side of financial advice and investment coaching.

Perhaps Dad likes being surrounded by lots of people because he grew up in a big family. He also loves having servants just like in the old days: people fussing around him and over him, working for him even when they're out of sight. He is deeply satisfied by his place at the top of this hierarchy, referring to himself as 'God' and 'the King'. He laughs and jokes and does a little jig. 'I am the King, I am the King,' he sings. He always gets a laugh. 'Everyone thinks I'm great.' He can be entertaining and endearing. 'They like me, they like me. I am the King.'

So when a real-life prince comes to stay at our 4.5-star backpacker accommodation, Dad recognises an opportunity.

An African prince on a worldwide adventure happens upon a sign at Perth airport. It boasts that Mandarin Gardens has a 25-metre pool plus a long list of other appealing offerings. The accommodation has a 5-star rating with a disclaimer in fine print: *restaurant application pending*. It's near the beach, and there's a free airport shuttle.

'Take me to this place known as Mandarin Gardens,' says the prince. The shuttle-bus driver today is Dad himself, and by the time they reach Mandarin Gardens, the prince has agreed to 'help out' in his office. The prince says he has studied commerce law.

What a catch, thinks Dad.

When a few days later Dad discovers the prince is a prince, he cannot believe his luck. 'I really *am* king now,' he says. 'I have a prince working for me.' The prince laughs because he finds it funny, doesn't understand or is being polite. When my father introduces the prince to people as his 'houseboy', the prince doesn't say anything.

At the same time the prince is staying at Mandarin Gardens, two of the local ducks – after landing on the next-door swamp for years – begin to land on our pool. Dad considers adding 'Australian wildlife' to the list of attractions. But when the ducks do their business in the pool, he decides they're not to be encouraged.

He waits until the pool is deserted and observes, from a balcony, the ducks paddling contentedly in the over-chlorinated water. *That's another thing*, he thinks. *They're costing me money because I have to sanitise their mess*. He raises his shotgun, rests it on the balustrade, angles it skyward and fires. The birds get the fright of their lives and fly off. But the very next day they are back. Francis brings out his shotgun again.

Police knock at our door, which I open. 'Yes?' I say calmly. I have a lot of experience with saying that Dad isn't home when police or people serving court summonses come to call. I've also had practice with tax investigators and health inspectors. 'Sorry, Dad isn't at home,' I say if I don't know them.

'We have reports of gunshots in the area,' one policeman says. 'Is your father home?'

Dad is watching through a keyhole inside our inner front door – he believes it's necessary to have two front doors for occasions such as this. Surprisingly, he opens the door and pushes past me. 'Hello, officers, how can I help?' He smiles.

'Mr Kwa, we've had reports of gunshots on your property. Do you know anything about this?'

Dad looks them straight in the eye. 'No, no, no. I never heard it. Actually, yes, yes, yes – I think I heard some car backfiring lately. I think that is what it must be. The car backfiring.'

The officers don't look like they buy it, but they have only telephone complaints to go on. 'You do understand, Mr Kwa, that with so many people staying on your property at any one time, it would be an extreme public safety risk to keep a gun here.' The officer looks at me, and I look down.

'No gun here, no gun here,' Dad says. 'Mimi, go inside. This is grown-up business.' A minute later, he comes inside. 'Buddy cops. Buddy ducks.'

The prince has been making himself useful to Dad, filing and carrying out general admin in return for free rent. Not that the prince needs free rent, mind you – I expect it's all part of his adventure.

The next day, Dad strikes up a conversation with him about 'back in Africa' and 'back at home'. 'Back in your palace you must go hunting. Hunting. You know hunting? Bang,

bang, gun.' The prince nods. 'So let's have duck for dinner. Hahahaha.'

That afternoon, the prince takes aim and shoots one of the ducks dead, first go. The other one flaps its wings violently and escapes before a second shot can be fired. Dad instructs the prince to pluck the dead duck, then eats it for dinner. 'Good idea, good idea,' Francis congratulates himself.

We never see the other duck again.

'Steve Jobs – see, that's me, that's me. And Bill Gates, I'm Bill Gates.' Dad enjoys using his electrical engineering skills to tinker with voltage. He has wired up an in-house video channel that sends a signal from his upstairs study to each of the apartments and bunkhouses. Anyone can watch Video One on Channel Five and Video Two on Channel Six. It's two dollars to rent a video, and whoever pays is basically paying for all the other guests to watch the movie as well, because the signal goes to everyone.

Dad has rigged up two VHS recorders to copy movies from one to the other. He sends me to the video shop on our street, where I rent videos using one of the lifetime's worth of free vouchers Dad has accumulated. The vouchers don't have an expiry date – a major oversight but a plus for us. I borrow movies like *Gremlins*, *Ghostbusters*, *Stand by Me* and the *Nightmare on Elm Street*. Mandarin Gardens copies all the classics.

All I have to do is insert a movie into VCR One and press a sequence of buttons to record it onto a blank videotape in VCR Two. If a guest happens to be flicking through TV channels when I'm pirating movies, they get to watch that one for free. Two dollars is a lot in 1987, and definitely a lot for a backpacker who's already paying ten dollars per night for their accommodation. (Although if they pay for six nights up front, they get the seventh free in a year-round promotion.)

It's my job to keep the movie list updated. I've saved it on a floppy disk so I can make additions between printing it out for new guests to take away with them at check-in. There are animated arguments between backpackers over what movie to watch. With two channels to share between a hundred guests, it's a case of first in, best dressed. I am the booking agent, often staying up late to put on a new video. Sometimes I fall asleep, and we get complaints the next day. And sometimes the video doesn't play right through to the end or reception is bad or the VCR eats the tape and I have to gently tug to untangle it, using a toothbrush handle to wind it back into place.

Dad teaches me to apologise profusely and say it has never happened before, even though it has. He tells me that's good business. But there are an awful lot of complaints about our video service, so he puts up a sign: 'NO REFUNDS on in-house movies.'

We build up quite a collection of films, a big investment of my time. Dad manufactures two large trundle drawers to hide the hundreds of tapes under his and Angela's bed. They are concealed by the fabric skirting along the bed base. When authorities knock on our front door, asking me if I know anything about pirated videos on the premises, I say, 'No, I don't.' When they ask if they can speak to an adult, I say, of course, 'Sorry, Dad isn't here.'

During the summer months we're so overbooked some weeks that we pitch tents on the expanse of lumpy dry lawn. An enormous pine tree between the main apartment block and the bunkhouses drops pine needles all over the grass. Dad calls them 'monkey tails', and raking them up is often on my list of jobs to do.

One weekend, Dad and Angela leave me in charge for a day. I 'man' the front desk, where a revolving door of people check in and out, make enquiries about this and that, and file their complaints. I field them all.

Dad has bought a bigger bus so he can take backpackers on sightseeing tours. When he got his bus licence he added this to our list of amenities. Unfortunately it doesn't increase our 4.5-star rating, but it sounds impressive, and a full bus of thirty passengers at thirty dollars per ticket is a $900 day.

'It is a hotel, I own a hotel,' Dad says. His passengers laugh at his jokes, and they drive off merrily to discover Western Australia. Today he's taking them to one of the state's premier destinations: thousands of weathered limestone pillars in Nambung National Park, two hours north of Perth, called the Pinnacles.

For me, the day should be fairly standard: collect rent, change sheets, and empty cash from our public telephone box, washing machine and dryer, then count it. So I can get through Angela's list and simultaneously take care of guest enquiries, I carry a cordless phone with a retractable metal aerial whenever I leave the front office, pasting an apologetic sign with our phone number on the sliding door. When the phone rings, it vibrates because the ringer has been set permanently at its loudest volume so I never miss important calls.

I'm raking up monkey tails when the cordless phone has its usual conniption – it's Dad calling me from a pay phone. He tells me his bus has broken down after he reversed into a Pinnacle. The Pinnacles are a protected national treasure, between twenty-five and thirty thousand years old, and you are not allowed to climb on them, let alone drive into them.

'Buddy hell! Just do as told.' Dad wants his Royal Automobile Club card number, not my questions. He is angry that his day hasn't gone to plan. To make it worse, he's lost two backpackers. Dad says they went off into the 17,500-hectare park to find a quiet place to shag, and haven't returned.

With Dad and Angela joining the search party and waiting for the RAC, my stint in the office will now be overnight. We're in between managers at the moment, so it's just me in a small desk alcove in front of a tiny black-and-white TV. It's mid-afternoon, Dad and thirty backpackers are two hundred kilometres away, and I don't know how long the RAC will take to fix the bus or if the ancient rock Dad crashed into will ever be the same.

Kevin, a blond British backpacker, slides open the office door. He's in his early twenties – an age I approve of for a backpacker. He's wearing sunglasses on top of his head and torn-off denim shorts. Three other backpackers step in behind him: two boys and a girl. They all speak at once, and it's a while before I work out what's going on.

'We've caught him red-handed, we found him, we know who it is,' Kevin says proudly.

'But now he's locked himself in,' the girl in a red striped bikini adds. 'He's going mental. He's not coming out.'

Over the past week, personal belongings have gone missing: first a Walkman, then two Walkmans, then a passport, then two – a steady stream of 'lost' property reports at a much higher rate than usual. Speculation that there's a thief among us, finger pointing and mistrust have all added to the usual undercurrent of drama at the hostel. There are no secure lockers at Mandarin Gardens, so it's the responsibility of each backpacker to arrange to store valuables in our office safe, but as there's a small fee for this, most don't bother. Besides, travellers need passports almost daily for trip bookings, checking in and out, admission to pubs and clubs, opening bank accounts, and applying for jobs. It's a hassle to leave valuables in our safe, so our lost property list has become a stolen property one.

The thief is an older guy, about forty – an inappropriate age for a 'backpacker', in my opinion. We find out later he is a career kleptomaniac. He hotel hops and travels the world with stolen money, passports, and … ladies' stockings.

'Yep,' says Kevin, 'we caught him going through Annabelle's backpack, then we all confronted him and tipped his bag upside down. *All* the stolen stuff is there, even my passport, *and* some stockings that went missing from the girls' bags.'

Am I dealing with a cross-dressing, foot fetishist career kleptomaniac?

The bikini girl chips in. 'Now he's gone bananas. He flipped out when we confronted him and shouted us out of the room. He's locked himself in there. You've got to call the police.'

I may be fourteen, but I'm nobody's fool; I want to verify what they're telling me before I call the police – Dad doesn't like anyone in uniform snooping around.

I walk down to Bunkhouse Two – my childhood home – to find a crowd of a dozen backpackers standing outside my old bedroom door. 'You don't know fuck,' the thief is shouting from inside. 'I'll kill you! Fuck off, fuck off.'

I'm used to the collision between the relics of my old life, before the backpackers existed, and my new life with strangers inhabiting every personal space, but this is still weird – a grown man is in my old bedroom, having a fit.

When the police arrive, the man is screaming, 'I have a syringe. I'll give you all AIDS.' The officers call an ambulance, and I wait out front to show in the men in white coats.

An hour later, Dad calls again. The bus is fixed, but the two backpackers are still missing. Dad isn't a good driver at night, so I will need to 'hold the fort' until tomorrow. Just another ordinary day at Mandarin Gardens.

I have school in the morning and homework due, so I study at the front desk and eventually crawl under it to fall asleep.

GALAGA AND
SLASHED TYRES

It's a challenge to hang on to the Hong Kong feeling when I'm home at the youth hostel with Dad, or by the Swan River with Paw Paw, Granddad and Mum. None of my lives could be more seismically different to those of my friends and classmates, or of most adults I meet. Hong Kong is my secret life, and I discover more and more of it each time I go.

Aunty Theresa and I are drying off after our swim in Repulse Bay. She removes her bright-pink flower swim cap, tousles her short black hair back to life and applies a red Elizabeth Arden lipstick. 'I don't like you going with this boy without Brigit to follow.'

Later that day we're at the club – eating club sandwiches, I am always thrilled to have *club at the club* – and I straighten up my posture on the blue striped bench cushion to give an impression of being older.

'Mimi, you are a scholarship girl. I introduce you to many nice, intelligent people with handsome sons and pretty daughters for you to play.' Aunty speaks with her mouth full, which she would never do around anyone else but me – and my cousins,

I expect. 'This boy should come in to meet me at least. And have some tea.' Chew, chew, chew. 'I am a very good judge of character.' Chew, chew. She smacks her lips. 'Waiter, one more sandwich, please.' She winks at me. 'We can be a little bit fat and still look like the super model.' Aunty does a wiggle, purses her lips and tilts her head from side to side like she's the cat's pyjamas.

The boy Aunty is talking about is Felix, who I met on my last trip to Hong Kong.

On the first day of that trip, Dad had an argument with Aunty. They – mostly Dad – did a lot of Cantonese shouting in Aunty's study, and when he came out he insisted I stay with him at the Park Lane Hotel.

I admit that at the hotel, I proceeded to eat the Pringles and KitKats, but only because I had to be there and they were there too. I also replaced them with 7-Eleven items. I don't mind it at the Park Lane, but I do much prefer to stay with Aunty and Brigit.

In the morning, I watched hundreds of locals doing Tai Chi in the park below my seventh-storey balcony. It was as though they were all connected, facing the same direction, moving in unison, each dancing with their invisible partner. Their flat palms twisted gently, guiding energy around them.

That night Dad gave me a hundred Hong Kong dollars so I could wander around Causeway Bay on my own after dark in a way Aunty would never have allowed. It was exciting to walk among thousands of Hong Kongers, everyone going somewhere. I joined the foot traffic flowing towards SOGO department store, then walked past G2000 clothing and up a slight incline to Jardine's Bazaar, passing by the bus stop where I usually got off if I was coming down from Aunty's place.

A group of older teenage boys fell into step with me. 'Hello, beautiful.' I smiled and kept walking. They didn't have much more English to say than that, so they awkwardly jostled with one another, laughing. 'Bye, beautiful.'

I can't go anywhere in Hong Kong without stares and advances, but I'm used it, and I kind of like it because I don't feel very pretty at home.

'You want bag?' I sidestepped a collection of leather handbags swinging towards me.

'You want watch?' A man showcased a display of copy watches, like *The Price Is Right* host Ian Turpie. 'Very nice price.'

His voice followed me as I pushed my way through the hawkers to a trinkets alley that widened to reveal my favourite clothing shops, tucked away in miniature garages. I rummaged through rails of jackets, skirts and tops, as a group of men and women stood around watching me.

The thick black sky was impossible to see as I walked back towards G2000 and SOGO with the light of neon signs in my eyes. In my ears was Cantonese and the rattling of trams. Laughter, car horns and video games.

Video games! I followed the sound down an alley I hadn't explored before. Beeping and blipping musical scales were coming from beyond an open door. 'GAME OVER!' An Atari Alien glowed, strobed and blacked out on the wall like it was clinging to life, before lighting up again. I descended the stairs, one Dunlop Volley at a time, to electric applause – the sound effects of a *Hyper Olympic* game – as I arrived in a room full of video games and teenagers. It was so dark and noisy, no one noticed the outsider. I exchanged notes for coins with a cashier, instantly recognising *Donkey Kong, Wonder Boy* and *1943*.

Then I noticed a boy playing my favourite game, *Galaga*. I put a coin on the glass ridge above the control panel to indicate my turn behind the owners of two coins in front of mine, and waited.

It amazed me that the same video games existed in Hong Kong as at Happy Granny's down at Scarborough Beach. This arcade had the same grungy feel about it, too: young men smoking, pretty girls with too much make-up and too few clothes, everyone just standing around. But not one of them was scruffy and unwashed like the beach bums at home. They were wearing spotless white T-shirts, jeans with custom rips, sparkling earrings, slicked-back hair and ponytails. They leaned on the walls and games.

It seemed I was the only female in the room who was actually playing the games and not just acting like decoration. A bunch of girls whispered and laughed behind their hands, and the body language of the boys indicated I was an unworthy opponent; they appeared extremely uninterested when it was my turn. I fired at the bugs and ships and aliens with my trigger finger, quickly approaching level thirty-two. I'd never got past that stage, but I had an audience now, so I tried harder. From the corner of my eye I could see the girls and boys looking from the screen to me, bewildered.

Afterwards I went to the park with a few of the boys and girls to drink liquor and smoke. The boys performed some kind of fight club, probably to impress the girls. The toughest boy was wearing a grey muscle singlet, jeans and an open shirt rolled at the sleeves, a packet of Lucky Strikes peeping out from his pocket.

'He is doing the push-up to impressive you,' said an older boy who was sitting beside me, the most clean-cut of them all. He was wearing tan chinos and a collared shirt with brilliant white sneakers and a broad toothy smile to match. 'I'm Felix.' He offered me a cigarette. 'Like the cat.'

He was the only one in the group who spoke English well. When I learned he was a nineteen-year-old real estate leasing agent, I suddenly realised these kids were all much older than me. But none of that mattered – Felix made me feel welcome, and it was a good feeling to be with people closer to my age than Dad. Felix translated their questions about me and about Australia, and my questions about what each of them did, where they lived, and what they wanted to do in the future.

One worked at G2000, which explained her outfit, and the tough boy was a mechanic, which explained his.

So, that's how I met Felix. I never saw the others again, but he became a friend, never too shy to call up to my hotel from the lobby and ask me out for a meal.

On this trip he calls me at Aunty's place. 'Meee-meee,' Brigit sings each time, 'it's the Mr Felix on the telephone.'

When he finally comes to tea with Aunty, he's wearing a suit and tie, and he bows and says 'yes, Aunty' a lot. The two break off into Cantonese, and I wonder what they're talking about.

When Felix and I head out after tea for a daytrip, I see that he has borrowed his boss's Audi convertible and parked it next to Aunty's neighbours' Jaguars and Rolls-Royces.

The Chanel scarf that she has given me for the ride streams backwards with my hair, and Felix puts on a Cantonese pop CD and sings along loudly. I laugh at what a contrast all of this is to life back home.

We drive to Stanley for lunch, and Felix enjoys showing me around. Although I've been many times, it's refreshing to see it through the eyes of someone new. He buys me a gift: a *Felix the Cat* T-shirt. 'I probably not see you again. This is to remember me.'

I wonder what Aunty said to him. I'm going back to Perth in a couple of days anyway, so who knows what will happen to our friendship? Felix must sense that too. Monkey left, Lukin left, now it's my turn to leave a friend, although he's the one letting go first.

The weather is balmy, and it's exhilarating to see tropical jungle foliage rush by as we climb Tai Hang Road with the top down, back to Aunty's place at Peace Mansion.

Felix flashes his toothy smile. 'It's like I'm driving the movie star.'

* * *

Back home in Perth, on another stiflingly warm summer afternoon I'm riding with Dad in our Volvo. Dad wears his signature checked shirt over a white singlet tucked into his brown-and-black sarong, tied nappy style. He has deck shoes on, and a thick gold chain dangles around his neck. A black cotton cord with a clip at one end is tethered to a leather coin pouch in one pocket, while a number of pens – along with a highlighter, just in case – peep over the top of the other one.

Dad drives his Kwa Car slowly – and dangerously. He's singing his favourite line from the song 'Just Born to Be Your Baby', about lumberjacks and kings. As our Volvo has KWA on its numberplates, there's no escaping identification, no matter how embarrassed I am. Dad's driving is neither aggressive nor defensive; he just appears to be completely oblivious to the cars around him, the cogs in his head turning on his next court case or get-rich-quick scheme.

'Dad. Dad! Watch out!'

We swerve to miss a family of ducks crossing the road alongside Herdsman Lake.

'Buddy Hell. Jee-sussss Christ. Buddy ducks.'

We swerve back into our lane as oncoming traffic is forced into chaos by Dad's last-minute manoeuvre.

'Omigod, Dad!'

A small stone hurtles directly towards us, connecting with our windscreen. Horns toot and there are a few shouts of 'fucking Asian driver!' as we pull over to the side of the road. I watch the family of ducks slide into the lake.

The windscreen is completely shattered in a crazy-paving safety-glass pattern, but somehow it remains intact. 'I can't see now,' says Dad.

I watch him eye off the rear-view mirror stuck to the cracked windscreen. 'No! Dad!'

But it's too late – he yanks the mirror inward, bringing thousands of glass fragments tumbling onto us both. 'Now I can see.' He laughs his kookaburra laugh. 'Ahahahaha.'

I look down at the mountain of glass on my lap, caught in the folds of my skirt, in the sides of my sneakers and covering the floor.

'You can clean it up when we get home. Keep the glass on your lap. You can use your skirt to carry it to the bin. It will save time, save time.' He laughs again.

A few days later, a group of girlfriends are over at my place, giggling and carrying on like teenagers are prone to do. All nine of us pile into the Kwa Car so Dad can drive us to Swensen's, an ice-cream parlour down at the beach. We show little regard for seatbelts or passenger numbers, with five girls squashed across the back seat and three in the boot. My friend Attalie is on my lap in the front.

'Mim, have you got the air conditioner on? Mr Kwa, is the air con on?' Zarn asks.

Attalie, who is wriggling to get comfortable on my lap, reaches out towards the windscreen, her hand going right through. She is quite stoned and squeals as a breeze washes into the car, and our laughter intensifies as everyone realises there's no windscreen.

It's dusk and Dad starts to sing, winding down his window to 'let in some fresh air'. More uncontrollable laughter. He sings 'Moon River', ecstatic to have a captive audience, and we laugh even harder. 'Your dad is hysterical, Mim,' my friends always say.

BROTHERS AND BIKIES

ANGELA INSTRUCTS ME TO PLUNGE THE SOILED CLOTH NAPPIES of her first child into a large laundry drum and teaches me to rub a safety pin with soap so it will glide smoothly through the triangulated cloth nappies when I change him.

The new baby is my brother Adrian, an Earth Dragon born in a double lucky number eight year, 1988, and given the Chinese name Wai Lung.

I love him so, and Angela softens enough to let me hold him. I walk him around the 23-metre swimming pool and pat his back as he wails with a sore tummy. 'There, there. Shhh-shh-sh.' He is so tiny in my arms. I whisper to him that I wish I could protect him from the craziness he has been born into: the madness of Kwa.

Angela appreciates my help, but with a newborn on the scene, it's not long before she gives Dad an ultimatum: 'Her or me.'

Dad sets me up in an apartment of my own, next door, the same one Monkey and her parents used to live in. Dad has partitioned it in two so he can take over the living area as his 'legal office'. On my side I have two bedrooms, a bathroom and a kitchen with an empty fridge. I fill it with frozen stews and casseroles Mum cooks for me. Paw Paw buys me boxes of cereal, and Granddad gives me a weekly allowance so I can buy my own milk and eggs. I use the second bedroom as my living room.

It's lonely living alone, and to-do lists are still shoved under my front door.

My latest job is helping Dad with his legal 'work'. He has become notorious for suing anyone and everyone. He sues the insomnia-relief tablet brand Mogadon for keeping him awake, with no luck, and Berocca for the same thing – another loss. 'I lose some, I wins some,' Dad says. 'But I win more than I lose, so they can't kick me out.'

There's a large boulder on the verge outside our house in exactly the same spot it's been for twenty years. Dad has reversed his Kwa car past it every day for half that. But one day he misjudges the gap and ploughs into the rock, damaging his car and leading him to the next logical action: sue someone. He files in court against our neighbour, and it turns out the rock protrudes twenty centimetres onto council land. Both Dad and council staff measure it, confirming he's right.

This is a win for Dad but just one of many weekly cases involving Mr Kwa, who these days attends court like it's his full-time job. A faulty product, bad service, poor design, 'I just don't like it' – these are all the sorts of things to put a bee in Francis Kwa's bonnet. Look at Dad the wrong way and you can surely expect a summons.

Soon, in the Year of the Metal Horse, Angela and Dad have another baby, Jerome, who is also adorable beyond belief.

Mandarin Gardens gets a new lease on life when new managers Don and Sarah move in with grand plans and dreams to enhance the backpackers' community spirit. They live in the unit beneath mine and begin hosting regular BBQ events, including Christmas lunch. The couple take me under their wing, becoming my good friends. I'm sixteen now, up to my final year of high school; Sarah is only nineteen and Don at least twenty years older.

Down by the pool, Don builds a bar and sets up a TV. Whenever I scrub clean the pool tiles with a toothbrush, one of the jobs on my list, I sit up at the bench with him to watch the Gulf War unfold.

One day, Angela screams at Dad, 'They've ripped out a page of the book. They're stealing from us!' She's talking about the ledger where we record rent paid in cash.

Don and Sarah plead with Dad, but he is resolute, so they pack their belongings, clothes and few pieces of furniture. Two more people gone, along with our sabotaged friendships.

I know they didn't steal from us, but by the time I find the missing page hidden in Dad's study, confirming their innocence, it's too late for me to go into battle. They've already been gone a month, during which Dad said Don slashed his minibus tyres in a wholesale supermarket carpark and grabbed Dad by the throat in the toilet paper aisle. According to Dad, Don threatened to kill him, so Dad filed a court action. Not long afterwards, Sarah left Don.

Mandarin Gardens is their undoing, and they are ours. The 4.5-star backpacker travellers' resort begins an accelerated decline.

Dad and Don go to court over the accusations. Dad sues over the death threats, and Don over unfair dismissal; Dad countersues for theft, and Don for slander.

Don contacts me to ask if I'll testify as a witness for him, but in the end, when the hammer comes down, I choose family. Kwa blood runs thick, and I side with Dad as I always do. In a letter to Don I say how sorry I am – and, understanding what a difficult position I'm in, he forgives me for turning him down. I am 'still a kid', he says, 'don't worry'.

* * *

In summer, Mandarin Gardens still promises sexual opportunity for twenty-somethings traversing the world on life's big adventure. I never know what combination of people each day will hold or what they'll do: what friendships, confrontations, altercations and alienations will transpire. Many of our guests confide in me like I'm Oprah living in a soap opera, and even when they don't, I still overhear a great deal. I never know what life-changing lesson a day at the biggest youth hostel in the Southern Hemisphere will teach me. There's constant excitement and abandonment, new friends coming and going, and promises of postcards and staying in touch. I grow accustomed to getting close and letting go, but I long to be normal like my private school meat-and-three-veg friends. They think my life is exciting, but all I want is theirs.

It's a typical Perth day, beautiful and thirty-five degrees, an ideal pool day. Today there's a bikie gang in the hood, looking for their own fun. They've been trawling the steaming streets of Scarborough in their leathers and chains and tattooed badges of honour. Wickedness on wheels. But even wicked people get hot around the collar on a 35-degree day, and as they head down to cool off at the beach, they happen past Mandarin Gardens. The leader on his Harley-Davidson looks left as he rides down the Wheatcroft Street hill. *Screeeeeeeeeech*. He slams on the brakes; his gang slam on their brakes.

The leader raises an arm for them all to reverse a few metres up the hill again, which they do in unison – a beautiful bikie ballet. The group look at what their leader has seen, and there it is, calling to them: a gleaming clear blue swimming pool. It looks as though it must be twenty-five metres, at least.

The bikies park, unsaddle and head down the red-brick driveway to the pool, one of them courteously holding the safety gate open for the others.

Dad is in his office. By the time he hears a commotion down at the pool, the other guests have made themselves scarce. Not wanting to offend the ruffians, no one has stuck around to watch them swim. Exposed backs and chests covered in tattoos and scars recline on sun lounges. One of the men rests his gun on a cushion while he strips off, as other bikies bomb into the water, cheering and shouting, drinking cans of whisky and cola.

Dad is incensed and, dressed in his white singlet and brown-and-black sarong, he strides through the safety gate to the pool. 'Hey-hey-hey-hey,' he says half jovially, half authoritatively, 'this is private property. You can't swim here.'

The dozen men in Y-fronts and couple of women in black lace underwear stop and stare for a while before their leader bursts out laughing. Then they all burst out laughing. 'Hello, little Chinaman.' They laugh some more. 'Oh well, if we can't swim here, how about you go for a swim?'

Two bikies – men you would not want to meet down a dark alley – walk towards Dad.

Angela and I keep watch from the balcony, bobbing down so we're out of sight, as Dad wags a finger at the bikies. Angela starts to giggle; his bravery or stupidity in the face of these armed strangers is comical. He's still telling them off and wagging a finger at them as two burly blokes pick him up by the ankles and under the arms. They swing him once, twice, three times and hurl him high into the air. His back smacks down on the water's surface, his singlet riding up in the ordeal. A red welt forms on his skin.

He's submerged for a moment then resurfaces, wildly gesticulating, telling off the bikies as if his monologue hadn't been interrupted. Finally, 'I'll call the police,' is the last thing the gang want to hear, so they collect their things – clothes, shoes, chains and guns – and head out through the safety gate in a line of wet inked figures up our driveway.

I start to laugh too, and Angela and I make eye contact and laugh together for the first time ever. I make a mental note never to forget this shared moment. Bikies are known for bombings, stabbings, setting people alight and the odd dabble in drugs, nothing funny about that — but as they uniformly reverse their polished vehicles to proceed down Wheatcroft Street, we are smiling.

Dad thinks they're gone and, suddenly regaining his mojo, runs to the middle of the street. 'And don't you come back,' he shouts.

The bikies screech to a halt and reverse up the hill. Dad runs, terrified, to hide under the stairs. The gang squawk with laughter as they ride off for good this time, while Angela and I are still giggling.

POT PLANT AND SKYSCRAPER

IN MY FINAL YEAR AT SCHOOL, I'M VOTED IN AS ARTS captain for my house. I had wanted to be a prefect and, according to the girls who helped count the votes, I may have been close. But the headmistress would have vetoed me anyway; I'm too unpredictable, and my family is too volatile. Arts captain it is instead, the perfect role for me. I'm so excited about the upcoming house drama competition that I lie awake much of the night trying to come up with the perfect choice of play.

I visit the State Library of Western Australia to do some research. When I look up at the brutalist grey entrance of the institution for the very first time, I feel as though I'm at university. The lobby is cavernous compared to anything at school.

Sitting at a long oak table, I leaf through pages and pages of texts, determined to find the perfect drama to win us the prize. In the end I settle on a flimsy little book. Once I've read it through three times, I know it's exactly what I'm after.

I've brought a pocketful of twenty-cent pieces to push into the photocopy machine in return for A4 replicas of the book's pages, but I choke a bit when I read a sign that *only 10 per cent of any publication may be copied before copyright laws apply.* This is unexpected. I weigh up my options.

Because I don't want to break copyright infringement laws, I decide to steal the book instead. How much harder can it be than shoplifting bubblegum and clothes? Or lying to the police for Dad.

The front entrance of the library is an empty space, after which there's the front desk with a rather stern woman seated behind it. Security plinths stand either side of the automatic door exit. I have a leather-tassel hippy satchel slung across my body.

An hour later, police escort me from the building.

I dropped the book in a pot plant next to the security plinths, planning to retrieve it from the other side once I was through – but when I reached for it the sensors picked it up anyway, and an embarrassing alarm filled the building. The librarian called the police, who arrived in a flash.

In the security room, we all watch the footage of my attempted theft. All I can do is tell the truth: I'm an arts captain at a well-known private girls' school, and all I wanted was a book for the school play, and if this is reported to school I may lose my scholarship. The police are as perplexed as I am by my story, and by how articulate and genuinely remorseful I am, so they let me go with a warning and wish me the best of luck with the play.

I take up a library membership, borrow the book and photocopy it at home – technically breaching copyright law, but surely this isn't as bad as the pirated videos – then give the play to all the girls performing. We have sleepovers in one of the empty bunkhouses, my old house, to rehearse.

When we win I almost knock Mrs Jackson out as I hoist the trophy in triumph. She smiles at me knowingly. 'I always knew you would come through, Mimi.'

Given his own obsession with the law, Dad is adamant that I should become a lawyer, so I apply to do my two weeks of work experience at the Supreme Court.

The first person I meet is a tall, curly-haired clerk called Anthony. 'Mimi KWA,' he says. 'Hey, you're not related to Francis KWA, are you?'

I'm flattered. 'Yes,' I say proudly. 'Yes, I am.'

He cocks his head and narrows his eyes behind his black rectangular glasses. 'He's quite well known around here, you know. A vexatious litigant.'

I'm thrilled. 'Yes, yes, he is,' I say enthusiastically.

I have no idea what he means, but later when I look it up I am mortified to find that it's someone who sues people regardless of the merit of the case, often just to harass them. I find out later that Dad isn't actually a vexatious litigant, as there has never been a court order against him. But now I know why the clerk laughed and walked off, and for the remainder of my two-week secondment I use my first name only, distancing myself from Kwa.

I attend quite a few court cases that fortnight, listening to the harrowing and brutal testimony of rape and murder trials, but the biggest court case in my life – the all-consuming one – is an ongoing battle of Dad's that I've been helping him work on at home for about half a decade.

Dad is suing our local council, the City of Stirling, with the demand that they permit him to build a twenty-storey highrise on our block. His precedent, a few streets away, is the Observation City Hotel, built when the America's Cup came to Perth in 1987. Alan Bond – or Bondy, as he's popularly known – was the mogul behind the hotel. And the minute the plan was announced, Dad wanted to do the same thing on our residential street.

'I'm just like Alan Bond,' Dad says. 'Bondy. He's my mate. I am Bondy.' Dad has only seen Bondy from a distance once, but he is so inspired by Observation City, a nineteen-storey hotel revised down from Bondy's original 24-storey plan, it keeps him awake at night. City of Stirling approved the smaller skyscraper despite mass protests. 'If my mate Bondy can build a skyscraper,' says Dad, 'so can I.'

Dad applies to rezone Mandarin Gardens for a highrise like Bondy's. When the council says no, he unleashes a series of court cases like I have never seen before. These multiple related cases become a drain on the public purse. There are so many he literally runs from court to court some days, skidding into courtrooms and filing sessions while always apologising profusely: 'Your Honourable Honour, I am humbly sorry for being late.'

When these Honourable Honours don't see things the Kwa way, Dad decides to go for 'a promotion' from the Supreme to the High Court – because he's 'not getting a fair trial' in the 'buddy Supreme Court'. But legal work of this sort is always protracted, and it will be more than a year before Dad can be heard.

With no one managing Mandarin Gardens, and Dad spending even more time than usual on his court cases against the City of Stirling, the hostel further deteriorates. So too does Dad's second marriage.

My world is in flux, and I struggle to keep my head above water. I can't stand to live next door to Dad anymore, or to stay with Mum. I finish high school and spend a couple of months living in a tiny flat with my friend Narelle, both of us on the dole and still sharing our secret handshake from when we were eleven and twelve. It's a boozed-up period, and I scald my ankle on a bar heater, causing a third-degree burn.

Rather than spiral further out of control, I defer university and make a plan to run away to England for a gap year. I'll fund it with the money Aunty Mary Cinderella left me in the hope I would travel the world. At seventeen, I'm very fortunate to be able to abscond with a small fortune, and put distance between me and my messed-up life. Dad isn't paying, so he's fine with it, and Mum supports me whatever I decide, or is too ill to know. Paw Paw and Granddad are quietly pleased I am getting away and plan to meet me in London for a couple of weeks at some stage.

Kwa looking after Kwa, Aunty Mary knew I'd need to escape one day.

FENG SHUI AND CAT'S PYJAMAS

First stop on my 1991 gap-year adventure is Sydney, where I stay with model friends in Rose Bay, attend Mardi Gras and get a taste of independence. Next I head to Hong Kong on my way to England, and after that I plan to explore Europe.

Over the years I've grown close to my cousin David, one of Clara's sons, so I'm pleased he's free to meet up in Hong Kong's bar district, Lan Kwai Fong.

'Oh hyellow, Mimi,' he enthuses as we lightly embrace and fake-kiss, European style, on both cheeks. I love it – so much more sophisticated than my bogan life in Perth.

David guides me down alleyways, along cobbled paths, through unmarked doorways and down dark staircases. We end up sipping cocktails in a small bar called Petticoat Lane, where little birdcages hang from lattice laced with ivy. I'm still underage but no one checks; being Eurasian I can look fifteen or fifty.

I show off to impress my older cousin, boasting about modelling jobs and television ambitions, but he has one up on me: he reveals he was scouted to be a big bank billboard model – seriously scouted on the street, just like in the movies. My cousin David! I can't contain my excitement.

'Ooooooh,' he says, 'didn't you know I was the HSBC pin-up boy? Oh, it was nothing.' He gestures in mock modesty as I sit on the edge of my seat.

'You should write a book,' I tell him.

David is a lawyer now. He rolls his eyes theatrically, giving the impression his current job is a little ho-hum compared to the bright lights of fame. We both know it's the opposite, though: David always has a new serial-killer story to keep me awake at night.

David reminds me about the time Dad took him to the ocean liner terminal at Tsim Sha Tsui to tour the boat that Dad had sailed to Australia on. The story has become family legend. David was just a little boy then, handsome in plaid shorts and braces, his hair slicked down. He made a cardboard replica of the ship to give to Francis, but when David played up, Francis whacked him hard on the backside, and the model ship was left behind. Francis had criticised it for being inaccurate, anyway. David was around six or seven then, a pipsqueak next to his Uncle Francis. Now David the man stands at least a foot taller than Dad.

We seldom get to see each other, but David and I have developed a unique bond over uncanny coincidences in our parallel lives. Francis and Clara could almost be the same person in the stories we tell, both of us attributing 'not turning out too bad' to growing up under the auspices of Aunty Theresa.

It's as though Theresa has been swapping one of us for the other. Throughout much of our childhoods we barely knew of each other's existence. I walked in one door while David exited through another, but when we speak it's like looking into a mirror. We both experienced the haircuts Theresa would take us for, and get entirely wrong; the scolding to sit up straight and to keep everything folded and neat; the memorable lavish meals; the walks along Repulse Bay – David following behind Aunty, me following behind Aunty – her consistent letter writing and, of course, thoughtful gifts. The unwavering care of Aunty.

David's references to his partner over the years turned out to be references to his ever-chipper Chinese boyfriend, Sam. No one was surprised, but Clara likes the arrangement not at all. To neutralise Clara's acidic approach, Theresa has welcomed Sam into the family with open arms, deliberately appearing in many photographs together with David and Sam to publicly embrace their relationship for Clara's benefit. But for Clara it remains a sore point. The gesture Theresa makes towards Sam might not sound like much, but in Chinese culture for her generation, it is significant. She also includes Sam in her will, again thoughtful and a very big deal; she knows it may raise the ire of Francis and Clara, but she does it anyway.

As David and I talk late into the night, drinking cocktails, our storytelling about our parents goes deeper and comparisons grow. Clara's scathing response to David being gay; Francis's scathing response to me not being born a boy. And so much more. Cousin to cousin, we see that you can take his mother and my father out of Hong Kong, but you can't take Hong Kong out of either of them.

When we stand up to say goodbye, I am swaying and he's not. My lack of coordination has everything to do with body mass and capacity, nothing to do with not being able to handle my grog, I assure myself. David is going to meet Sam, and I will navigate my way back to Aunty Theresa's place. We cousins European air kiss a wobbly farewell.

The next day, Aunty Theresa and I enter the magnificent foyer of the HSBC building, designed by British architect Norman Foster. 'Look at this.' She waves her hand upwards, and I take in the enormity of the complex modern masterpiece. 'On top he designed cannons,' she says like she knows Foster personally – maybe she does. 'Feng shui design to protect the money.' She nods at a staffer ushering us towards a long marble reception desk. 'And do you know what the Bank of China do with their building design?' I can't say I do. 'They build it like a knife. A knife to cut their competitor. To counteract the cannons pointed at them.' She makes two pistols with her hands. 'You look. I will take you to the China Club. It is a good view from there, and you will see. Fighting, fighting, the two bank are fighting.' She moves her fists as if she's preparing for a boxing match, tells a receptionist who we're here to see, and turns back to me. 'Even the building are fighting, Mimi. But it is peaceful fighting. It is feng shui.'

We are offered tea and more tea, but I accept a soft drink. While we wait at a desk for the banker to come, Aunty reaches into her Louis Vuitton handbag. 'This was a gift from' – she looks up and thinks – 'from the Duchess of … Oh, I forget the place. She gave everyone at the party this, in Milan.' Aunty rifles inside the crocodile-leather pouch. 'Her castle is very hard to maintain now. It costs her so much, she has to let go many of the staff so is not so comfortable to visit anymore, I prefer not to go. Better to meet somewhere to catch up.'

A Caucasian expat man in a three-piece pinstriped suit approaches us.

'But, Mimi, a copy is just as good if you do not receive as a gift.' She pats the crocodile and flashes her charming smile at the banker. 'This is my very beautiful niece, Mimi.' I blush and look down. 'She is a beneficiary of my very beautiful late sister Mary's estate.'

I smile at the thought of Aunty Mary's high rosy cheeks and infectious good nature, and my memories of her playing Aunty Mary Cinderella with me at Bicton, her warm embrace as she lifted and spun me around at the park or on the beach.

'As the executor, I will need to close this account and transfer all of it to this one – Mimi's account.' Aunty points to various documents she has neatly laid out to face the banker.

'Of course, Miss Kwa. Not a problem.' He excuses himself to finalise the paperwork.

'Mimi' – Aunty shifts her position and angles towards me – 'this is a big amount. As you know, your Aunty Mary left the same to all her nieces and nephews because she wants you to travel and have good life.' Someone places a plate of cookies in front of us; Aunty winks at me, taking one. 'They always look after me here. I know the top, top banker.' She does a little cat's pyjamas wiggle in her chair.

The amount Aunty Mary has left me is enough to travel for a year and put a deposit on a house – I am extremely lucky.

Aunty Theresa and I exit the HSBC building to hat tipping and bows, then her driver pulls up at the entrance as though to complete the fairytale scene.

'Mimi, I know you will be frugal and careful. You don't flash your money in the wrong places. Just like I don't flash my diamonds if I am in the poor area.' She holds up a hand to admire her rings encrusted with rubies, emeralds and diamonds. 'It is good to show compassion. If you can give, give. I always like to help others. But do not put yourself in a position where people will rob you. They will not care what you have in your heart, only what is in your purse.' She tips the driveway attendant as he closes the car door for us, then rests her crocodile bag in the back seat between us as we drive away. 'And never boast, Mimi.'

For lunch, as promised, Aunty takes me to the China Club in order to show me the feng shui stand-off between the banks. A tall, elegant woman in a cheongsam checks her clipboard for our booking. The China Club appears much older than the ones we usually visit, the American Club or the Royal Hong Kong Yacht Club, but it's actually brand new. There's a small framed photo of Princess Diana walking up the same staircase we're walking up now. Famous artworks and signed photos of patrons make for a fascinating trip to the top floor.

Aunty doesn't have a booking, of course. 'My friend always says whenever I want I can sign in under his membership.' Then she whispers, 'It's one hundred and fifty thousand Hong Kong to join.' We sit down at a table for four; Aunty hasn't planned to meet anyone else but has asked for extra seats 'just in case we bump into some friends'. She loves to say, 'More people, more food!'

The place is like a museum. Pictures of Chairman Mao and Tiananmen Square observe us from the wall above.

'The man who started this club is David Tang, a very nice man. He likes silks and the old style, the one like I sell in my shop. The one like your grandfather make and sell all over the world. All the corners, from Philippines to England – your family was the best in this business for silk. My uncle – who you would call Grandfather if he was alive, but he is actually your grandfather's brother – kept the business after your grandfather die.'

She picks up the menus and pretends to read while she talks. 'He – my uncle – helped your grandfather start the Swatow Lace business on Pedder Street. A long time ago. Your grandfather, my father, joined Uncle when he move from China with Second and Third Mother. Your grandmother is Wife Number Three, you know, so we call her Third Mother.'

I nod as I do whenever she tells this story.

'So when your grandfather die, in the war, his brother take over the business. During the war the brother was stranded in Shanghai.' She puts down the menu. 'And we, your grandfather and me, the children and his wife – we helped to keep the business running under the Japanese even though we must stop many our operation, and the Japanese taking most of the earnings. So then, I have the little Swatow Lace shop at the

Mandarin Hotel in honour of your family. And Mr Tang' – she looks around to make sure no one is listening – 'Mr Tang is going to open a shop where your family shop was, on Pedder Street. He wants to call it Shanghai Tang. Swatow Lace, our family business, was at 16 Pedder Street, remember I have taken you past there. He is going to open at number 12. You see, you have a connection to all of Hong Kong, Mimi. Everywhere, just look around and you will see.' She traces her finger down the menu, really reading it this time.

I contemplate the enormity of our Chinese and Hong Kong Kwa history, the smoke from Great-Grandfather's pipe disappearing down alleyways, curling up tall buildings, wending its way into the wallpaper pattern here at the China Club.

'You want a club sandwich?' Aunty asks. 'You know you love a club, at the club.' She laughs at our in-joke.

I nod and smile. 'Yes please, Aunty.'

NOW KWA

虎穴龙潭

Dragon pool, tiger den
– Chinese idiom

MONKEYS AND ZOO

I LEFT AUSTRALIA A CHILD OF SEVENTEEN AND RETURN A legal adult a year later. Dad leased my old apartment the moment I moved out with Narelle after school, so it's no surprise he has kept tenants in there with no intention of evicting them. What's left of Aunty Mary's money is enough for a minimum deposit on a unit, which Dad puts in his name, across the road from Mandarin Gardens. I live there rent-free, and he uses the property as an asset to borrow against, digging further into debt.

Dad continues to take legal action against the City of Stirling, and this becomes his main focus as his empire crumbles. He enjoys having me live directly across the road because I'm nearby enough to proofread his legal documents at no notice and far enough away that my problems are not his.

Angela is living in her own Mandarin Gardens apartment now, out of his hair. Divorce is imminent, and she seems unhappy. She will let me babysit my beloved little brothers, but she doesn't like them getting too close to me.

Despite returning from my travel adventures stronger and wiser, having experienced both the exhilaration and fright of freedom, I slip back into old patterns. I project my pain by coddling my brothers, taking them to the movies and museums, giving them presents in boxes that burst with helium balloons; I'm overcompensating for what I missed out on in Dad's Kwa compound, and what they must be missing out on now. I can see history repeating and know the psychological consequences because I'm experiencing them myself. My brothers are facing some of the same obstacles that I have had to confront, as well as some unique to them. Although the parallels of our journey end at Angela – who loves them dearly – I will never give up on my relationship with these boys, no matter how many walls divide us.

My old school friend Emma has moved in with me and while she prepares to visit the Philippines to meet her biological parents for the first time in her life, I make some last-minute tweaks to my academic timetable. I have decided to study Architecture at the University of Western Australia, with a minor in Drama and Asian Studies. Drawing boards were everywhere at Dad's place growing up and I was always rather surprised when other families didn't have one or two lying around themselves, or when my friends found it a novelty to drift my set square ruler on its parallel slider. But my choice is a great disappointment to Dad, who had his sights set on law for me, and an unspoken disappointment for my mother who, I sense, knows that I'm an artist at heart. But 'there's no money being an artist,' as Dad says. Architecture is a compromise because there is design involved and, hopefully, an income.

To be honest, I really don't know what I want to be, and Architecture makes sense because Dad is an engineer and frequently says he is an architect, so I hear that word all the time. Mind you, I also hear 'lawyer' a lot. I have secret aspirations to write and report, but believe I must take a conventional career path supported by a 'proper degree'. As a little girl, I watched *60 Minutes* hosts Jana, Mike and Ray scaling buildings and reporting hunched behind walls with mortar fire in the background or interviewing world leaders and superstars, and I thought, *I'd like to do that one day*. I can't seem to get a vision in my head of being an architect, but I always dream about being a journalist and newsreader on TV. Jana Wendt is the only woman on national television with a non-Anglo background, and she is not blonde so that does give me hope but, as there are no Asians on air, deep down, I don't like my chances.

In 1993, there is no university qualification for 'TV host' so I spend no time trying to figure out another way to become one. My primary school friend Michelle gets me a job as a photographer at Boat Torque Cruises, taking photos of passengers embarking on their wine tours and party river jaunts, racing back to a photo lab to develop the films and leaping into the arms of the crew across more than a metre of water sometimes, as we re-board the boats. Then we do a roaring trade selling the printed photos to drunk patrons.

One afternoon, I drop my brothers off at Mandarin Gardens after taking them to the zoo. I park the car, then hug and kiss the boys goodbye before they dash upstairs to show Angela what goodies they've brought home. At the end of our outings, we usually go for fast food – Hungry Jacks or KFC. If Adrian wants one thing and Jerome another, we go to the drive-through at both restaurants because I love to make them happy.

My window is up to make the most of the half-hearted air conditioning that I'll switch on once the engine is running again, and I'm wondering if I should wind it down a crack, to let in a bit of air first, when I see something extraordinary.

From across the carpark, about thirty metres away, Angela is walking straight towards me. I brace in panic, my chest tightening as I dig my nails into my palm. Experience tells me this can only mean a confrontation. As the slight figure with a formidable presence heads my way, I freeze and hold my breath.

Maybe she's upset with me for buying the boys junk food – or is she angry at me for not coming in to see her before I collected them from Dad? Whatever has upset her, I'm terrified she will stop me from seeing my little brothers again. In the seconds it takes her to cross the carpark, all possible outcomes are freight trains through my head, and some are really catastrophic.

I'm frozen in fear as she taps on the window, but then I suddenly spring to life as if jumping to attention for an army commander. Awkwardly I grapple with the manual winder to lower the glass. I gaze up at Angela, dumbfounded and nervous.

'I just wanted to say …' She doesn't quite look me in the eye. 'I just wanted to say thank you. I know you really love the boys.'

'Yes, yes, of course,' is all I can manage, but she is already walking away. I start the engine and drive off, numb with the adult realisation that she was just as nervous as me.

STRIPES AND BOMBS

I VISIT GRANDDAD ONE MORNING AT MOUNT HOSPITAL, A private facility in a picturesque part of Perth. His room overlooks the Mounts Bay Road estuary, a stone's throw from my Boat Torque job.

Recovery for standard prostate surgery should be only a few days, but due to Granddad's age and the leg pain he's been experiencing, they're keeping him in for a bit longer. No cancer was detected, but he opted for the surgery as a precaution. I open a window in Granddad's room, letting in a gust of fresh air. Below, I can see ducks gliding on the water and weeping willows skimming the surface. 'Architecture's going well,' I lie. 'But I'm not sure I want to be an architect anymore. I think I might want to be a journalist.' I turn to face Granddad, who is propped up with pillows in bed.

'Oh,' he says. 'Are you sure? You've changed course a few times, haven't you, young'un? I thought your year abroad inspired you to do architecture. Remember when Paw Paw and I came to see you? We all enjoyed our time on the Thames, looking at the buildings of London.'

Yes, of course I remember; it was only two years ago.

'And I told you all about the Blitz and the part I played in the war.'

Granddad pointed out where the bombs hit and the fires burned, remembering the events as if they'd happened yesterday. I wish my grandparents and I did more together in London, but after a few days of tours and high tea I had to be back at my job down in Cornwall, and they were due for a visit with Paw Paw's brother in the north.

I want to give Granddad a big hug, but he looks fragile under the sheets and thin cotton blanket, so instead I sit on the edge of his bed, my Doc Martens barely reaching the floor. We're deep in conversation when I realise the time – I'm late for a lecture but would much rather stay here. I stand up from his hospital bed and, like a bird, gently swoop in to kiss my favourite man on the forehead. Then I am gone.

In the afternoon, Mum and Paw Paw call me from Granddad's bedside. 'There's been a complication, Mimi. You need to come.'

I return and park next to the estuary and stride past the pond, the water like glass. As I pick up the pace, a startled duck lifts off leaving ripples behind. My chest tightens, and I break into a run. In the elevator I reason with myself. *It's just a complication. I'm sure he's fine. I just saw him this morning.* I press a fingernail into my palm; the familiar pain comforts me, keeping my anxiety at bay as I take a deep breath and step out of the lift.

Mum and Paw Paw turn to me with tear-streaked faces as I walk into the room. The bed is empty. 'No, no!' I scream. 'No.' I run out and take three steps at a time down the fire-escape stairs to the street, Paw Paw and Mum yelling after me from the open third-storey window. I drive away half-blinded by tears, hitting the steering wheel and screaming in despair.

Granddad's heart gave way. The doctors had thought the pain in his legs was from old war injuries, but he was having a heart attack right there in the hospital – right under their noses, where you might expect such a thing to be picked up. The elective surgery and anaesthetic put too much stress on his body, they said.

Paw Paw is so grief-stricken, the last thing she can think about is filing a complaint. 'The nursing staff thought it was his parachuting injuries playing up,' she says. 'They weren't to know.'

I look at her, incredulous. 'They are medical staff, Paw Paw. If they can't detect a heart attack, who can?'

For the hundredth time, we hold each other and cry.

'When we met,' she says, 'your grandfather and I, he went to the ballet just to please me, and he courted me with a warning. He said, "I am ten years older than you. If you marry me I will die before you." We were young, and it seemed such a silly thing to worry about. But he was right, Mimi. He was right.' We weep some more. Granddad was seventy-nine.

I keep Granddad alive by recounting his war hero stories to anyone who will listen, and I unexpectedly burst into tears in all sorts of places: a friend's car, a university lecture theatre, walking Whisky. I turn to friends, and Mum retreats further into her voices. I host a series of wild parties with my housemate Emma and, at one of them, our friend Danny Green, a boxing protégé, swallows my pet goldfish. That was right before one girl, Widge, swings Zarn around as they're dancing to *The Cure* and she falls and breaks her arm on the kitchen tiles. Never a dull moment. People have sex on car bonnets and light joints like they're cigarettes.

But one day, when I host a 'hat party' and my girlfriend Nina instead wears pictures of nude women stuck on an ice-cream container on her head, I decide things have gone too far. I am after all, a feminist.

Then I meet John – handsome and funny, from a normal family of meat-and-three-veg Catholics. He has no idea what he's getting into, and we fall madly in love.

'Your dad keeps asking me what my dad does,' John says one night. 'Remind me, why can't I tell him?'

John and I are locked in an embrace on the bed in my unit across the road from Mandarin Gardens. We're at the stage where we can barely keep our hands off each other. Young love!

'Because,' I tickle his chin and kiss him lightly, 'if my dad finds out your dad is a magistrate, he'll be over there quicker than you can say, "My dad's a magistrate." Your dad will *never* hear the end of it.' We laugh.

'Is that so?' John asks and kisses me.

'I think we should live together.' I roll on top of him.

'What will we tell our parents?'

I nestle into his shoulder. 'We've been together six months. They'll be fine.'

'Mimi, your mother and I, we're worried John is too old for you. You know what your grandfather said to me about being older. And he was right. He did die first.'

Mum is holed up, as usual, in her basement room, but Paw Paw uses 'we' for leverage.

'Paw Paw, he's only three years older.' I have a stupid 'I'm in love' smile on my face.

'Oh, I didn't realise. He looks much older than that.'

Now I laugh. 'He does not!' I know she's worrying about me, and I appreciatively throw my arms around her in the bearhug I wish I'd given Granddad the day he died. 'I love you, Paw Paw.'

She holds me out from herself to see me better, a twinkle in her eye. 'Well, if this is what you want, I am happy for you.'

'Mi, you still haven't told me what his father does.'

I go against my own counsel, exhausted by the question. 'He's a magistrate, Dad. John's dad is a magistrate. He comes from a very good family. We haven't taken the decision for him to move in here lightly.' Then I tell a lie: 'His parents are fine with it.'

'Right, well, I want their number. I want to talk to them.'

Just as I feared. 'I don't have it, Dad,' I lie again.

'They live in Morley, right? If John is Roberts then his father is Len Roberts. I know all the magistrates, ahahaha.'

I roll my eyes. 'Dad, I'm twenty. We're not getting married – I really don't think you need to talk to them.'

But it's too late: Dad is already scouring the White Pages telephone book and before I can stop him, he's revving his Kwa Car up the hill on his way to Morley. I am utterly mortified. I dig my fingernails into my hand and focus on that pain instead.

When he arrives at the unsuspecting Roberts household, Dad asks immediately for legal advice – on the grounds John's parents are virtually related to him now – and when John's dad mentions he has a sore back and asks to be excused, Dad insists that Len lie on the floor so he can walk on the magistrate's back, cracking it in two places. 'I am an expert in the chiropractic, you know.' Len's back never recovers.

Not long after this incident, John moves in with me as planned. He has brought a few humble possessions from the bachelor pad he shared with two friends, among them a Holden HD station wagon, 1966 – an iconic car that he intends to fix up one day. It's unroadworthy and unregistered, so he parks it outside our unit.

'Francis,' he says to Dad, 'perhaps you could advise me on how to bring my car back to life.' John is half serious, half buttering Dad up.

'Yes, yes,' Dad replies, 'I am a tup-tup-tup mechanic. I can show you. Yes, I can fix it.'

A few weeks later the car vanishes, and John and I are at a loss until I open our mail and unfold a council bill for towing and impounding fees. I call the council, and the person at the other end checks a file on the curious incident of the disappearing car. 'It says here a Mr Francis Kwa called to have the car towed, because it was an eyesore.'

We can't afford to bail out John's beloved Commodore, so all he has left are pangs of nostalgia. We do see the funny side, though, and I'm thankful for the sense of humour my new partner brings to the table – after all, this is one of countless Francis Kwa incidents John will no doubt endure by my side.

Whenever my tiger stripes are shadows tightening around me, I turn to John, my rock in the storm.

When I tell Aunty Theresa about my new-found love, she flies out to inspect the relationship and gives it a cat's pyjamas two-thumbs-up stamp of approval. She even meets John's parents and, to my relief, somewhat redeems the Kwa name with them in a way only Aunty can do.

At yum cha with Dad, John, Adrian and Jerome, Theresa announces she is moving to Manila to escape the handover of Hong Kong, which is coming up in 1997, marking the end of Britain's 99-year lease, which extended their administration there from 1898. She isn't taking any chances, keen to get her money out before China takes the territory back. In Brigit's home city, Aunty can be cared for in her old age without fearing her maid may leave her. Aunty has dual Australian–British citizenship, and we've tried for years – without any luck – to get a visa for Brigit to migrate to Australia as Aunty's companion, so this is the next best option. Aunty plans to visit Hong Kong regularly.

Ocean Palace is Perth's biggest Chinese restaurant, seating two hundred, and the maître d' has assigned us a standard round table covered with a white cloth under the lazy Susan in the middle. We order san choy bau and spring rolls, plus stir-fry noodles for the boys. Considering this is a Kwa event, everything is going well so far.

But when chicken feet come out for Dad, so do a pair of surgical gloves from his pocket. He slides them over his hands, and snaps the latex on as if he's in an operating theatre. Dad Wombled a whole pallet of these gloves and uses them at every possible opportunity – and, apparently, even when there isn't one.

Aunty looks at her brother, horrified. Dad helps himself to food with his gloved hands and eats, and I kick him under the table. Adrian and Jerome excuse themselves and go outside in teenage shame, while John – who is becoming accustomed to Kwa eccentricities by now – keeps eating.

'What?' Dad looks at me as if I'm insane. 'They are free. No need chopstick. What's wrong with you?'

Everyone in the restaurant seems to be staring as I die of embarrassment, and Aunty tut-tuts, frowning her disapproval.

Dad eats with his gloves on for the whole meal. 'It's a good idea, good idea. No washing up. No washing up. Ahhahahahahahah.'

John doesn't speak to Angela out of respect for me. 'I can't understand why you're nice to her,' he says.

'I do it for my brothers, you know that,' I reply.

Plus, the little girl in me still craves acceptance and love from this woman. Why do I hang on when it makes more sense to let go? My grandparents never gave up on Mum, or me. Aunty Theresa would never give up on Dad, and I won't ever give up on my brothers, or Dad either. So for Adrian and Jerome's sake I keep making an effort with Angela.

Kwa blood is thicker than pain. It washes over wounds and warnings, whispering, 'You are Kwa. You will never walk away.'

CLOUDS AND ANCHOR

IT'S 9.30 AM ON WEDNESDAY, 20 NOVEMBER 1996, AND AFTER many years as a litigant and hundreds of free court applications, Dad finally has a group of rather bemused and confused council lawyers exactly where he wants them: awaiting his late arrival at the High Court of Australia.

He tousles his hair and adjusts his bow tie to sit crooked as I hand him his stack of files. 'Watch this. Watch this. The master at work.' His eyes gleam, and he half hobbles, half shuffles into the courtroom, leaving me to find my own way to a seat in the gallery.

A High Court judge appears via satellite link-up from Canberra. I have barely sat down before Dad does his deliberate tripping act, dropping his stack of files and scrambling to gather them up. 'Your Honour, Your Most Gracious Honour. So sorry, Your Honour. I am so tired from up all night preparing, Your Honour. So sorry, Your Honour.'

The Honourable Judge Toohey waits patiently.

HIS HONOUR: Yes, thank you. Yes, Mr Kwa?

MR KWA: Yes. I just lost a bit of paper.

HIS HONOUR: Just before you start, Mr Kwa, let me just point out a couple of matters to you. One is that this is a motion to remove a matter that is before the Supreme Court into this court.

His Honour explains that Dad is applying to change the entire national constitution and that the facts of the case need to be sorted out in the Supreme Court before that can be considered.

Dad says he has grounds to change the entire national constitution and that it will only take five to ten minutes.

HIS HONOUR: I will hear from you.

MR KWA: If you could hear from me.

His Honour tells Dad he has already said that he will.

HIS HONOUR: Can I just say something else before you start, Mr Kwa, and that is that there is a considerable amount of documentary material that has been filed in this matter, filed on your behalf.

MR KWA: Yes.

HIS HONOUR: And most of it, I have to say, seems to me to have nothing to do with the application at all.

His Honour explains he is yet to find a relevant document among the files Dad has submitted.

MR KWA: It is entirely irrelevant as far as giving evidence is concerned.

HIS HONOUR: Well, if it is irrelevant it is a bit of a pity that it arrived in the court.

Dad goes on to tell the judge that the court is biased. Then he reads from the Bible.

MR KWA: I would like to refer to the Holy Gospel according to Matthew 22:1–14, which says: 'Many are called but few are chosen.' Meaning that many may apply but few are chosen. In this regard I pray that I have sufficient merit as to be chosen. In further postulating, Your Honour, that I should be chosen, I again refer to the Holy Gospel. I read according to Matthew 22:1–13, which reflects that: in order to be chosen one must be wise and devote particular effort for their preparation. I pray that I have demonstrated this in my paper, which I submit to record now.

Dad tells His Honour about a case the judge himself presided over – Dad even gives the court staff a transcript.

HIS HONOUR: I am sufficiently familiar with that case, Mr Kwa.

The City of Stirling is as perplexed as the judge. There's a team of six lawyers on the council's side; on Dad's, just him and me.

CITY OF STIRLING: Your Honour, I have not been provided with copies of any of this information Mr Kwa is handing up at the moment.

HIS HONOUR: Well, it is not information.

MR KWA: I know that this is not criminal law but everybody is entitled to a fair trial. That is my belief.

HIS HONOUR: But, Mr Kwa … your action is against the City of Stirling. It is an action brought in a State Court and on the face of it involves no Commonwealth matter. This is the High Court.

MR KWA: My pleading, Your Honour, is that it is a fair trial. I am Australian citizen. I am entitled to a fair trial regardless. Now, constitution …

His Honour appears to be in a degree of pain as he entertains Dad's longwinded presentation, and I am unable to locate a suitable rock to hide under.

HIS HONOUR: Those are your submissions, are they?

MR KWA: Yes. Thank you, Your Honour.

HIS HONOUR: Yes. Thank you, Mr Kwa.

MR KWA: Thank you, Your Honour.

HIS HONOUR: Yes. Thank you, Mr Kwa.

MR KWA: Yes. Thank you, Your Honour.

The judge grits his teeth and hands down his decision, throwing Dad's case out.

Outside court, Dad is jubilant. 'Did you see me? Did you see me? It's the High Court. He likes me. I get along very well with judges. All the judges. We have the same thinking, see. Better than average brain.'

I help him with his files. 'Dad, I don't think you won in there.'

He shakes his head. 'Oh, I won alright. I won alright. The High Court of Australia saw Francis Tak Lau Kwa!'

By now I've swapped architecture for broadcast journalism, finally following my dream to become a TV news anchor, having discovered a university that's just begun offering their long-established course as an actual degree.

In 1997, a year into my new study stream at the WA Academy of Performing Arts, I try out for an ABC cadetship, just for practice, along with three thousand other applicants. We jump through exam and interview hoops, and then, as the numbers are culled, more interviews and screen tests. It's obvious I won't get in.

I'm at my old high school, walking towards the school's second-hand swap shop to finally hand over my old blazer, skirts, shirts and dresses, when my little red Nokia mobile phone rings. An ABC cadet recruiter is on the other end. 'Mimi, how do you feel about moving to Melbourne?'

I sit down in the middle of the oval and fall back to lie down on the soft green lawn, watching white clouds shift across an endless blue sky, euphoric with the realisation that my life is about to change.

I had planned to defer uni and move to Kuala Lumpur with John for his new job, but now I can only stay a few months before my cadetship begins. In the new KL office that his Perth boss is renting, John and I paint dull partitioned walls white and the doors a cheerful mint-green. I carry in plants to feng shui the energy, and John sets about managing local staff. It's summer and I don't want to leave him here, but I do. A few months later, he follows me to Melbourne.

A year after, I defect from the ABC to Channel Nine.

'You're the first non-WASP I've ever put on TV. The first Asian.' My formidable commercial news boss is gruff, with a terrifying reputation for cutting off neckties he dislikes and leaving around diet books as hints for female presenters. 'Don't get any fatter in the face,' he tells me, then walks away.

I feng shui my desk with plants to deflect bad vibes, as well as the excessive electrical energy from the news feeds streaming on rows of TVs bolted to the wall above me. They show every channel simultaneously, and we're also permanently tuned in to emergency service radio transmitters and news wires. Four fax machines spit press releases, and phones ring off the hook – the eye of the storm of daily news.

After a disastrous first shift ambushing Russell Crowe, I gradually win over my commercial colleagues and attract only the occasional derisive 'ABC' comment from my chief of staff.

I haven't been assigned a story today, so I lean back in my chair, casually scanning the screens for a yarn to chase.

'Oh God. That's my house.' I sit bolt upright with alarm.

'Police are yet to comment,' says the newsreader on the screen. 'We'll bring you more on this breaking news in our next update in an hour.'

I'm already on the phone. 'Dad, what's going on? Mandarin Gardens is on the news.'

Dad is pumped. 'Yes, yes. All the televisions are here. It's famous. I'm famous. All the televisions are here.'

I take a deep breath. 'Dad, I realise that, but what is going on?'

I recognise the familiar sound of journos trying to get Dad's attention. 'There is a fight in the bunkhouse. Someone dead.'

I try to keep him engaged. 'What do you mean "someone dead"? What happened?'

'Yes, a man, dead. I have to go. Very busy.'

'Dad. Tell me what happened.'

'I tell you already. Buddy hell. There is man. He come in and stealing things from the backpackers. The police kill him.'

'Dad, what man?'

'I don't know, he's not here anymore.'

'So who is dead?'

'One of the backpacker.'

'Dad, this is very confusing.'

'The news is here. I have to go. I tell you everything already. Buddy hell.'

'Dad, do not speak to the news. Do not speak to anyone. If you do, make sure it's only Channel Nine, and I can try to manage it from here. But ... actually, Dad, it's just best you don't speak to anyone at all. Okay?'

'Yes, yes, okay, daughter. Know-it-all daughter. Yes, yes, whatever you say.'

I hang up and look on the wires: the exclusive channel where news agencies share information.

Police are investigating the death of a backpacker at a Perth youth hostel. The yet-to-be-named man allegedly carried out a number of thefts at Scarborough Beach backpacker hostel Mandarin Gardens. Police tried to restrain the man who is now deceased.

My chief of staff shouts across the newsroom, 'We're getting the feed from Seven, for the updates. Mimi, news exchange, now. Shot list what comes through from Perth on the backpacker thing. We're pooling.' This is just shorthand for the fact that Channel Nine has a deal to share footage with Channel Seven.

I head into news exchange and say, 'That's where I grew up. That's my dad.'

The eighteen-year-old news edit assistant, who has spent seventy-two hours straight in this tiny room filled with small screens, looks up from a couch in the corner. 'That's your dad? Really?'

Dad is adjusting his position in front of the camera. He's on the balcony outside his front office. 'Have you got the pool in?' Dad asks the crew. 'Have you got the pool in?' They are rolling, and the pool is in shot over Dad's left shoulder. 'At the moment we have a special deal,' he says. 'You stay six nights and get the seventh night free.'

I watch in horror as newsroom colleagues come to see 'Mimi's dad' on TV. This part isn't going to air, of course – it's only raw footage shared between networks – but still!

I notice he has the wireless phone on him, the loud one with the tall aerial, so I call him again. 'Dad, what on earth are you doing? I just saw you doing an interview with Seven. I told you not to talk to anyone.'

'Daughter, you don't understand about the media. Daughter – oh, daughter. You do not understand. In Perth, Channel Seven is the highest rating. See. See. Good publicity. Everybody likes me. Free advertise.'

I put down the phone just in time to see the tail end of Dad on the feed: 'Yes, yes, yes. And we have a tennis table and twenty-five metres pool.'

GOLDFISH AND RATS

Mandarin Gardens is falling apart. The pool has grown mouldy, and the bathrooms I once cleaned are blackening with grime. Monkey tails litter an overgrown lawn, and four and a half stars drop to three. Dad's proud list of amenities grows yellow, with guests hardly recognising Mandarin Gardens from the glossy brochures anymore and posting poor reviews on something called the 'internet'.

The Australian Youth Hostels Association drops Dad's membership, so he sues them in the Federal Court. The judge, unable to see any reason for the case, orders Francis to pay the YHA's legal bill and cites the parallel lawsuit against the YHA Dad is running in the Supreme Court. 'Buddy hell. Buddy judge. He doesn't understand. Buddy hell. I'll show them. I'm a lawyer. I know better than buddy most of them buddy monkeys in the courts.'

Tenancy at Mandarin Gardens wanes to the point that utilities and the mortgage go unpaid. Eventually, the sheriff arrives to repossess all four and a half thousand square metres of land. The few backpackers still in residence demand refunds, and Francis stows a few things in a garbage bag as police barricade the property. Later, he returns with my twelve-year-old brother,

Jerome, who squeezes through a gap in the padlocked fence to rescue his goldfish with a plastic bag. The boys move into a flat with Angela, and Dad couch-surfs with friends.

When the latest Supreme Court verdict is handed down, Francis actually wins his thirteen-year fight against the City of Stirling to rezone and build a highrise on the Mandarin Gardens site. But the verdict has come way too late, applying to a property Francis Kwa no longer owns. It's a sad end to Dad's dream. The bank sells Mandarin Gardens to a developer, who plans to build a four-storey retirement village, and Francis has to start again.

He's resilient, though, and quickly finds work as a chartered engineer – his pre-hostel profession. He also has his other sidelines – wedding celebrant, migration agent, arbitrator. After the bank takes its money from the sale of Mandarin Gardens, Francis uses the remainder to put a deposit on a house in Floreat, a major step up from Scarborough.

His new neighbours are judges and surgeons and, two doors down, a professor, and it doesn't take long for him to alienate most of the street by turning his place into a derelict property. He crams his quarter-acre block with stuff – an accumulation of junk so extreme it makes the papers.

'Rat Infested Property.' Dad sends me a colour photocopy of the article. 'Look, look. I'm on the front page.' He shares his excitement over the phone and by letter. *Look. Look. This is me*, he jots in the corner of the article, the address highlighted in yellow in case I have any doubt. According to the article, neighbours have been complaining to the City of Cambridge about Francis's hoarding for months.

'No, no,' he says. 'My neighbours love me.'

Photos in the article appear to have been taken from over the fence by those loving neighbours.

'Whenever I need legal advice, the retired judge agrees with me. They all love me. Everyone loves me. Everyone thinks I'm right.'

I remember what it was like at our youth hostel, with Dad reusing everything. He was ahead of his time waging a War on Waste. 'No waste, no waste' is Aunty Theresa's motto for food, whereas it is Dad's motto for everything.

I had the job of unravelling plastic wrap from around the three newspapers flung over our wall each day. I would peel back the outer layer along the length of the rolled-up newspaper, little by little so as not to tear it, pulling the plastic free about an inch all the way along. Then I'd press the edge onto the stair rail.

We used the plastic wrap for leftovers and my school lunches, but over the years we accumulated hundreds of layers around the balustrade, much more than we would ever need. When I rolled off the cling film, I'd quickly scan the news headlines before taking the papers to Dad.

Visitors must have found it odd to walk into a roll of cling film as soon as they entered our front door. But that sight was possibly not as odd as the mirrors Dad attached with rusted wire either side of the staircase, or the mirror at the top of the stairs – when you got to the landing, you'd almost topple backwards and break your neck. This was his version of feng shui, but it wasn't very good luck. Meeting my reflection every time I walked up to my room took some getting used to; the first time, I got disoriented and cut my hand on a rusted wire. I sucked on the blood and wondered out loud if I might need a tetanus shot.

'You'll be okay.' Dad said. 'Mirrors good idea. Good idea. You just clumsy. And fat. Ahahahahahhahah.'

Dad's Floreat house is overrun with Mandarin Gardens junk, but most of it was packed into shipping containers and sent to a farm far north of Perth. 'Storage is cheap. Cheaper than throwing away. You never know when I might need it.' He loses track of what's in the containers and where they are, but manages to locate one worth bringing home so he can advertise its contents on Gumtree: dozens of heaters, toasters, bunk beds and taps, among other things – he ripped out whatever he could. He spends months fielding enquiries for twenty-dollar items.

Various international university students rent rooms in Dad's house. They clamber around and over stuff, wedging themselves in wherever they can find space.

Dad has sold a lot, but still stuff multiplies like cancer cells. The house, propped on stilts, has dozens of plastic tubs shoved under it. In them are items like duvets, cheese graters, chopping boards – 'I might need them one day' – hotel toothbrushes, empty shampoo bottles – 'You never know' – framed yellowing prints, remote controls and mousetraps. They all live under the house with the spiders and famous rats from the front page of the local rag.

I fly from Melbourne to visit Dad. It takes me a while to make it through his complicated gate system: a pulley attached to a wire, metal bar and latch. I walk under a sailcloth that forms the carport, past a garage filled with anvils and motorcycles, old tools and welding machines, then past a mezzanine floor with a ladder – no doubt there's a lodger up there – and clothes racks, kettles, a set of hair curlers, incomplete card decks, two pianos, old brochures and jars of pens that don't work, and finally I find the front door.

Inside, I squeeze past three photocopiers. Pictures of Dad are dotted around in newspaper articles, laminated photos alongside magnetic calendars dating back to the 1970s. On a table awkwardly arranged in a small galley kitchen, where a table should definitely not be, I find a small bubblegum dispenser containing odd socks and a tape measure. I shimmy past, sidling up to the fridge. A four-foot stuffed crocodile watches me from the top of cupboards coated in cooking residue, presumably from the four woks and two rice cookers collecting grime underneath. There are two overflowing plastic-bag holders attached to the wall, but alarmingly no stair rail for plastic wrap from newspapers.

Dad is praying to his ancestors in a lounge room overcrowded with furniture. He has put castor wheels on the antique chair legs so he can move around freely in the one square metre of available space. Joss sticks are burning, but the serenity is sabotaged by a loud and constant whirring; Dad has installed a rangehood in the lounge room above his ancestral shrine to suck up the smoke. It's the first time I've seen a rangehood in a lounge room.

'Good idea, good idea,' says Dad. 'Look. No smoke, no smoke.'

I can hardly hear him above the din of the extractor fan.

In the same room, Dad has a massage chair with a mirrored bathroom cabinet above it, where he hides his jade and gold treasures. It's the first time I've seen a bathroom cabinet in a lounge room.

Dad has attached a magnifying glass to a concertina arm on the wall above his dining table. 'All the better to read the newspaper – it's a good idea. See. I can read with close up, whenever I want.'

Also attached to the wall is a bracket holding Dad's headphones, the cord running up the wall and along a cornice to an enormous television mounted next to the rangehood in the opposite corner. 'So I can hear the TV.' The television is just two metres away.

There's a shaving mirror attached to the wall too. 'It's angled perfectly to reflect the ceiling light onto my newspaper position. See, so I can read. Here, look.'

Dad has a cherished picture of Mandarin Gardens framed and hanging above a door with an inscription that reads, *I did it my way*. Even though it has been repossessed, closed down and demolished, Mandarin Gardens will always be Francis's masterpiece. Five pictures are glued together in a panoramic series, overlapping and not quite matching up to form the perfect image. A bit like life. Dad has signed and dated it anyway, for authenticity. I imagine him sticky-taping its corners, framing it and polishing the glass with a dirty tea towel, threading wire through staples on the back of the frame, hammering a nail above the door and hanging the memory of his kingdom. *I did it my way.*

Dad brings out a vinyl album. He's sitting on an antique Chinese carved wooden dining chair on castor wheels. 'So convenient,' he says as he scoots from dining table to record player. He lifts and places the needle, and the recording crackles to life: it's Dad singing 'Moon River' with the Melbourne Symphony Orchestra at the Malvern Town Hall, a lifetime ago. He closes his eyes and listens to the young man, and dreams of Mandarin Gardens.

My teenage brothers were living with Dad in among the paying lodgers until recently. When more students moved in, Dad decided that it was time for my brothers to move out. The boys are in high school, and Dad knows they don't have jobs or any money, but they move back in with Angela in her one-bedroom apartment. Dad has now installed four more students in my brothers' old room. Their Matchbox cars are still in plastic tubs under the tenants' beds.

When I ask Dad why they've moved home, he says, 'Darling daughter, I told the boys if they pay rent they can stay. They said "no" so they go. Simple. Their choice. No hard feeling.'

Dad never ceases to amaze me.

I never cease to amaze Dad. 'They can work. Buddy no-hopers. I worked when I was seven years old.'

ALLIGATOR AND SAFARI

I LONG TO SEE AUNTY. SHE OFTEN WRITES AND I SAVOUR HER letters, usually calling her back right away instead of taking the time to handwrite my thoughts. A letter from Theresa is like stardust, a sprinkle of magic every time.

I imagine her sitting at her mahogany desk. 'Brigit, Brigit,' she calls out, 'I'm writing to Mimi.'

Brigit brings in a cup of Chinese tea and sets it beside Aunty. 'Now, what's for lunch? Once I finish writing, I will eat.'

Brigit feigns dismay as she always does with this routine. 'But, ma'am, you tell me you are on a diet, and you have a dinner party with the professor vice-chancellor peoples tonight, so you wanted no lunch.'

Aunty rubs her belly and laughs. 'Okay. Okay then, just a little snack then, so I don't get fat.'

Brigit rolls her eyes. 'Oh, ma'am.' And she prepares a three-course lunch, knowing Theresa will change her mind and want a big meal after all.

I open the latest letter from Theresa, unfolding the rice-paper-thin blue paper. The cheapest way to send a letter overseas involves writing it within the folds of the custom envelope. I've kept dozens of these fine foolscap sheets filled with elegant curls and wisps, versions of copperplate only Aunty and my grandparents' generation knows. I have to take great care to open her letter, gently tearing the correct edges in two with a knife, careful not to butcher any of those beautiful words.

Aunty and Paw Paw each own ornate letter openers. Paw Paw's is brass and shaped like a sword, a scholarly male figure sculpted on the handle; it's a wartime souvenir from the Netherlands, near the border with Belgium. Theresa's letter opener is ivory, a souvenir from a Kenyan safari when she would visit with BOAC to join celebrity and distinguished passengers on hunting trips. Ernest Hemingway made safaris fashionable in the 1950s, and as the world recovered from the war, stars such as John Wayne and Katharine Hepburn filmed movies in Africa, which opened a wellspring of flight paths for Theresa to explore.

In her letter just arrived, Aunty shares news of Hong Kong. She was just there and is, as usual, staying in her aristocratic German friends' place. It seems they are never there, and they're more than happy for Aunty to occupy their home for months on end, treating their villa as her own. This includes their staff: a driver, and a maid who doubles as cook. *The gym in the building is so-so*, she writes. *So I visit the tennis club where the baroness still includes my signature on her membership.*

I picture us crossing the road after a swim at the beach, Aunty with her flip-flops and tasselled terry-towelling poncho and me trying to keep up, wearing the terry shorts and varsity printed T-shirt she bought for me on our shopping spree the day before. 'You are such a good shopper. Good shopper.' Aunty had clapped her hands with glee every time I emerged from the change room modelling something new.

I read on. Aunty has drawn a little smiley face with slanted eyes. *Do you remember the club sandwiches?* she writes. *How is baby Royston? How is John? How is your mother?* Aunty has filled the entire page, keeping flourishes to a minimum to fit in all her news. I turn it over, and her words occupy every available space on the back too, though she has shown great care not to stray onto the glue flaps.

I can come to see you, but why don't you come up here to Manila to stay for a while? I have many, many new friends here. One lady owns a whole university. All of it. You can meet her. Brigit can cook for you. My new driver will pick you up.

Much love, Aunty Theresa xx

This is the call of Kwa.

John and I decide to take a trip to Manila and bring thirteen-month-old Royston on his first trip overseas.

I'm used to people staring at my mixed-race looks in Australia, Hong Kong and everywhere else in the world – belonging and not belonging anywhere – and I know the kind of reception John gets when we travel too, standing out in China, Thailand and the Philippines, where there are few expats: a tall, rugged white man with his mixed-up girlfriend. Schoolgirls on a bubble-car ride behind us at the Window of the World theme park, in far southern China's Shenzhen, ran up to John with notepads one time, calling out, 'Bluce Lillous!' But these experiences didn't prepare us for the attention Royston would receive.

Our little blond boy squeals with delight as John carries him off the plane, and we're enveloped by the soggy humidity as maintenance workers stop what they're doing to stare at my child. A sea of local ground crew flood the lounge entrance, move out of the way, and then, realising there's a baby, surround John and Royston while I follow with our bags. 'Ooooh, he's so cute.' A young worker touches Royston's chubby hand, bouncing it up and down in hers. 'Yes, he's so cute, mister,' a man says to John. 'May I touch the hair? The hair is so white.' By the time we arrive at the gate, having collected our check-in luggage, Royston has been fanfared the length of the terminal.

We head for arrival gate K for Kwa, where we find Aunty Theresa's driver holding a small whiteboard that says *MISS KWA*. Aunty is so excited about our visit that she has travelled with her driver to greet us – not all Aunty's guests receive such a welcome. I fling my arms around her for a warm hug. She beams, claps her hands, and bobs up and down to elicit a smile from Royston. 'Aunty Theresa,' I say. 'Aunty Teessah,' he repeats.

I am elated. As I sink into the leather car seat, I feel I've come home. This is Manila, of course, not Hong Kong, but Aunty is here, and that's home to me.

The air conditioning is on, but beads of sweat still run down our faces. It's hotter than Hong Kong, so Aunty gives John the front seat to be nearer the air con, and she sits in the back with me – to be nearer Royston. Aunty chuckles, holding my son's tiny hand and then pulling hers away, hiding it beside her so he can't see it beyond the booster seat she has so thoughtfully arranged. He laughs as he and Aunty play this game all the way home.

I watch the scenery change out the window: shantytown, slum, condominiums, highrise; shantytown, slum, condominiums, highrise. We stop at traffic lights, and a boy, six or seven years old, knocks on my window, holding up a bunch of bananas and nodding at me expectantly. I shake my head. Another child, this time a little girl, skips across the main road between cyclists and mopeds with a cotton bag, slung across her body, holding mangoes.

'You want?' Aunty says.

'No thanks, Aunty.'

A young man in a grubby and torn singlet top, fit and shining in the heat, walks between two lanes of traffic and stops momentarily at each car. He's selling water. 'Water, water,'

Aunty says to her driver. He pops open the ashtray and reaches for a few coins before winding down his window just enough to make the exchange. He is ex-military; in the Philippines, most personal drivers are. They double as security guards in troubled Manila where the elite feel they must protect themselves from being robbed or kidnapped or worse.

Every time I visit, there has just been a spate of Chinese abductions, according to Aunty, so I must be very careful never to go out of her driver's sight unless I'm at a shopping centre. Most of the high-end malls are off limits to locals unless they look rich; the security guards can tell, I'm told. To me it's a bizarre feeling to walk through a familiar shopping-centre entrance when the person behind you gets turned away or their bag is searched because they don't look like they can afford anything inside. Security can always tell I'm a tourist and usher me to the left, bypassing the metal detector and bag search that even a Chinese Filipino in head-to-toe Gucci can't avoid.

When we arrive at Aunty's condo, a guard in the sentry box tips his cap, recognising our car, while another circles us and peers in the windows. 'My niece, my niece,' Aunty says. The expressionless guard nods us through, and we drive into a cavernous carpark then stop alongside a marbled lift well. Another guard, this one friendlier, helps our driver with our cases. 'I can take that,' I offer.

'No, no, no, let them do it,' Aunty insists. 'Here, you live it up. Live it up.'

I'm familiar with Aunty's routine, having grown up shadowing her over so many school holidays: massage, gym, swim, eat, sleep, usually a couple of times a day and sometimes punctuated by shopping. We've been at her place three days now, and I am copying her routine as closely as I can. Royston adds to the schedule by sliding on his tummy across the parquetry floor. It's almost a mirror, Brigit has polished it so well.

'Mimi,' Brigit says with a laugh, 'why you don't let me get that for you?' She's referring to the orange juice I'm helping myself to from the fridge. No other guest would ever even be allowed in the kitchen, let alone into the laundry behind it, or Brigit's tiny room beyond that.

'Mimi' – she takes the bottle from me – 'I juice you a fresh one. Off you go.' I am shooed out, laughing.

Brigit perfectly pulps the orange and serves it to me in a glass nestled in a white doily cupholder, before peeling grapes for John and Royston. John raises an eyebrow at me as if to say, *She's peeled our grapes*, and I laugh. This is ludicrous and luxurious compared to our lives in Australia. It's new to John, but I've been existing across galaxies since I was born.

Today Aunty's friend picks us up and takes us to a resort. The friend owns the resort, or has shares in it – with Aunty I can never quite tell who owns what or what title belongs to whom, as she has a way of stringing several connections and references into her pre-introductory briefings: 'She's the daughter of the magnate who owns the main Telco. Her daughter is a professor in the best university. She is an owner in the island we are going to. Maaaany famous movie stars go there – even the European prince comes for a holiday. But when her son married the owner of the biscuit company – you know the one, Arnott or Nabisco or something – that was a mistake. They are divorce now. She didn't like her, anyway. Now he has the marketing degree and he works in the head of the marketing at the biggest bank in Philippines. Maaaaany people know him. She's a good friend. So generous. You will like her.'

In Aunty's orbit, it can be difficult to place who is who, but it's highly entertaining to try. And one thing is certain: just like me, they all adore her and would do anything for her.

After a bumpy two-hour ride in Aunty's very nice friend's luxury van, we emerge at a Spanish-style resort. It's hard to imagine how the manicured lawns and trimmed hedges can survive in this heat, but they must like the humidity because the foliage is lush. We swim in a lagoon-style pool looking out over a private golf course set before a picturesque rolling landscape. I turn towards the jungle and wonder about the locals living in villages nearby, forbidden from ever setting foot in here without a worker's uniform.

'Ma'am.' A waiter brings drinks to the edge of the pool, and John and I glide over, leaving Royston in Aunty's arms. She's wearing her signature bright-pink flower swim cap and a broad smile; at seventy-five, she is radiant. Royston splashes as Aunty laughs and holds him out from her, pulling him back again with an arm wrapped around his waist. He keeps splashing to the enthusiastic applause of a line-up of staff, each wearing white-and-tan uniforms with dark edging at the collar pockets and seemingly happy dispositions on their sleeves, despite their life of servitude.

'Little prince, little prince,' Aunty sings.

A few days later, temperatures are soaring. Although our time is spent in air conditioning or the pool, the thick humid envelope of air in between is bearable for a few minutes at most. When the generator at Aunty's condo breaks down, we feel it instantly. Royston cries, his little pink face flushed; it must be forty-five degrees in here.

Brigit's sister has come up from their village home to stay for a while and help out, and maybe find a city boyfriend. She's beautiful and like an elk crouching by Royston's cot, fanning him with a magazine, singing to him in her T-shirt and jeans. How on earth can she be wearing jeans?

'They are used to it.' Aunty reads my mind, standing beside me in the doorway to Royston's room. All the power is out now, and Aunty is carrying a flashlight; I've been using the one on my mobile phone. John is downstairs in the bath-warm pool when Aunty says, 'I've sent Brigit to tell your husband to get ready. Grab your overnight bag. We are leaving.'

We walk into the Shangri-La Hotel foyer looking like drowned rats, and Royston stops crying the minute the air con hits us. Aunty pays for three rooms: one for John and me, an adjoining one for Royston, and one for herself. 'Live it up.' She winks at me.

Once I've settled Royston into a blissful sleep and John's nodded off, I slip out into the corridor wearing my hotel robe and slippers and tap lightly on Aunty's door.

'Alligatorrrr,' I hear. To Aunty, 'See you later, alligator' can be abbreviated to 'alligator' as shorthand for 'see you later' and 'hello' and 'welcome'. 'Alligator. Alligator.' She is so happy. 'Now, what would you like? I get you something. Thirsty? Hungry?' She's wearing her hotel robe too and leans back in an armchair, perusing a menu before swinging her legs up to sit cross-legged and dial room service. 'Why not.' She smiles broadly and winks. Champagne and club sandwiches soon arrive, and Aunty watches my delight. 'Eat, eat,' she commands. 'Hmm, this is good.' Her mouth is full, so it sounds more like 'HMM-rthmisoud', but I can understand her. I always have.

I wipe crumbs from my chin. 'You've worked so hard, Aunty Theresa.' I replace the starched white linen napkin on the tray.

'No, not really.' She folds her own napkin and lies my glass flute down too, as one might expect of cabin crew when they collect your empty plate. 'I am very lazy.'

Laughing, she picks up the tray and carries it across the room to leave outside the door. She comes back and sits down, cross-legged again, her expression now serious. 'I have had a good life, Mimi.' For a moment she looks reflective, as though she has sailed off somewhere far away. 'Really, Mimi, I am so very lucky.'

COFFIN AND WOLF

'MIMI, I WAS SO EMBARRASSED WHEN THE DELIVERY BOY brought the flowers up the path. That big 80 on the balloon was bobbing up and down for all the neighbours to see!' Paw Paw is laughing; she's tickled pink with the flowers.

I wish I was there for her birthday. It's the same day as Dad's, which is strange – for two Geminis, they couldn't be more different. Except for my sixth birthday party, Dad never celebrates them. 'Doesn't matter, doesn't matter,' he says. He did give me a half-eaten packet of biscuits wrapped in Christmas paper for my eleventh birthday, and for my twelfth he gave me golf balls knowing I didn't play golf. As a child, I was so upset by his attempts at birthday celebrations, he gave up in subsequent years.

Paw Paw, on the other hand, is a birthday and Christmas professional. On Boxing Day she follows a tradition of leaving money in a box for the milkman, postman and newspaper boy, and in the lead-up to Christmas she wraps dozens and dozens of presents from every family member including the dog, guinea pigs and two budgerigars to every other family member – including the dog, guinea pigs and two budgerigars.

'Oh, Mimi.' I'm in Melbourne but I feel her warmth emanate all the way from Perth. 'Mimi, I just love the flowers. I wish I could give you a big hug.'

I try not to cry. 'I do too, Paw Paw. I do too.'

I haven't seen Paw Paw since she came to Melbourne a couple of months ago. We toured around, went to the theatre and had a lovely time together.

I had a few work shifts in between, but not for Channel Nine anymore. I spent five years there chasing 'bad guys' for a nightly current affairs program, where my boss was fond of telling me how I would never amount to anything, whenever I was eligible for a pay review. I covered news stories and diet stories, and interviewed celebrities like Serena Williams, Russell Crowe (we reconciled after my appalling ambush), Pierce Brosnan and Kylie Minogue. Then there were the weekly helicopter rides; the series of stories with Chopper Read; an investigation into psychics and another into police brutality; the girl who didn't know she was pregnant when she gave birth at full term; and the boy, Chris, who aged at ten times the normal rate and died at nineteen soon after I'd spent weeks filming with him. I never knew what story I'd be thrown on next. It was exciting and fun, confronting and sad, but after having Royston, the idea of going back to long hours and spontaneous trips away – sometimes for days at no notice – didn't make sense, so instead I return to my dream job at the ABC: anchoring news. No more last-minute chartered flights, screaming bosses or chequebook journalism – sitting behind a news desk is exactly where I want to be.

'John,' I call out, after hanging up the phone, 'I'm worried about Paw Paw. She says she's too old to travel overseas anymore. She lives to travel.'

John walks down the hall to the kitchen. We live in a single-fronted cottage on a pretty street in the Melbourne suburb of Prahran. 'Well, let's visit again soon, before this one comes along.' He pats the curve of my belly where our second child grows while Royston masters walking.

'Okay,' I say, grateful for John's unwavering support, 'that would be good.'

A few days later I receive a frantic phone call.

'Mimi, Mimi,' my mum cries, 'I'm taking Paw Paw to the hospital. She's having a heart attack.'

The world goes into slow motion, like when my mum flew down a corridor and threw herself in front of a car.

'Let me speak to her,' I say.

For the first time in my life, I hear Paw Paw swear. 'Shit,' she says, 'I can't get my seatbelt on.'

Mum hangs up. I don't call back straight away; I don't want to delay them getting to the hospital. I'm numb for a moment. Then, all of a sudden, I have questions. Why haven't they called an ambulance? Why even worry about the seatbelt?

I never get to ask. When Mum calls me from Paw Paw's bedside, she holds the phone to Paw Paw's ear for me to say goodbye, but all I hear is the rushing of oxygen through tubes, the beeping of machines, and a voice that says, 'Clear,' and again, 'Clear!'

Mum drops the phone and I hyperventilate, feeling I might lose the baby. I can hardly breathe, and if he can feel my sorrow I am sorry, but I can't help convulsing with grief. I hold my stomach, and the baby gives a little kick. In my mind I hear Paw Paw's words, *The show must go on*, so I breathe to bring the oxygen back into my bloodstream for the baby, to stop the panic attack. I breathe.

Mum and I sit crouched against a wall at the funeral parlour. Paw Paw is in the open coffin in front of us. We have cried all we can cry today. I flew in on the soonest flight and haven't had dry eyes since touching down.

Aunty Zora sings a song from her musical theatre days, 'You Don't Bring Me Flowers', and dances around the coffin, the trill of her voice filling the empty hall. Mum and I giggle, breaking the tension for a moment; there will be plenty of time for being serious.

It's hard to know what to do now our matriarch is gone. Paw Paw was mother to us all.

The day of the funeral comes, and as Paw Paw is lowered into her grave, shared with Granddad, we play Vivaldi. I have to stop from flinging myself into the hole with her, just like I had to at Granddad's service ten years ago.

There is no one to brush Mum's 'condition' under the carpet anymore, and before my eyes she deteriorates rapidly at the thought she will now be alone.

'John,' I say over the phone to him at home in Melbourne, where he stayed to look after Royston, 'I can't leave my mum here.'

'Ms Bryce, we are doctors. If you open the door we can help you. We are not going to hurt you.'

Mum, who lives with us in Prahran now, has barricaded herself in her room.

'She just wants my money,' Mum screams at the CATT team. 'She wants me locked up so she can take my money.'

I'm pressed against the wall between large pieces of antique furniture from Bicton, so heavily pregnant now that I can barely get past Mum's things in the hallway. We brought truck loads over from Western Australia when she moved into a small cottage, identical to ours, next door. The supposedly God-fearing landlord, who is well known in the community, demanded six months' rent in advance, and I was so desperate that I agreed.

'Ms Bryce. Mela. We have assessed you as a threat to your own safety. You can come with us voluntarily, or we will use force.' A medic puts on white latex gloves and prepares a syringe.

'Mum,' I say, 'please come out.'

'Shut up. Go away. Leave me alone.'

The CATT team are about to force the door when it opens. Mum steps out, shaky and frightened. Then she spits, 'It's her! She just wants to see the back of me.'

I hold my belly, and the team squeeze past me with Mum, two leading the way, two walking behind. There are police on the footpath too, as not everyone could fit inside with Mum's hoard of belongings.

I ride in the front of the ambulance, listening to my mum scream about me and at me. I breathe deeply and rub my round belly reassuringly. 'It's okay. It's going to be okay.'

Lately the episodes have been overwhelming, and I've got no idea how Paw Paw and Granddad managed it for so many decades, how on earth they coped. I couldn't go on, so I approached a family friend, Professor Allan Fels. He's from Western Australia too, and there's always a Perth connection, but this one is surprisingly close – he took John's mum to a debutante ball, and I've interviewed him on TV a few times.

After I called him about my mother, the professor met up with me at Fawkner Park during one of my darkest hours. We sat on a bench, the Alfred hospital looming behind us. The professor is on the board of directors there, and his daughter's battle with mental illness is publicly known.

'I don't think I can do it,' I said.

The professor took my hand. 'Don't worry, Mimi. I will help you.'

With his support it came to pass, and now Mum is being led from the ambulance into the Alfred psychiatric unit. I feel sick to be doing this to her, but I just couldn't have my children growing up the way I did. This time it would be me and John wrestling with Mum in the night, dragging her home from shouting at neighbours, tending her wounds when it got too much, or finding her dead.

Stepping into Paw Paw and Granddad's shoes is incomprehensible – I can't do it. I promised them I would always look after Mum and I meant it, but I didn't mean hiding her from the world and pretending there's nothing wrong. I have to look after her my way.

Days turn into six weeks; solitary isolation, 'for her own safety', evolves into art therapy classes on the main ward. I visit Mum every day. Usually she displays some distrust when she sees me, but sometimes she's pleased, which gives me hope. Sometimes, though, she refuses to see me at all.

When Mum turns a corner, she asks that I bring in the photo essay I made for her in the days before the CATT team arrived to take her away. It was my last-ditch attempt to persuade her to see a psychiatrist. On each page there were photos of Mum with me, Royston and John. Under each picture I wrote how much we love her, and that she can have a happy life with us, along with a meaningful role in our family, and she doesn't have to hear 'the voices' anymore. I was letting her know she could be well, but she ripped it up and screamed at me.

Now she wants me to bring it in to show her doctors. I have to tape the pages back together, but her willingness to read it and the fact she mentioned it to them are great signs.

Then Mum is ready to come home. She has been diagnosed with chronic and acute schizophrenia and treated accordingly. 'Mela has responded well to the medication. Not all patients maintain their dosage. How will you handle that?'

'She never ever lies,' I said. 'So if she's promised to take her medication, she will.'

By the expressions on the doctors' faces, I don't think they've ever heard such conviction and optimism about maintaining dosages at home. But I know I can rely on Mum to take the pills. She will do it because now she's able to enjoy a day without the voices, and she appreciates what she has to lose if she slips up with her tablets.

I finally read the torrent of historical personal and legal letters sent back and forth between Mum's camp and Dad's. Doctors' assessments. Character references and assassinations. Pages and pages of desperation – over me. Folders of medical reports and lawyer fees reopen vast wounds – in me. I keep most of them; I might need them some day. But there is one file I can never bear to share.

Because of all the blame my grandparents dished out on my dad for the accident, it has taken me decades to shed the resentment I harbour towards him over it – maybe I still haven't finished. Then someone asks me, 'Are you sure the brakes failed?' And I realise something: Mum might have put the car in the path of that truck deliberately. The 'voices' were at their most persuasive back then.

I take a copper wastepaper bin, which used to belong at Bicton, into my Melbourne garden. It's strangely satisfying to strike a match and watch as the forty-year-old medical and legal files containing my mother's confessions of deeply disturbing thoughts wrestle with the heat, twist and contort, curl, burn, blacken and succumb. The glow of the flames flickers across my face as John and the children sleep. Mum's living-room light is on, and classical music drifts over to me from her radio.

Someone close said to me once, 'You're doing the right thing, Mimi, looking after your mother,' and I thought, *But isn't it the only thing?*

''Mimmmiiii Kwaaaaaaa!' my tall friend Foxy waves me over to a check-in counter. I'm a mother of two now. My own mum has made steady improvements and John has given me a leave pass for a girls' getaway in Hong Kong. On board, we find we're seated apart, so I reshuffle strangers' seats. Two crew members stop and stare as I make a health announcement to the entire cabin in my best television voice. 'My friend is highly allergic to peanuts.' Foxy turns bright scarlet and hides under an aeroplane blanket.

When we arrive, I spot a walking stick furiously waving in the air. A bejewelled hand is on the end of it. It points to me and a male flight attendant pushes a wheelchair hastily over.

'Aunteeeee!' I throw my arms around her neck and beam at my friends. I couldn't be more proud to have these two worlds collide at last.

'Welcome to Hong Kong.' Aunty pulls herself to her feet and shoos the steward playfully away. 'Let's have some fun!'

We enjoy dumplings, dinner and drinks each day. 'More people. More dishes.'

Aunty leaves nothing to waste. 'Waiter please wrap up this duck carcass. I take away for my cook to make broth.' She smiles and lowers her spectacles to look at a menu. 'So much food to eat. Four day, you here not long enough. Not long enough for all this food.'

'*Jiao ao zhi yuan*,' she says when I'm alone with her. 'You make Aunty proud. You have nice friends and you have good husband. A beautiful family. Good career. You are veeeeery lucky. You can still become a diplomat, you know. Never too late. Never too late.'

At our hotel, Aunty lays out a silk suit bag on a bed in our room for three, and I undo the zip. My girlfriends and I gasp. 'Ohhh, wow!'

I run my hands over a blanket of long soft fur. It's stunning.

'It's a wolf.' Aunty says matter of factly. 'I wore it in Europe. But Asia? Too hot. Much too hot. I give your cousin Jojo my mink. You remember I selected the live mink individually at the farm.' The gift is a rite of passage. Aunty is of another time.

To her great satisfaction I admire myself in the dresser mirror like a 1950s movie star, hugging the fur collar close to my face, pouting. It's entirely glamorous, but at the same time, of course, entirely wrong by today's standards and I will never be able to wear it.

'Perfect for Melbourne weather.' Aunty adjusts the fur to sit squarely on my shoulders. 'You put red lipstick and you look just like Joan Crawford.' She opens one side of the coat revealing a striped silk lining and a monogrammed pocket which reads TWC KWA then, taking an Elizabeth Arden lipstick from her black quilted Chanel handbag with gold chain strap, she slips it into the wolf's pocket.

On the flight home to Melbourne, a Chinese woman sits next to me and I find out she's about to become an internet bride. She is keen on a visa to live in Australia, but not so keen on marrying.

'I need a housekeeper if you would like to stay with me,' I offer.

So, I 'bring home a stray', as my friends put it. We are out of earshot of my new housekeeper as we wait for our luggage and Foxy and George peel with laughter. 'Mimi Kwa, you cannot get on an aeroplane without recruiting staff! You're just like Aunty.' Or like my dad. I smile — either way it's a very Kwa thing to do.

As John and the children run up the driveway to greet me, a petite Chinese woman follows a few steps behind. Given we've had Columbian, South Korean and Taiwanese students, as well as German, Swiss and Canadian au pairs living with us over the years, John isn't the least bit surprised. He understands you can take the girl out of Mandarin Gardens, but you can't take Mandarin Gardens out of the girl.

CARAVAN AND SAINT

You really can't take Mandarin Gardens out of the man. Relics of the Kwa compound still litter Dad's house. His panorama of the hostel is more yellow than last time I visited, faded and peeling, hanging by twisted, rusted wire on rusted nails embedded in the doorframe.

'I'm okay,' Dad tells me. 'They can't keep me down. I lost everything. Now I build myself up again. I am rich again. Engineers make a lot of money. Look, look, look, and I have all the engineers working for me.'

A Chinese engineering student peers over a stack of folders on an overcrowded desk.

'You look good, Dad,' I say with a smile.

'I do. I do. Yes, I do, don't I? Do you know what is my secret to youth? Do you know?'

I narrow my eyes. He's always looked younger than his age, and lately – after two eye lifts to cut away saggy lids – it's as though he's shaved off another decade. He exercises and can still make one beer last a week, sometimes two.

'Ah, I've got it! It's your hair, Dad. You've dyed your hair.'

He does a little dance, much like Rumpelstiltskin might when the miller's daughter fails to guess his name. 'You are wrong. You do not know my secret. Yes, it's a different colour. No grey. No grey. But is it dyed? Is it dyed? No. No, it is not. Ahhhahaha.'

I look closer and see sooty specks on his tartan shirt. 'Dad, what is that?'

He does his little dance again. 'Well, you see, I happened to be given some boxes of boot polish.'

'Dad! You'll poison yourself. You can't put boot polish in your hair.'

He tells me that of course he can. He has dozens of cans of black boot polish in his laundry – he needs to get through them. 'I use the surgical gloves to put it in every morning. Same as hair dye. Looks good, isn't it? And it's free. Good idea. Good idea. Your father is veeeery clever man, you know. Very clever.' I note the white glove tied to his belt with different denomination coins in the fingers and thumb and am reminded of the futility of arguing.

Dad is still finding inventive ways to use his apparently never-ending supply of surgical gloves and I had almost forgotten that fact by the time he brings my teenage brothers to Melbourne for a visit. We are shopping on Acland Street, St Kilda, me a few paces in front, when I see a friend from work. 'Seamus, hi.' Dad and the boys stop behind me.

Seamus hesitates. 'How are you?' he says, his eyes flitting to the side. What is he looking at? It's disconcerting. Seamus seems quite distracted.

'Oh,' I say realising it's me being rude – I should introduce my family. 'Seamus this is my ...' I turn around to see my brothers cringing and Dad holding up a surgical glove, dropping coins into each finger. Twenty cents – pointer, fifty cents – thumb, dollar – ring. Two dollar – pinky.

'What?' Dad stares at us, staring at him, as if we are idiots. 'What? It's a good idea. Look, I can arrange all my coins. It's very handy. Only I can think of this. I am very clever you know. Veeeeerry clever.' He knots the latex glove to his waist, stretching it around his belt, then tugging on it to make sure it's secure. Then, Dad walks off, as if there is nothing odd at all about the glove bouncing up and down against his hip. 'It's my new wallet. See. I'm very clever you know,' he says to no one in particular. 'The coins fits like a glove. Ahahahahaha. See. See I'm funny too. A glove. Get it.'

Dad's first wife was ill, and his second wife was angry. So just like his father, Ying Kam, Francis goes for a third.

I'm on the phone to Dad for one of our marathon conversations that usually go nowhere, when he breaks the news.

Francis met Karen when she applied for accommodation at his place. He already had Madonna and Michelle living in Adrian and Jerome's old room, and Madonna introduced Karen to Francis. Madonna is the daughter of the late Ng Yuk's former maid, and Madonna and Karen have student visas to study religion. Karen needed somewhere to stay, so Francis offered her a rusted-out Wombled old caravan for only a hundred dollars per week.

Francis parked Karen's accommodation on the median strip at the front of his property, causing another neighbourhood conniption in gentrified Floreat – he hoped it might lead to another front page. He connected three extension cords to one another and ran them through the laundry window into the house to a power point, with the other end connecting to a power board in the caravan, so Karen could plug in her microwave, toaster and kettle. The cord swung over the public footpath between caravan and fence, looping past Dad's three-storey recycled metal 'Christmas tree' pyramid that stays up all year round in the front yard.

Despite the visual atrocities Dad brings to the neighbourhood, Karen's innocent, caring and friendly demeanour has endeared her to most of the community. She brings home-cooked noodles to the elderly and walks their dogs. The white-collared street has grown fond of her.

Francis gives me a week's notice of the wedding, knowing I can't attend as my fourth child is coincidentally due the very same day.

'Dad, you knew I wouldn't be able to come.'

Flashback: finding photos of Dad and Angela's wedding on the kitchen table. Why would I think he'd behave differently this time?

As well as a migration agent, engineer, arbitrator and serial litigant, Dad is a marriage celebrant – a service he also offered during our Mandarin Gardens era – and laments he cannot conduct his own wedding. Karen's farmer father flies in from Malaysia and wears a flannelette shirt and gumboots to the ceremony as he has no other outfit and has never had reason to travel outside his village before. My in-laws, Len and Kathleen, are invited but decline because of the back-cracking incident. John's brother, Steve, attends, and my brothers – Dad's sons – are there too, although Dad seats them at a 'visitors' table at the very back.

Adrian and Jerome call me after the event. 'Mimi, he had complete strangers on the bridal table, and on all the tables in front of us.'

Karen isn't much older than me, and I cannot imagine why a woman my age would want to marry Dad, but I write to say thank you for looking after my father because, quite honestly, it saves me from having to do it – which, incidentally, I would if I had to. If Kwa called to Kwa, I would heed.

Karen is a saint. I tell her in a letter how grateful I am. Dad intercepts her mail so she never knows I wrote, and I accept that she has made her choice.

COCONUTS AND HUBCAPS

Since Theresa's move to the Philippines, Francis is frequently in Manila on 'very important business'. His focus, like mine, has shifted from Hong Kong.

As he checks in three plastic garbage bags at the luggage counter, the attendant expresses concern over their durability. This invites Francis's slow explanation — as if she is stupid — that the bags are 'layered three inside one another' and are 'the most expensive tough bin bags available outside hazardous chemical disposal bags'. The airline employee calls over her supervisor.

'Look,' Francis says when they continue to question the bags' suitability, 'I am an engineer and a lawyer and I'm telling you, these are as strong as an ordinary suitcase.' He explains that by reinforcing the bags with packing tape and string, they may be even more impervious to opening than, say, a 'faulty zip or buckle on a factory-made case'. He reaches behind him to check in one more thing: a bulging, battered and broken suit 'case — in point'. 'See,' he says, 'this suitcase is faulty, and yet I have made it strong, just like the plastic bags.' The zip is broken, and the case is held together with wire threaded and wound at strategic intervals. 'I am an engineer and a lawyer.'

* * *

Francis arrives in Manila raring to go with his latest 'important business' idea. He's also looking forward to the pampering his sister offers when he comes to stay: a driver at his beck and call, not to mention the four- and five-course daily meals by Brigit.

'She is a chef,' Theresa remarked proudly, the last time Francis visited. 'She is better than that. Such a good cook.'

Brigit blushed at the praise. 'Awww, ma'aaaam,' she said modestly.

'It's alright,' Francis said. 'Karen can cook better.' He burst out laughing. 'Only joking, only joking.'

Theresa's latest driver, Viner, is on time to pick up Francis from the airport. He drives him straight to his favourite shopping haunt, Greenhills, so he can browse the mall before seeing his sister. Francis is constantly on the lookout for new business opportunities, and there may be a product or invention he can bring back to Australia.

Last time he was in Manila, he observed that Filipinos consume high numbers of coconuts and decided he would export coconut husks to Australia for use in roadworks that contain soil on median strips and beside freeways. The high moisture absorbency and long fibres of coconut husks make them useful for all sorts of applications, such as netting to prevent erosion. *Perfect*, thought Francis. *One of the biggest coconut producers in the Philippines throws away nine billion husks a year.* But when he teed up a meeting to explain to that producer he could help turn their waste into profit, unfortunately none of the organisations in charge of Australian road construction were as excited about the idea as he was. He lamented being ahead of his time, then immediately moved on to the next big thing.

Viner unloads the three black garbage bags from the boot of Theresa's Mercedes-Benz. In the back seat, the suitcase is on a blanket that protects the leather upholstery from the wire that has poked through the airline's attempt to tape it down.

Francis gestures to the case. 'Leave it, leave it there for now. We will take it with us on an adventure tomorrow.'

After a sumptuous meal cooked by Brigit, Francis partakes in customary banter with Theresa, who is familiar with his eccentricities, even grubby garbage bags full of clothes and travel items. She has patiently watched over Francis like a guardian angel since he was born, and her love is unwavering.

In the morning, Theresa needs Viner to take her to the gym, after which Francis will commandeer the driver for his own errand.

'Bijit, Bijit, Bijit.' Francis corners the maid in the tiny kitchen. 'Give me your brother's phone number and work address. I can't seem to find it.' He licks his index finger – the crooked one irreparably damaged from when the thief threw the gold phone at him – and flips through a pocket-sized black address book he reserves for Philippines contacts. 'Ah. No, I got it. Here it is. Is he still at this place?'

Brigit nods. 'Yes, Mr Kwa. But he did tell you last time that he is really very busy in the mechanic workshop and he does not think he can make the time for your business plans.'

Francis growls, 'You don't understand. I will make him very rich. Very rich. I will go to see him today.'

Viner and Francis have been on the road for almost two hours when they finally arrive at Success Servicing and Auto.

Brigit's brother Marco wipes his oily palm on a rag before shaking Francis's hand. They're standing out front of a village workshop where Marco repairs motorbikes and cars. He does well, and business is stable.

Over the past forty years, Brigit has been helping her family to be comfortable with the money she's earned from Theresa, and donations from Miss Kwa made building the village church possible. Brigit's mother and younger sister run a small shop, also thanks to Theresa's generosity, and Marco has an obligation to Francis because he is Theresa's brother.

Theresa's car is surrounded by local children clamouring for a glimpse inside – a Mercedes-Benz is a rare sight. Viner shoos the kids away before hauling the battered suitcase from the back seat over to Francis and Marco.

'Look. Look. Look at this business proposition I have brought for you.' Francis beams.

The suitcase makes a dull thud as it hits the dirt, then the wire holding it together gives way. The case falls open and a dozen or so silvery circles of assorted sizes spill out everywhere. Hubcaps – like rolling, spinning, toppling, seesawing giant coins. Children gather round, fascinated by the rich man in the fancy car who has brought an old broken suitcase full of dirty used hubcaps.

'Hubcaps,' Marco says, deadpan.

'Yes, yes, yes,' Francis says excitedly. 'I will import used hubcaps from Australia.' He claps, unable to contain his glee. 'No one wants old hubcaps in Australia. You can sell them to your people here, and we will both make money. It's a good idea. I will make you rich.'

Disappointingly, after half an hour Francis is unable to convince Marco of the benefits of his hubcap scheme. Before agreeing to go, he makes one last-ditch attempt. 'Viner agrees with me – don't you, Viner?'

Viner is uncomfortable but tries to flatter his boss's brother. 'Mr Kwa, you are very clever.'

'See. See. Viner knows I'm right. This is a good opportunity for you, Marco.'

Marco and Viner revert to Tagalog between them, and after a few exchanges Marco says to Francis, 'I am very honoured you have come so far to visit me and to bring this opportunity, but I am sorry it is not something I can do. I have no time, and

I do not think the Philippines people can be willing to buy old hubcaps from Australia.'

Francis insists on leaving the pile of hubcaps behind. 'You let me know how you go with them, and I will bring many more next time.' As Viner opens the car door, Francis calls over his shoulder, 'I will make you rich.'

Francis is pleased with himself; the meeting went well.

Children chase the Mercedes in a trail of dust, while Marco absent-mindedly wipes his hands, shaking his head at the pile of scrap metal. A small child rolls a hubcap around in the dirt for play, before other children join in the game.

Time spent driving to various meetings with Viner gives Francis more ideas.

At the Greenhills mall, shopkeepers and stallholders are amused by this frequent browser who seldom spends any money. Francis jokes and laughs with staff, bartering for discounts on already cheap items. His manner is so charming, and the disposition of many Filipinos so accommodating, Francis frequently walks away with free things.

'Look, Viner. Look, they love me. Look, they give me this bracelet.' He holds up plastic beads threaded with elastic, a children's bracelet useful for no one he knows. 'And they changed my watch battery for nothing. You know, Viner, I think we are good team.' Francis has been sitting on an idea involving the driver for a while. 'Viner' – he pats the man's shoulder – 'how would you like to come live in Australia?

I visit Aunty in Manila on my own, relishing the opportunity to have quality Aunty time, a virtual impossibility since starting a family.

She's in her study preparing her will, yet again. Another day, another will, my cousin David and I often joke. Aunty is obsessed with leaving everyone she knows just the right thing and just the right amount, tweaking this fine equation over and over. She uses my last day with her to refine her latest edition, so I can add it to the pile of wills in my safe back in Melbourne. As she works, I stare out through her lounge-room window, which looks over a courtyard ten storeys below.

'Don't read it now, Mimi. Open it on the plane and take it home and lock in your safe.' Aunty and I warmly embrace, and she pinches my cheek. 'Still cute,' she laughs, and I go.

As I settle in for my flight, I prioritise ordering champagne before turning my mind to Aunty's latest will. I slide the document out of its carefully sealed envelope. Aunty has waxed and stamped the flap at the back with her chop.

Francis is waiting at Perth airport. 'You drive.' He hands Viner the keys and sits in the back seat.

'I can't believe Francis has convinced Viner to move to Perth. He didn't even call to tell me!' Aunty is clearly upset. 'Viner resigned, saying he was flying to Perth to find work, and I had to call Francis to find out what is going on. Mimi! Why has he done this? What should I do?'

I haven't heard Aunty this distressed since a Viennese baroness died, leaving Theresa part of her estate. Lawyers called in the middle of the night, instructing her to go to the castle immediately or the family would swallow up the items left to her.

'Should I go?' she asked when she called me at 1 am.

'I think by the time you get there it might all be over, Aunty. What did she leave you?'

'Oh, some painting and statue and a mirror or something.'

I rolled over a little more in bed, trying not to wake John. 'Just get the lawyers to seize the things on your behalf, and they can sell them for you and send the proceeds.'

Often my advice works out for Aunty, so in the case of my father's 'theft of Viner' – as she puts it – I may be able to help.

I call Dad to tell him how cross I am about what he has done. I also plead with Viner to go back, but they both ignore me.

Eventually, after Viner endures the searing Australian summer in a tin shed, he writes to Theresa apologising and asking for his old job back. But by the time he returns to Manila without a penny to his name, Aunty has replaced him and has decided to rewrite her will. She writes her final edition then applies her signature and Chinese chop for safe measure.

Eighteen per cent to each of her siblings, and nineteen to Brigit – just one per cent more this time, to make her point. *Subtle*, Theresa congratulates herself, unaware this may be more damaging to House of Kwa than she could imagine.

Brigit has been dedicated and loyal, sacrificing her opportunity to have a husband and children. She rises before sunrise so her parents and siblings may prosper from the money she earns. What she and Theresa share after all these decades can only be described as companionship. Theresa is well cared for by a woman she trusts, in an unequal yet amicable and respectful transaction. And a mighty thorn in the Kwa dragon claw.

TEXTS AND TEARS

Aunty Theresa is in hospital in Manila. 'Routine tests,' Dad says. 'She will be fine.' He first appears unconcerned about her sudden slip in health, then he becomes impossible to get hold of. I keep ringing, and he keeps not answering – it's infuriating. I call him again but no answer. I feel the weight of centuries, I feel it coming. Aunty is not long for this world.

I text him: *Hi Dad, Do you have hospital or Brigit's mobile? She's not picking up at home.*

Dad texts, *Under control. Watching my favourite one hour movie MacGyver.*

We text back and forth, as usual getting nowhere. He says things like 'old man knows best', 'you are young and stupid' and 'the real Boss has spoken'. He's bamboozling me, and it works.

Dad's last message for the day, *Three blind monkey*, refers to me, Adrian and Jerome.

Dad arrives in Manila. I text him again.

Hi Dad, I would just like to speak to Aunty. I was devastated you didn't take me to hk to see or say goodbye to Aunty Mary before she died. I would like it very much if you could help me and not obstruct me getting in touch with Aunty Theresa now.

Dad: *Miss Kwa is not allowed to talk to anyone. Re Mary Kwa. Please get your fact straight. If I had taken you there what could you have done anyway? I do not expect a medical problem with Miss Kwa. Water on duck's back.*

Dad gets the expression wrong as well as Aunty's diagnosis, and after this he doesn't call or answer calls, text or answer texts.

So I call my cousin David, wishing I had done so sooner. 'David, what's going on? Have you spoken to Brigit?'

'No, she doesn't answer. I got through to the hospital but got cut off, and your father doesn't return my calls. He keeps sending me messages that Aunty is completely fine.'

David shares Brigit's number with me, and she picks up first time.

'Hello, Meeee-meeee.' It's wonderful to hear her voice. 'I asked your father to get you to call me, Mimi.'

'You did?'

'Yes, your aunty, so, so sick, you must come. I don't know what to do, Mimi. It is the cancer, Mimi. It is the cancer.'

All I can hear is sobbing over the phone now. I'm around the side of the house, away from the kids, and I sit down on the concrete and cry with her. 'I am coming, Brigit. I will be there soon.'

The summer day is a scorcher, but I stay outside. I dial David again and pace up and down the driveway shared with our neighbours. Their autistic son sways by their washing line, watching me with interest. The other neighbour's dogs bark through the fence at me, and I try to shush them.

'I'm on the next plane already,' David says. 'I board in an hour.'

I am so relieved he'll be there with Aunty, and I won't be far behind. It will give Aunty such comfort having him there, her closest nephew.

It seems there's nothing for me to do but wait until my flight departs in the morning. But in the middle of the bedtime drill, my phone pings with a text.

Dad: *This is very expensive message to send you from Philippine. Your Aunty is pass away.*

Mason, who is seven, thinks I have fallen over and hurt myself. 'Are you okay, Mummy?'

I feel numb. My flight is at 7 am and already I'm too late for Aunty. The dragon plagues my nightmares.

Before the sun rises, I kiss the kids goodbye as they sleep. John wakes to ask if I'm sure he can't take me to the airport; my mum could mind the kids. 'No. I love you.' I need to be alone in my grief.

The only thing that buoys me up is knowing David must have made it in time. His flight only took two hours, so he will have been by Aunty's side – holding her hand, whispering funny memories, comforting her, telling her, 'It's going be alright.'

There's been a light shower overnight, in the middle of summer. I look out the taxi window at a rainbow. It's Aunty.

In the Qantas lounge, someone kind ushers me to a private partitioned room, and they also shuffle the seating arrangement on the plane to make sure I'm as far from other passengers as possible so my grief can be quarantined.

I emerge from the gate at Manila airport, but there's no whiteboard sign with my name written on it. I scour the drivers' faces, but none are looking for me. Outside, in the stinking hot blanket of humidity, I call Dad. No answer, so I text.

After I've waited over an hour, not sure whether to smoke, drink or both, a new driver of Aunty's walks towards me. He is teary and introduces himself as Jay. We shake hands and walk to the car in silence, his shoulders slumped in exhaustion, presumably from ferrying everyone around. He opens the passenger side door.

'Get in, get in,' says Dad.

'Dad, what happened? Aunty has died. Tell me about last night. What happened? Did she speak to you and David? Was she in pain? What happened? How did she die?'

'I wasn't with her. I was at Greenhills. It's the shopping mall. I was getting my watch fixed.'

'You were *what*?'

'I had to get my watch fixed.'

'Dad.' I am in utter disbelief. 'Okay, so David was with her, then. Please tell me she had David with her. '

'No. David didn't make it in time.'

I look in the rear-view mirror at Jay. He is crying and shaking.

We're on our way to the chapel. Manila traffic, excruciating at the best of times, seems to slow even more during this personal crisis. How anyone gets anything done here is beyond me. We pass shantytowns where babies are being bathed in ice-cream tubs on the side of the road. I continue to stare out the window while Dad spends the hour-long ride trying to butter me up by telling me Aunty Theresa has left me everything. I should have twigged by now that he is up to something, but I'm too distraught that Aunty died without family around her.

At the Roman Catholic 'chapel of rest', I go straight to the mourning room where Aunty must lie in an open casket – in state – for five days while friends and family keep up a twenty-four hour vigil by her side. The room is filled with more than a dozen people I don't know. Then I see Brigit. Embracing, we sob inconsolably for what seems like years but in reality is only a minute. I stand by the elaborate coffin, almost too scared to look in.

People sidle up to me and offer, 'Isn't she beautiful?' and 'Doesn't she look peaceful?' And I feel like retorting, 'No. She looks dead and nothing like herself at all. I would like to grieve alone.' Then I want to shout, 'She wasn't your aunty. She was mine. I loved her more than you did. I don't want to share her with you. Go away.' Instead, I smile and nod politely. The strangers are staying whether Aunty and I want them there or not.

She really doesn't look at all like herself – she would never do her hair and make-up like that. What would BOAC say about this Imelda Marcos look? She does seem younger, I'll admit that, but that dress and those white stockings ... and why are her shoes off? I stare at her feet, and a stranger interrupts my inner voice to jovially tell me, 'She must not wear shoes in the casket because her spirit may need to wear the shoes so we can hear it walk around in the night.'

Oh, of course. That makes sense. 'Thank you.' I smile and nod. Why is everyone so goddamned happy?

I catch sight of David, and for a moment we stare at each other, needing no words; she meant just as much to both of us.

As he fills me in on Aunty's last hours, how he left Sam in Hong Kong tied up with work and rushed here on the first flight only to wait more than an hour to be collected from the airport, I have another slow-motion, surreal moment of disbelief. Like me, David was left waiting at the arrivals terminal for Jay the driver, only at that stage Aunty was still alive. 'Uncle Francis was getting his watch fixed at Greenhills, and he insisted Jay wait for him.'

The pain of not being there with Aunty in her last hours rips through me, repeatedly. I'm flooded with memories of me, a little girl, following Aunty along the beach, copying her dainty swagger, both of us in bikinis, Aunty attracting admiring looks wherever she went, the club, the club sandwiches, the shop and the hotel. The woman who showed me the world through her eyes and who never stopped having dreams for her niece.

* * *

Dad and I take food from the wake back to Aunty's condo, where Dad has been staying for days. In the lift, a well-meaning stranger gives some cheery advice. 'It's bad luck to bring food home from the open-casket room. A pit stop en route is absolutely necessary to shake off any spirits you may have picked up from the coffin. I hope your driver told you.' Too late now. In Aunty's bathroom I roll my eyes at myself in the mirror. How will I get through this? I shower to get rid of the bad luck and spirits, then go straight to sleep.

Brigit is the most dedicated of us all, staying with Aunty's body around the clock, twenty-four seven, for five days. Members of Brigit's family, here from her village to lend support, take over from her whenever she comes home briefly to wash and change into fresh clothes. No one is allowed to brush their hair in the room with Aunty – if they do, they will die – so obviously Brigit must come home to brush her hair too. I don't tell her I brought food back without making a pit stop; that might well and truly tip her over the edge, she's so fragile. I'm bound to break another rule and end up dead or plagued with coffin spirits for eternity.

Dad's wife, Karen, will arrive tomorrow. They're checking in to a hotel, at my insistence, which is a huge relief. I want the whole funeral, and Aunty, to myself – to grieve alone in her house, surrounded by everything that reminds me of her.

Dad is hung up on that 'one per cent more' for Brigit in Aunty's will.

The dragon circles, trouble brews, and I pace with anxiety. Aunty was trying to send a message from the grave to her siblings about Brigit. The one per cent more is a sign of Aunty's love – a cryptic Kwa show of respect – but to Francis it's a ticking time bomb. If Theresa was using her Last Will and Testament to give Brigit the last word, it is not working out how Aunty planned.

The executors swoop in: two trusted friends appointed by Theresa to manage her Philippines estate. Letty is the dean of a prestigious ladies' college, while Tessie heads a corporation employing tens of thousands of staff. They are highly respected, super-accomplished women, undoubtedly Aunty's link to the diocese archbishop who blessed her before she died. Yet however well connected these executors are, they are not well versed in House of Kwa.

Aunty was neurotic about her things ending up in the right hands. Not only did she rewrite her will repeatedly, she has three of them: one for her Hong Kong estate, one for her estate in the Philippines, and one for an apartment in Perth. Three wills like her father's three wives. I am her executor in Australia, and David is her trusted overseer in Hong Kong. She changed her wills so frequently in the two decades before she died, she would have been an estate lawyer's dream but for the free legal advice available within the family. David and his brother Steven, both lawyers, would roll their eyes as they opened each new revision – another of dear Aunty's wills to proof. After my cousins were done, she would send me copies to put in my safe.

Brigit takes me through the condo, room by room, outlining Aunty's wishes for various items. The painting above her bed is to go to a particular nun in Italy, a small Ming Dynasty urn is for a professor in Thailand, a doctor in Hong Kong was promised the antique jade lion, and so on. Aunty wanted David to have her monogrammed silver cutlery, and promised that Brigit could keep the sewing machine and Jay the stereo.

Letty and Tessie agree that Theresa had indeed told them Brigit would know which decorative items should go to whom. But the will refers to a list of wishes no one can find: photographs of furniture, ornaments and jewellery with names of intended recipients written on the back. I search all the rooms and then revisit them, opening cupboards and draws, fossicking through the same things again and again like a madwoman.

I find photo albums, old negatives and newspaper clippings: marvellous windows to Aunty's life, and to Dad's, Mary's and Clara's. Theresa looks so glamorous in these black-and-white shots, and I hadn't known about the magazine and newspaper articles in which she features. There's even a six-page spread on Hong Kong with Theresa as the travel guide. And it's in the May 1965 British *Woman's Weekly*, the Western world's most widely read magazine at the time – with all the articles written by men.

I sip on a glass of bad wine that teetotaller Aunty had hidden in a glass case: *Break in case of emergency*. Well, Aunty, this is an emergency.

I marvel at the breadth of her career. She never walked me through her life the way I'm walking through it now.

The more awful wine I consume, the more self-indulgent this exercise becomes. I recall how Aunty would kick me under the table if I wasn't sitting straight, only needing to look at me sharply for a nanosecond to let me know I'd said too much or spoken too emotively. 'Don't smile too much – you want to stay smooth, smooth,' she would coach, rubbing my forehead with her thumb. Expression lines were a big no-no of Aunty's. She tried her very best to help me to behave in a dignified manner: kind, patient, smart and well turned out. Poor Aunty, hoping the hopes she had for us all. What disappointments we must have been.

I chuckle again.

'You can be a diplomat or a politician,' she would tell me. Only last year, she reassured me my career in journalism could still lead to something 'more respectable'. From her study in Manila, Aunty would watch me read the world news out of Melbourne. 'That lipstick really is too red,' she once called to tell me, just as I came off air from anchoring the live international bulletin that reached forty countries, including the Philippines; she added that 'this trunk call is very expensive, very expensive', but that it was certainly 'very important'. A gross lipstick misdemeanour would have cost Theresa her job at BOAC. 'How can it be you will be invited back to read the news with lipstick so bright?' I laugh out loud again at the memory. She sent me jewellery and scarves to wear on air, our secret sign as I presented to audiences across the globe, though I only ever felt I was talking to her.

It's getting late, and the wine remains terrible no matter how much I drink. The funeral is tomorrow. I need to write Aunty's eulogy.

Francis Tak Lau Kwa and Clara Wai Mui Kwa, Ng Yuk's last remaining of thirty-two brothers and sisters, are about to be reunited over their beloved sister Theresa's dead body.

SOMBREROS AND BELLHOP

EVERYONE IS ON THEIR BEST BEHAVIOUR BEFORE AUNTY IS put to rest, even Dad. The coffin-side circus continues as more random people show up – distant relatives of Brigit, friends of friends – the wake room a revolving door of well-wishers keen to honour Theresa's departure for the next life. It's the festival of Theresa with a packed audience and standing room only. The lucky eight rows of plastic chairs are all taken. Garlands and posies line the walls, while ribboned boxes of cumbersome and constrained flower arrangements adorn a number of trestle tables.

Theresa looks out from her portrait beside her coffin. She's on a yacht, wearing a white windcheater and a smile. Through her lightly tinted sunglasses her eyes are visible, crinkled in the corners. In this moment she is free.

Some visitors have been paying their respects by camping out with the vigil stalwarts as per local custom, inhabiting an annex off the main room with its bleak brown wallpaper. Maroon vinyl cushions stick to the bare thighs of visitors in shorts. Brigit and her family have set up beds here too, their sleeping-bags and pillows strewn about for round-the-clock shifts.

Dad arrives with Karen. In the lead-up to the funeral, he came to Aunty's condo a couple of times in order to lord it over me. Now he sidles up to a man and, for the benefit of the whole room, tells him, 'It's all mine.' And ignoring my glare, Dad moves down the line to ensure no one misses out on his news. 'Everything, she leaves everything to me.'

I've had numerous meetings with funeral directors and Aunty's local executors, and I've pointed repeatedly to the clause in Aunty's will saying that she wants 'no service' and 'no fanfare' at all. 'No, nooooo,' the Filipinas say. 'Mimi, you muuuust give her a big send-off. She would loooove that. With music and a parade and a proper ceremony. Mimi, you cannot doooo that to your aunty. To ignore her like that and not do the proper send-off. Oh, Mimi, it is so wrong.'

In the end I agree to follow local custom and, in doing so, watch the bills stack up – an invoice for everything from entertainment and audiovisual equipment, to the urn for Aunty's ashes, not to mention commemorative programs and funeral DVDs for the hundreds of people who, I am assured, will demand a copy. The Filipina executors have made me the 'honorary decision-maker', so I can consent to all the choices they have already made. They are persuasive, and I am worn down. 'Mimiiii, we must have more flowers. More, more – of course we must.' And, 'Oooooooh, this urn is sooooo much nicer, don't you think?'

David provides me some solace in this upside-down place, and now Sam has arrived in Manila too, these days a cherished son-in-law to Clara after years of gentle petitioning succeeded in turning her homophobia around. Between sneaking off with me for cigarettes and emptying his hipflask into my orange juice, my cousin counsels me to stay calm and on track – which is good advice, given funeral proceedings are about to commence. I look over at David to see him watching his mum prattle on in a similar way to a stranger, and I remind myself he has his own Kwa to deal with.

Clara arrived from London last night after a long flight. She and her son walking arm in arm was a sight to behold; David is tall and handsome, six foot six, like his brother and father, and Clara is refined, beautiful and diminutive beside him. Thin yet strong, she's all in black with a single thick gold chain around her neck, her hair styled in a chic pixie cut straight from the '60s. She's a gorgeous, frail and elegant eighty-one-year-old beauty, and anyone uninitiated with Kwa would find it impossible to imagine what a both harsh and blessed life she has lived. Clara gestures to Sam, who is walking behind them, and he steps in to take her other arm. I think about how handsome Clara and Dad look, and how lost without Theresa they must feel.

A priest stands in front of Aunty's coffin, reciting a few words about God and about this lady he has never met.

I'm the only person wearing colour. First of all, in my hurry I forgot to pack anything black. Second, I'm not ready to raid Aunty's wardrobe just yet. And third, Aunty is wearing bright pink, and I always follow her lead. I don't want her to feel out of place or alone. If only we could be back tossing sand with our flip-flops on the Repulse Bay beach, making our way over to the club for its famed sandwiches, while Aunty graciously acknowledges cheeky wolf-whistles from old friends, me stumbling in her shadow to keep up.

Three guitarists in oversized sombreros begin singing a happy tune I can't make out. It floats and fades. Something about a señorita – it's all in Tagalog. I mustn't look at David, in case we burst out laughing. It's as though Aunty is being serenaded on her last voyage out to sea by three lovers.

As if the scene isn't bizarre enough, Dad stands up and starts swaying, his swagger growing into all-out dancing as he moves to the rhythm as though he's in a trance. He sweeps his arms over his sister's coffin and, like a man possessed, lifts his hands to the sky. The musicians up the tempo and – in what I believe may go down in history as an unprecedented creative collaboration – Dad concocts original lyrics in English, while the three accompanists do their very best to harmonise in Tagalog.

Dad waves his arms in the air as if we should all join in, and some do. He's suddenly a rock star clapping and geeing-up the crowd.

Before I have a chance to process all of this, he is dragging Clara from her seat.

'Ooooooh, okay,' she says, nodding enthusiastically as though she's been chosen to dance with a prince at a ball, elated to have been selected out of the crowd. She claps wildly, and brother and sister waltz beside their sister's corpse against a backdrop of obligatory grief-stricken wailing from Brigit's distant relatives – and from the wife of a masseuse Aunty once employed, and her family who never met Aunty.

The elderly siblings go for a dip, and I wince and peek through my fingers, imagining two more funerals if such behaviour continues. Even for these seasoned mourners, Dad and Clara are a spectacle. They manage to stabilise after the dip and steal their own show, spinning and dipping again. I'm grateful they haven't attempted a lift, and I'm completely unsure whether to be appalled or touched by the sentimentality of the moment. Tears well in my eyes.

It's time to carry the casket to the cremation chapel. David and I exchange disbelieving looks as we stifle uncomfortable giggles over our parents' behaviour, regaining composure only once we step away from each other while everyone files out of the mourning room.

Having David here is a great comfort to me, and I wonder if we may be the only sane people at the service. He moves closer to me again, looks down at me and whispers, 'Nothing matters much. Much matters little. In the end, nothing matters at all.' It's a saying he first told me in Hong Kong over a beer and champagne cocktail, one of his favourites. 'Don't worry,' he says and nudges me. He and I have always enjoyed drinking while comparing notes on our eccentric, narcissistic, entertaining parents. But now these two are the last survivors of their unique strand of Kwa, and I wonder if this will be the last memorable story about them we will have to tell.

In a haze of aftershave and perfume, David and I wait for the funeral procession to wend its way to the chapel. We're wedged between audacious hats and suits – and even tracksuits – in the sultry Manila heat, none of the dress choices making much sense to me.

I'm thinking about how our parallel childhoods revolved around beach walks and meals with Aunty, long yum chas and warm early evenings in her study, when the pallbearers appear. As Kwas and Bryans, we occupy the whole front row; we watch the coffin lowered before us and then chapel staff step forward to prop open the casket of a woman who has already lain in state for five days – she has to put up one last appearance. I give Aunty a nod of respect, followed by a quick apologetic glance because she has had to go through all this. All she wanted was a simple service and for her ashes to be scattered in the ocean.

Over Brigit's sobs and occasional wails, I read Aunty's eulogy. I talk about Aunty's work as an air hostess, then her gift shop, tucked in near reception at Hong Kong's most famous hotel. When Aunty appeared at the grand red carpet reopening of the Mandarin Oriental, David was on her arm as her date. Barry Humphries greeted them at the door, and the hotel manager made a beeline for Aunty. 'Miss Kwa, I am so pleased you could make it.' Now in charge of the entire building, this man had been a bellhop back in the day, and when others looked down their noses at him, Theresa was always kind. He never forgot that.

As I take my seat, I can see that David is trying not to cry.

Brigit rushes forward to drape herself across the coffin. She clings to it, moaning, and my heart goes out to her. 'Miss Kwa,' she wails, 'Miss Kwa.' She collapses to the floor. Three of her relatives lift her to her seat where she continues to sob, so loudly she almost drowns out David as he reads from the *Woman's Weekly* article featuring Aunty.

Now comes another custom, unfamiliar to me. Well-rehearsed assistants standing behind the casket swiftly cover it with a white bespoke coffin-shaped cardboard box and hand out permanent markers. The pens pass from one person to the next so that each of us can write a parting message or tribute, or, in some cases, just a name. It's like signing the cast of a school friend who has broken an arm, but this time the cast is for Theresa's irreparably broken life.

The coffin is jostled about and almost topples over as Dad pushes to the front, shoving a pen in Karen's hand and ordering her to write a prayer, after which he writes, *You always said I am 'the star' in my own movie*, and draws a star.

Immediate family members — blood relatives, Dad, Aunty Clara, David and me — are directed to an annex off the main room. Dad drags Karen in with us despite my protests. 'Theresa said all the time, "Karen is family." So she is family. She comes in.'

I end up squashed next to David, then I'm taken by surprise when I realise we're all crammed into a space the size of a small elevator, with a glass window on one side. It's a viewing room, just like in a maternity ward, only, eerily, at the other end of life. Huddled together, we watch the cremation team reveal the coffin, which is covered in hurried last words. Aunty is lying on top. Staff remove her jewellery and shroud her in a white sheet. A young man holds her pearl earrings up to the glass, slides them into a velvet pouch, and places it on a tray with her watch and necklace.

A woman points to a black button on our side of the glass. We are meant to press it and send Aunty into the fire.

The furnace door opens, and the woman gestures to the button again, more vigorously this time as she grows impatient, but none of us wants to do the deed. David suggests that 'it might be most fitting for brother and sister, Francis and Clara, to press it together'. I am so relieved it's not me; I couldn't agree more. They count to three and press it, springing the conveyor belt to life, sending their sister and mother figure into the inferno.

'You won't be able to wear those earrings,' Dad instructs me a moment later, referring to Aunty's pearls. 'It's bad luck to wear what she wore dead.'

Apparently, though, it's not such bad luck to wear the dead person themselves. I am horrified to learn that Aunty's ashes are being sold off – in quarter-teaspoon portions placed in glass vials shaped like crystal pendants – for anyone to keep. When all the mourners congregate in another building for tea and biscuits, I'm stunned to see so many strangers eagerly lining up to wear Aunty around their necks. I selected the urn for her ashes when we went through the 'extras' package options, but I certainly did not approve of this.

'It is tradition, Mimi,' Tessie says. 'You, no need to pay. Non-family must pay, but you can have for free, Mimi. Isn't that wonderful?' When it comes to religion and tradition, I see an unexpected side of this executor.

Cash flies from purses held high as mourners vie to be served, reminding me of the betting ring at the horseraces.

'That's not the point,' I say. 'She wants to be scattered in the ocean. It has to be all of her, not just what's left.'

Tessie appears not to compute.

'I am so sorry. So sorry.' I push through the crowd. 'I'm sooooo sorry,' I say to the strangers who want to carry Aunty around with them. 'No, no, no.' I take a fistful of money from the attendant selling Aunty off and return it to the lady at the front of the queue. 'We cannot separate the ashes today.' I bow repeatedly, begging forgiveness from the disappointed strangers, my hands together in an attempt to appear respectful, having used this tactic successfully on a number of less critical occasions. They look at me as though I've lost my marbles, but they put their money away.

Except Dad, who proceeds to the front, asks for five necklaces and instructs the attendant to 'put it on the bill'. I am dismayed, but he just shakes his head and frowns at me, scooping the ashes into the little vials: one for him, one for Clara, one for Karen, and two spares — because, according to Dad, keeping spares of anything is a good idea.

BLOOD AND LOCK

THE DAYS AFTER THE FUNERAL ARE SPENT ON THE administration of the will and sorting through belongings. Dad visits the condo often taking whatever he fancies and putting it into his large suitcase 'hidden' on the small balcony outside Aunty's guestroom. When he's sure no one's looking, I watch Dad take items from shelves and cupboards, his expression inscrutable, his selection between priceless figurines and worthless plastic indiscriminate. I don't mind him taking things, not at all. It's his sister and his grief, and hoarding as many of Aunty's things as possible is his way of trying to fill a hole. I totally get it, but his indifference to due process makes Letty's and Tessie's jobs hard.

'Today we've received disappointing information from friends in high places,' Letty says. 'Before Theresa's death, your father Francis was already visiting with lawyers to contest the will, and he instructed the legal firms to send bills for services to us!' Both executors are incensed. 'Your aunty would not want to pay her brother's legal fees to contest her own will.' They're so exasperated that their tolerance for Francis's squirrelling away of items evaporates instantly. Tessie and Letty put the apartment and its contents into 'total lockdown' and appoint me the sole person responsible to sort through Aunty's things. 'Mimi, you are the one Aunty told us we should trust and depend on.'

Letty draws the short straw to inform Francis he can no longer visit the apartment without her prior consent.

Francis is furious. 'You are the daughter. I am the king.' His dragon blood boils. 'YOU women will NOT tell ME what to do. Karen and I are VERY disappointed in you.'

I put down the phone.

Jay parks across from Dad's hotel. 'Will you be okay, ma'am?' His eyes brim with concern.

'Thank you, Jay. Of course I will.' I have a paper bag full of things I hope might help Dad feel better, and I ask the front desk to call him. He appears alone, and I can see his scales are still up, the tendons on his throat taut with rage.

We walk down a passage into the hotel's indoor pool area.

'You are the daughter and you DO AS TOLD.' He shakes a taloned wing. 'You let me INTO the apartment NOW to take what I want or you will PAY.'

'Dad,' I say, trying to shift the subject, 'I have brought the necklace for Karen. I know Aunty would have liked Karen to have it. Could you call Karen down please, Dad? I'd like to smooth things over with her.'

'Give me that!' He seizes the pouch, pulls out the necklace, examines it and squints at me. 'Theresa said to me on her deathbed she wanted Karen to have ALL her jewellery.'

'Dad, we can only go by what Aunty's will stipulates. We can't just make it up.'

'You will DO. AS. TOLD.' He breathes fire and shouts.

I am a tiger crouched on the tiles, waiting for the flames to die down. Through tears, I offer, 'Please, Dad, just give Karen the necklace. I'm sorry for any confusion.'

'You WILL be sorry. You do NOT tell me what to do. I tell YOU what to do. You will arrange a meeting with the executors, and you will make them let me into the apartment. That is an ORDER!'

A security guard walks in to see if I'm okay. 'I'm fine,' I say. I try to breathe and calm myself. 'There are some photo albums I thought you might like to look through, Dad, to reminisce. Some albums Aunty put together are dedicated to you.'

He snorts. 'They are ALL mine anyway. I will show you.' He waves a clenched fist at me, and it would almost be comical if I didn't feel so sad that it has come to this.

I leave the hotel, dazed, my eyes red from crying. Then Jay says he has bad news: Brigit can't locate the spare keys to Aunty's apartment, and Dad is the most likely person to have them.

I arrange for an emergency locksmith to come over, and the building's security guards pin up photos of Dad in their patrol booths.

DIAMONDS AND DRUNKS

Aunty Clara has been oblivious to the commotion going on behind the scenes and is quite uninterested in the will or her dead sister's valuables. But when Francis invites her to be his ally in claiming the jewellery Theresa has left to me and my cousin Josephine, he awakens a dormant Kwa spirit in Clara. She decides she suddenly cares very much about the jewels after all.

Unaware of our parents' plan, David and I meet in the executive lounge on the thirty-sixth floor of the Shangri-La Hotel. He and his boyfriend, Sam, are staying here. David and I air-kiss before he guides me to an armchair in the corner and orders drinks. I welcome the chair's embrace after a long day with Tessie and Letty; we were visiting safety deposit boxes to collect Aunty's precious gems, which involved a lot of security checks and paperwork. When we returned to the condo, Brigit was not back from market, so I carefully stashed the jewels high up in Aunty's study.

'Mimi,' David says, 'what do you intend to do with the jewels?'

'The executors just said I could deal with the distribution.'

He sits upright and orders more drinks. 'Mimi, you cannot keep the jewellery to yourself. There is no inventory, and you can't find the photos or Aunty's letter of wishes.'

I nod in agreement.

'Your father and my mother are going to want to take control of the situation, and that could mean a big mess.'

'Yes, it could.'

'So, we need a plan, and we need to make it happen as quickly as possible.'

First we call Josephine in London. David and his sister talk for a while, then Jo tells me, 'Mimi, I'm very happy for David to represent me and for you both to decide what we each should have. Aunty did always say she wanted me to have the Russian emeralds, which she said once belonged to the Tzar. I hope that will be okay?' I remember that Aunty had always said that, and she'd promised me her eternity rings, so we agree and hang up.

David and I decide to go through the jewellery piece by piece. Apart from the emeralds and eternity rings, we'll take turns choosing from remaining items. Simple.

'We trust you implicitly, Brigit,' I assure her as she sobs on the other end of the phone line. 'You can do this. It's okay.' She reluctantly agrees to bring the jewels to the hotel right away.

Half an hour later, she calls me from the foyer to announce her arrival.

Brigit puts down the concierge phone, sweating. She is carrying hundreds of thousands of dollars' worth of irreplaceable, highly sentimental jewellery. The pressure is so intense, she is close to fainting and cannot wait to hand the bags over to me.

Then something very unexpected happens, beyond any of the catastrophic scenarios Brigit thought of on her way here. The enormous foyer appeared almost empty when she arrived, with just doormen, receptionists and a couple over there on the lounge – Francis!

He strides over, quicker than she can find an escape route. 'Brigit, what are *you* doing here?'

She looks around desperately, clasping the bags so tightly to her sides she might seriously have a heart attack. 'Oh, Mr Kwa, I just came to see your daughter, Mimi. She will be down in a minute.' He squints and eyes the bags in her white-knuckled grip. Her heart pounds, and sweat pours from her forehead despite the air conditioning.

Francis takes Brigit's shaking arm with a firm grip and guides her to the seat where Karen is waiting. 'Look who's here, Karen. It's Brigit. And what have we got here?' He gestures to the bags Brigit is clinging to for dear life.

Just then, I step out of the elevator with a spring in my step. I go left and stride into the foyer near the safety deposit box desk, the word *Cashier* printed in gold on its suspended sign. A hotel staff member greets me, but instead of smiling back I stop dead in my tracks.

Brigit is sitting on a striped satin settee with my father and Karen; two bags are on the chair between them. She looks tense. They all do.

They haven't seen me. My heart bursting out of my chest, I use the cashier's phone to call up to David, who soon appears beside me with his game face on.

As I walk with my cousin under a dozen chandeliers towards the settee, Dad sees us and stands up, a grim look on his face.

'Uncle Francis,' David says, 'what a *wonderful* surprise to see you. Why don't you join us in the *executive* lounge for a drink? First we'll go upstairs to invite my mother, of course. You must have come to see her. Yes?'

Francis straightens up to a stature befitting an 'executive'.

Brigit steps towards me and thrusts both bags into my arms — live bombs. She is still trembling.

'And, Karen,' says David, 'of course you must join us too.' His tall, imposing figure stoops to corral the elders. He gives me a nod as they walk off to the lifts.

'I'm so sorry, Brigit.' I hug her. 'I had no idea Dad would be here.'

Brigit sobs uncontrollably; how she has any tears left, I don't know. 'I was so frightened, Mimi. I was really so frightened.'

While David walks ahead and gives Francis and Karen a personal tour of the hotel – recounting facts about artworks, the building and Manila in general – I say goodbye to Brigit and head to a different lift well in order to beat the others to the executive lounge.

At a table near the corner, Sam is the only guest there, tapping away on his laptop. As I approach, he looks up and smiles a broad, charismatic smile. I slide two bags under his table, where they're concealed by a floor-length white cloth, and he grins and nods knowingly, a Cheshire cat. Like most people, he finds the Kwa family both perplexing and entertaining.

Soon, we're joined by David, Aunty Clara, Dad and Karen, and the five of us sit at another table while Sam keeps working. For the next couple of hours, David and I speak loudly to our elders about nothing much. We gloss over the few indirect mutterings from Francis and Clara about 'family jewellery' and bags belonging to 'the family'. We exchange fond memories of Theresa, and David carefully drops obvious hints into the conversation, such as, 'Aunty Theresa would really want her wishes to be honoured, wouldn't she?'

I nod in furious agreement.

David continues, 'Uncle Francis and Mother, she truly wanted to save you both any headache to do with her estate. It's such a complicated process to apply for probate and to administer a will. And there's all that longwinded and expensive talk with lawyers and government departments.' He yawns dramatically. 'Oh, what a bore. Aunty Theresa thought better to let the younger ones take care of the hard work while you two can relax. Right?'

I'm the only one nodding. Sam keeps tapping away at his computer. Karen sips her twelfth cup of Chinese tea, not having said a single thing this entire time; I wonder what on earth she must think of all this.

It's late. David indicates he's ready for bed with more dramatic yawning and stretching. We've drunk and small-talked the old siblings under the table, and we breathe a sigh of relief as Clara, Francis and Karen leave.

Sam looks up from his laptop and smiles. 'Can I stop standing guard now? I really need to go to the bathroom.'

In David and Sam's hotel room, we lay out Aunty's jewels on the bedspread. David has another brilliant idea, but before he's able to share it the phone rings.

It's Clara. 'David, David, where are the jewels?'

David takes a very deep breath. 'Mother, don't worry, they are all very secure. In fact, they're locked up in the safe downstairs at reception under my and Mimi's joint names so only we can access it. So it is all very safe. Just have a good night's rest, and we'll speak tomorrow.'

David gestures for Sam to pour more wine, and his eyes roll in my direction as his mother continues ranting in his ear.

'Yes, Mother dear, Mimi has gone home. We thought we would sort out the jewels tomorrow when we are fresh ... Ohhhh, *you* would like to be there to sort through them? Right. But Theresa said they are for Josephine and Mimi to share, so they must be the ones to do it ... Yes, I understand that you and Francis are older, but Jo and Mimi are adults now, they are not children ... Yes, Mother, I realise that Josephine is your child, but she is not "a" child ... Yes, Mother, but Jo has asked me to sort out her share ... Yes, Mummy, you are right, you should be there when we sort it all out. Okay, I'll call you when Mimi gets here in the morning. Okay? ... Alright, Mother. Very tired now.' Dramatic yawn. 'Good night.'

Clara keeps talking as David hangs up, his clever idea now solidified.

'We will allocate the real rings and necklaces, brooches and pearls to you and Jo, Mimi, and leave just enough costume jewellery for Mother to go through with you that she will be convinced of her inclusion. We will re-stage this event again in the morning, for her benefit.'

DISC AND DUMPLINGS

I WAKE UP WITH A THUMPING HEADACHE. I'M NOT LOOKING forward to going back to the Shangri-La at ten, to go through the costume jewellery with Aunty Clara. Running my hand over the bag of my inherited precious adornments, I wonder if it will be safe here at the condo. What if Dad gets past the guards while I'm gone? What if he bullies Brigit or Jay into letting him in without me here?

As I'm eating breakfast, Tessie calls to tell me my father has requested a meeting with her and Letty that afternoon. Can I please attend at Letty's apartment? Light lunch will be served. Of course, I agree.

I decide to wear a gold disc pendant Clara gave me two years ago. She put the 24-carat chain around my neck and fastened the clasp, looked me in the eye, squeezed my hands and said, 'You are Kwa. You remember that. Kwa is strong. Kwa is good. You are Kwa. True Kwa. You have the name, but I also see the Kwa in you.' She held my hands and my gaze for some time, and I was deeply touched by both her generosity and remark. Today I hope the necklace will be a sign of peace, and I fasten the chain carefully to make sure the small gold Chinese symbol faces outwards. 'It means happy – happy and good luck,' Clara said with my hands in hers. 'You are happy. You are Kwa. I love you.'

Aunty Theresa's condo is right across the road from the Shangri-La. She chose the location so she could use the hotel gym and pool, but as there isn't anywhere to cross safely and traffic is so bad, it takes a full twenty minutes to drive around the block to the hotel entrance. As guards sweep the car for bombs I think of John and the kids, wondering what they're doing now, glad they're not here to see Kwa at its worst.

A doorman helps me out, then sashays ahead to join his colleague at the entrance. Together they open two heavy glass doors, just as the Sikh men did for me at the Mandarin Oriental, when I would eagerly skip behind Aunty on our way to Swatow Lace.

'Could you kindly call up to Mr David Bryan's room and let him know Miss Mimi Kwa has arrived?' I ask the hotel attendant.

Her eyes widen. 'Oh. Miss Mimi Kwa?' Your parents Mrs Bryan and Mr Kwa were here this morning asking for access to your safe. When we told them there is no safety deposit under your name anyway, they became quite upset and shouted at us. I am very sorry to have caused them any inconveniences. Please can you send the hotel's apologies to them?'

It takes a moment for this to sink in.

She gestures in the direction of the restaurant. 'They went on for breakfast and billed it to David Bryan's room.'

When I arrive upstairs, Aunty Clara is already in David and Sam's room. We embrace, and Clara examines the gold disc pendant around my collar, 'Oh ho lang, ho lang. Very beautiful' she says and then the show begins. Sam adjusts a black velvet display tray identical to one you might find in a jeweller's shop. Aunty Clara paws through the first few items Sam has laid out.

'Now, Mother,' says David, 'you do realise you're choosing for Josephine, don't you? Not for yourself.'

'Myself, yes, myself,' she says absentmindedly. 'But where are all the diamonds and the precious stones?'

The duplicity in the room is a multilayered cake you could cut with a knife, and the icing is Aunty Clara's attempt to distract me from anything of potential value. 'Look, look at this, how it shines,' she gasps, holding up a cubic zirconia pendant that she and I both know perfectly well is not worth a penny. 'It is a beautiful diamond – *you* should have this.' There are a few real items that we left in the collection in the end, but this is not one of them.

She practises a little sleight of hand, shoving a genuine Rolex, with a fine black leather band, to her edge of the tray and concealing it under a flared sleeve – clearly worn for the occasion. She repeats this routine until she has accumulated too big a collection to hide, but she has gone too far to care. She puts on a gold bracelet and disappears into a reverie. 'It's a little big for me. I will need to have it resized. And this ring will need to be resized too.'

I head to the meeting with Tessie and Letty, Jay and I picking up Dad on the way. Like all chauffeurs, Jay bears silent witness and pretends not to listen in to Dad's rant. 'The executors are very cunning. They will make great difficulty for me. It is your duty to look after my interests. We are on the same side.' Dad is starting off with a friendly approach today, and I hope he won't go on the attack this time. The dragon narrows his eyes, dancing gracefully around his victim.

'Dad, the issue with Aunty's will is that it doesn't say you get everything like you are telling everyone. It just says furniture and fixtures.'

The dragon's blood ratchets up to a boil. 'Shut up. You do as I say! If you don't back me up, then everything is gone. They will take it all.'

Dad and I take the lift to Letty's apartment, travelling in silence. He seethes, and I recalibrate for the next round.

Letty and Tessie are on the balcony, sitting at a lavish stone dining table surrounded by succulents and statues. The view is of a condominium courtyard shared by elite Manila residents; it is even more gentrified than Aunty Theresa's wealthy neighbourhood. There is more of a Spanish influence at Letty's.

Two maids subtly bow and exit backwards as if I might be the Queen herself, and Dad and I sit down. The maids return with Chinese tea and plates of simply delicious dumplings.

Dad kicks me under the table. I lower my gaze. I had forgotten to assume a meek facade, my only way to get through lunch without fuss.

Dad speaks with the executors as if I'm not there, pontificating about seniority and asking Letty and Tessie their ages. 'I am at least ten years your senior. You are just young girls.'

The executors are looking to me for guidance.

'You do not understand,' Dad says, as we eat beautifully decorated, ornate desserts. 'It is *all* mine. You women do not understand the Kwa family.' I chew on a strap of mango garnish. 'You do not interfere in our House.' The chocolate fondant on the miniature cupcakes is delectable. 'And my daughter is only a girl, how could she know anything?'

At this point, the highly educated and successful women entertaining us have clearly had enough.

Dad shakes with anger in the lift as we leave. The dragon's eyes are red with rage. 'You know nothing, daughter. You do not know what you are dealing with.'

The doors open, and I get out before the fire breath can burn me more.

BANK AND BRIDGE

Obtaining probate is tedious. But I've jumped through the hoops before, as executor of Paw Paw's will, and I know what to do. It should be easy: the only thing in Aunty Theresa's Australian will is a property in South Perth, an established, upmarket riverside neighbourhood. She sold off all her other Perth assets, over the years, or Dad sold them for her, and I'm fortunate to have the least complicated of Aunty's wills to manage. Theresa bought her apartment in 1971, and now her investment of a few thousand dollars is worth over half a million and she wanted the proceeds shared between my brothers, Angela, my mum and me.

A couple, Allan and Maria, have rented Aunty's apartment since the early '90s. I call them and ask that they maintain payments into Theresa's account as usual. But once probate comes through and I pay a visit to Westpac bank, I find no rent money in Aunty's accounts.

Dad picks up my call. 'Oh, dear daughter. The tenants like me. I own the apartment. It was your Aunty's will. It is not your place to make decisions. You cannot and will not outsmart me.'

And just like that, I am plunged into a hell I thought I had escaped long ago, one I ran from and hid from in my career – and in my children, my husband, my friends – but there it is, here it is, the dragon's jaws open to swallow me, the tiger exhausted beneath the jungle canopy. The dragon circles and swoops; there was never going to be any escape.

I put the kids to bed, inhale half a bottle of wine, call John's dad – the magistrate – and cry. 'What do I do, Len? He's my dad, but Aunty left the apartment to my brothers and me, Angela and my mum – probably knowing Dad would never look after any of us.'

Ever since Francis walked on Len's back, claiming he was a 'Chinese doctor', and ever since Francis called Len day and night for legal advice that he never followed, Len has been rather unimpressed, so there is little to no convincing required for my father-in-law to help me. There was also the time Francis took Len out to a Chinese vegetarian restaurant where the chicken, beef and pork were all tofu; Len never got over that.

Len says my best bet is to file against Dad to recoup the rent, which if nothing else will keep him busy and off my case while I sell the apartment.

I fly secretly to Perth. It's only a secret from Dad, and it feels weird because usually I'm flying to Perth to see him but, instead, I must deal with the tenants in person. The little girl in me struggles with the weight and complexity of who we are to each other: I feel such a deep sense of obligation to him but he doesn't seem to have the same dutiful concern for me. The woman in me clings to a moral compass, magnetically twitching an arrow to 'right'.

I relate the whole Manila episode to my brothers and former stepmother, Angela, who is my host tonight at her rented villa in the fashionable suburb of Subiaco. She's happier than I've ever seen her, softened. She has prepared five dishes for our dinner, and regardless, I'm grateful for the effort. I drink wine and relax.

I'm looking out for Angela's interest in Aunty Theresa's will, but I cannot believe that's the only reason she embraced me when I arrived. The fact that Theresa left both Francis's ex-wives part of her estate is not lost on anyone. Great-Grandfather left First Mother behind in China and abandoned Number Two Wife and Number Three Wife for heaven, and Theresa wasn't letting that happen again.

We four share stories about Dad. We could write a book – and maybe I will one day, I think.

My brother Jerome has his feet up on the couch. He had a minor motorcycle accident yesterday. Angela picked me up and we rushed to the hospital because the only one he wanted to see was me, to sit there silently through injections and examinations. I held his hand just like I held Mama, Ng Yuk's, hand decades ago.

When Ng Yuk, Dad's mother, refused to go for blood tests in Hong Kong, I would go with her. She couldn't speak English but to say, 'Your daddy, no good. No good.' And I could not speak Chinese but to say, '*Mm goi*. Thank you.' We held hands as nurses took blood. 'Good boy,' Ng Yuk said to me in English. 'Good boy.' I watched Kwa blood fill the vial. Slowly rising.

When I was a teenager Mama celebrated her 86th birthday and Aunty Theresa reserved an entire floor of a Hong Kong restaurant to fit the hundreds of guests from around the world, Kwas paying their respects to the last living wife of Ying Kam. Ng Yuk wasn't actually eighty-six but it's custom to add a year for each generation after you, so she was really only eighty-three. I wasn't long out of primary school, and of all the guests, she wanted me to sit at her table. At her funeral a year later, I stood behind David in a long line of mourners to view Ng Yuk's open casket. Her frail body and tiny feet were finally at peace. Aunty Theresa asked for donations of blankets for the poor rather than flowers and, after the Catholic service, immediate family, like me, attended a Buddhist one where a monk cut the throat of a live chicken to protect Theresa as next of kin, after the almanac revealed it was double death day. I watched the red liquid drip onto the altar and pool on the floor.

I lodge Magistrates Court documents over Dad's rent collection, and predictably he is not happy. His text messages are like tiny swords.

I have Aunty's ashes in Melbourne and hope to hold a service somewhere in Australia once Dad has settled down. For now, all I can do is steel myself while he's on the warpath.

'I have plenty up my sleeve,' he rants. 'Don't think you know me. I will teach you.'

After a while, Dad perhaps becomes irritated by my numb responses – I am behind in his game – and out of sheer frustration throws me a bone. It's buried deep in a ten-screen-long text.

There is an ABSOLUTE CAVEAT on the title of your Aunty's apartment. This PROHIBITS you from selling it.

What?! That can't be right. I do some yoga stretches to help me absorb this information and call the titles office from a forward fold position.

'No, Madam, I cannot disclose the details of the title without proof of your grant of probate or evidence of your interest in the property.'

I stand upright and book another flight to Perth, this time to go to the land titles office.

'Hmmm, let me see.' A helpful elderly man looks at me over his spectacles. 'It'll just take me a minute.' He shuffles behind shelves and emerges with a folder. 'Yes. There is a caveat on that property. A title cannot be transferred with a caveat.' He smiles sympathetically.

'How did the caveat get there?'

The bespectacled man hands me a form, upon which is Dad's signature, dated three weeks before Theresa died.

There's no record of how Dad managed to prove a caveatable interest in his sister's property – maybe he took an old bank statement with his name on it, or old letters from Theresa mentioning maintenance – and it's at the discretion of the titles office clerk to decide if a caveat is warranted before they approve it. You only need to provide proof of an interest in the property then they record the caveat but not why it was placed.

Dad texts me. *You can never win. I am the King. It's all mine.*

I want the bitterness to wash from me to the furthest corners of existence, and most of all I want to relinquish my executorship. But if I die, John is the next in line, then Adrian, then Jerome, then five other people before any mention of Dad at all. Theresa did not want him in charge.

Dad gets even more furious when he goes to collect rent from Aunty's tenants and finds an empty apartment. He then sends essay-length messages on my birthday. I read his messages multiple times and feel depression creeping in.

Dad sends physical letters too. They arrive by the dozen: news articles highlighted in yellow to show Dad 'knows best', pages of prose to show Dad is 'all powerful', and notes to tell me, *You will never win.*

I resolve to fight back with love, compiling a beautiful hardcover hundred-page photo book filled with pictures of Dad and me and his grandchildren. This tactic helped to get Mum well, so maybe it'll work with Dad. I write of family and harmony, and Adrian delivers it to Dad.

Please lift the caveat. Please let me do what is right. Please let me be free to do the job Theresa has asked of me. You have four beautiful grandchildren, three loving children. Look around you. We don't need to fight.

Saying this in writing or in person has no effect. Dad's silence is stony, the dragon circling lower, aiming for the tiger's jugular. The tiger is lying down now, almost resolute that death would be easier than this torment.

Dad sends another letter. I leave it unopened for days. When I read it at last, the letter informs me that my father is suing me in the Supreme Court of Western Australia.

Kwa v Kwa

It's hard to breathe. It's hard not to breathe. I stare at the page as though I can alter the words somehow. My forehead pours with sweat, and that night I have trouble sleeping.

The following morning, when I peer into the bathroom mirror, I see that a thick sprig of my hair has turned grey overnight. The dragon hurtles towards the tiger, who can no longer hide. She searches for an exit and sees no option but to draw breath and face the flames.

No one seems surprised that he has escalated matters to court – of course he has. But I am. This is Dad who painted my bicycle with me, Dad who lugged my piano on stage to sing at school, Dad who I Wombled and collected junk with, Dad who I fired a rifle with, Dad who drove me and my friends to parties and who boasted about me behind my back to anyone who would listen – whenever I overheard, I would swell with pride. Dad taught me how to use a soldering iron, a hammer, pliers, a cement mixer and an electric saw. He built me a tractor-tyre swing and found me a trampoline, a swing set and a ping-pong table. He had a lolly cabinet just for me.

Despite the reality of the situation, I don't accept that Dad and I are about to go head-to-head in court. My heart is breaking. I am a little girl crushed.

* * *

At our Magistrate's hearing Dad says, 'My daughter is confused. She is young. I am upholding the will of my sister, and I ask that this trial be held over until the will is settled. It is before the Supreme Court.'

My chest tightens. I'm going to throw up. In the grip of a panic attack, I slide open a glass door, step outside and lean on a wall to steady myself. The garden sways. I breathe the fresh air into my lungs – deep, deep breaths – but I begin to hyperventilate. I sit cross-legged, lie down, sit up again, rock, just working it through. *It's going to be okay.* At home, I have a hot shower. The water rushes over me. *It's going to be okay.* I fend off dragon snarls.

Dad has a reputation with Perth judges as a serial litigant, but no matter what a nuisance he is, they've never been able to strike him out. Dad does win sometimes, so he is still part of the furniture. He dines out on being the first man to represent himself in the High Court of Australia since land rights activist Eddie Mabo won his historic case.

Acutely aware of the emotional toll this is all taking on me, John's dad finds me a lawyer: Johnson Kitto, a trusted, upstanding man whom people call on public radio for advice. My father-in-law gives him a resounding stamp of approval. 'Kitto was always straight. Always fair. I trust him.' Kitto takes my case and is undeterred and easily able to separate emotion from legal fact.

Fogged with fear and memories pushing aggressively forth to mar every experience by intruding on my thoughts – *The bench needs wiping; remember how you got in trouble for not wiping the bench? A child is crying; remember how you cried yourself to sleep? Hide the kitchen knives; remember how you were told your mother must not know where they are* – I'm unable to comprehend this fight will ever be over.

* * *

Since Aunty died, I've been drowning in House of Kwa. My husband and kids are almost losing sight of me beneath the waves that roll in.

In November 2013, a preliminary Supreme Court hearing works out whether the court will allow the full *Kwa v Kwa* case. Kitto appears for me, and Dad appears for himself.

In ten years, Dad has been to the Supreme Court countless times: against the Bank of Western Australia, the City of Stirling, the City of Cambridge, the Barrister's Board, the Engineers Association, pharmaceutical companies, the Australian Youth Hostels Association, and now me. Dad is confident in this familiar environment; I haven't been here since my work-experience days.

The whole case hinges on one thing I wouldn't have thought of in a million years. I watch in disbelief, from the public gallery of the Supreme Court, as Dad smugly tables a yellowing wad of paper – explosive ammunition the dragon has been sitting on all along. I'm horrified to hear that Theresa appointed Francis as her power of attorney in 1960, a decade and a half before I was born, to manage her Australian financial affairs.

The penny drops with the thud of a dragon foot. Dad used his power of attorney to put a caveat on the South Perth property. He took this same document to lawyers in the Philippines to contest the will there. I think I might faint.

'Your Honour, my daughter is deluded and believes that she is in charge. I do not blame her. I only wish to guide her. You see from the document I bring to you today that, in fact, I am the sole person responsible for my dear beloved departed sister's financial affairs.' Dad's hair is tousled and bow tie crooked, just like in the High Court years ago, his signature courtroom style.

'Thank you, Mr Kwa,' the judge says. 'Yes, Mr Kitto?'

I cannot bear the thought of how this will end. As Kitto rises to address the judge, I leave my body, a tiger perched up on the elaborate balustrade of the viewing confine; my tail and whiskers twitch, sizing up the scaled and cunning predator below and identifying the exits.

Then Kitto hurls a stick of dynamite that blows Francis's entire case apart.

'Miss Theresa Kwa cancelled the POA forty years ago.'

Kitto dramatically slaps down Aunty's letter cancelling Dad's rights over her affairs — it proves she had second thoughts over him handling her assets and that, having come to her senses, she rescinded his power after just a few weeks. My eyes look to heaven.

'Mimi,' says Kitto, 'it's done. You won. It's over.'

'But Dad is an expert at appeals.'

'No, Mimi. No, he cannot appeal. It's been thrown out.'

JUNK AND BRACE

WE ASSEMBLE ON A JUNK BOAT IN HONG KONG HARBOUR. It's Aunty Theresa's second funeral, and her ashes are finally to be laid to rest in the place she called home all her life. David and I have kept this ceremony small: close family and a few Chinese relatives who caught wind of it somehow.

Aunty Clara has made the trip from England. She wears black trousers and a black skivvy, her slight frame clinging to a table with outstretched arms gripping its edges.

Adrian and Jerome are here with their girlfriends, and Third Wife Karen keeps busy in the corner, arranging flowers to be thrown in the water to follow Theresa's ashes.

Francis opens the formalities. 'I have a photocopier.' He casts an eye around the intimate group. The boat rocks, and we hold on to the side or something bolted down so as not to keel over. 'Do you understand? I have a photocopier. You know? Photocopier?' Dad grips a pole with one hand, his notes in the other.

David charges to the toilet at the rear of the boat, retching violently in the background as we all keep swaying. Sam smiles sympathetically in David's direction, and then at all of us for having to hear.

Today is the first time I've seen Dad since the court case. We kissed on the cheek and embraced, then gazed silently for too long into each other's eyes; we have not mentioned the war. It feels strange to carry on as though nothing happened, as though blood taking a knife to blood never occurred, but it's the wisest and kindest choice – because if we don't choose this, Kwa would need to turn on Kwa again or, worse still, turn its back, and that, the unthinkable, could never happen. Kwa sticks together, even when battling itself. We are assembled to remember Theresa and won't let anything spoil that this time.

'I have a photocopier,' Dad repeats, for those who may not have heard. He is letting us know he is a big businessman because he is rich and important enough to actually *own* a photocopier – the type usually reserved for libraries and office blocks, never a home study.

Dad's message is lost, and the audience turns from sickly and sombre to sickly and confused. David returns momentarily, only to lurch for the less-than-modest amenities again, and I imagine the junk's loo sloshing from side to side.

Dad presses on. 'Here, I have photocopied words my sister wrote to me.'

I grab my brothers' hands and squeeze them tight as we sit in a row of Kwa siblings, our heads bowed.

This morning I took Aunty's decorative urn, filled with her remains, to a buffet breakfast at the Mandarin Oriental, her favourite hotel. I had booked a room so she could spend one last night there. The suites she designed have since been refurbished, but they appear in a coffee-table book I keep by my bed, along with a photo of her true love, Tony, looking over an architect's cardboard model of the hotel.

I wandered down its corridors with Aunty, speaking softly to her, on her last tour. If anyone thought I looked strange carrying around a black urn decorated in white opal, no one mentioned this. I ate the buffet breakfast on her behalf, then swanned out beneath the chandeliers and through the foyer, together for the last time. Two doormen opened the glass doors for us to leave. 'Miss Kwa.' I heard again. 'And little Miss Kwa.'

One of the reasons I didn't invite the hundreds of friends and family members in Aunty's address book to this second ceremony is that I couldn't tell who was a plumber she met only once or not at all, and who was a dear friend. Instead, I sent them all a poem Aunty chose: 'Don't grieve for me, for now I'm free'. Many people use this poem, which goes by many names, with no one able to agree who wrote it. Aunty asked for it to be her simple death notice, with no explanation.

I should have expected the outpouring of grief that was posted back, along with the questions: 'What happened?' 'How did she die?' And the requests for me to call South Africa, Canada, England and Hong Kong. 'I would so like to speak with you to understand more,' they would say most politely. She died at eighty-three but, in the minds of so many, Theresa was still a vivacious young woman serving drinks on BOAC flights, travelling the world, overseeing her shop, attending lavish events, walking on the beach and dining at clubs. Breaking hearts wherever she went.

But despite this outpouring of emotion from across continents, David and I decided on a small and intimate gathering, exactly as Theresa had wished – a humble, understated affair to make up for the Manila spectacle.

Francis hands out photocopies of the important excerpt from his eulogy – *You are the star in your own movie* – passing a wad of paper to Adrian to distribute along the row, then handing another fistful to a distant relative.

Adrian and Jerome each make their own tributes, and David does a reading. Then it's time to scatter Aunty's ashes.

There's a strong wind today, and I worry we'll end up with Aunty all over us if she blows back off the sea. Fortunately a large tube has been tied to the side of the vessel for such an occasion. Dad and Clara go first, ladling Aunty into the tube so she slides straight down into the water. Fish gather and call to their friends, ensuring Theresa will live on through the sea, maybe even ending up on a table in her favourite fish restaurant.

On the way to David and Sam's place in Admiralty we sit on the upper sundeck. Dad's beside me, talking about his latest court case. I take a selfie of us together; he admires my sunglasses and asks if they're real, and I admire his Don Johnson funeral look, although it's not much different to his normal style.

He holds up the pink chain on his sunglasses. 'Look, look, you need one of this, otherwise you'll lose your Ray-Ban overboard.'

I appreciate the good advice; it shows that he cares.

With the *Kwa v Kwa* episode behind us and Aunty's ashes out at sea, the tiger leaps from the flames into calm, cool waters, and the dragon has new priorities as he readies his Floreat place for a grand Perth renovation.

Dad welds while wearing a bicycle helmet, no goggles and no shoes. He walks on a slippery wet roof with no harness, and contravenes a lengthy list of safety regulations to get his renovation underway. It's clear he hasn't built what the council said he could; he has overstepped the agreed footprint and height, altered all the window sizes, and created an additional three bathrooms and three bedrooms. Another Francis Kwa dream emerges: a mini Mandarin Gardens.

Jerome is mortified and throws his hands in the air. 'He doesn't listen, Mimi.' As an 'actual' qualified architect, Jerome has spent months on Dad's 'project' only to be undermined at every stage. 'Sonny boy,' Dad says, 'you know nothing. I am far wiser than you. Do not tell your old man what to do.'

When I go upstairs one day during a visit from Melbourne, the balcony balustrade wobbles while Dad – busy assembling an IKEA drawer and hardly looking up – reassures me, 'Don't worry, don't worry.' He's trying to force the wrong screw into the wrong hole. 'It will be okay. Father knows best.' I'm careful not to lean on the rail again.

The picture of the proposed building on the fence looks nothing like the actual building behind it. 'I did it my way,' Dad sings.

The City of Cambridge issues a cease works notice ordering Francis to demolish unapproved parts of the building, so he sues them. Neighbours whose dogs Karen once walked and to whom she delivered meals are now estranged; Karen is sad that Francis won't let her see them anymore. Three couples on the street list their houses for sale in the same week, wanting as much distance from Dad as possible and hoping to sell fast before there's too much damage to their property prices.

My phone flashes with a text message: *Call me when convenient. I still care about your mother. Karen, my wife, accepts this. I am the boss.*

The last thing Mum needs in her life is Dad. She's doing just fine with us now. She takes her medication religiously, and she tutors students in all year levels and from every ethnic background. She looks after her grandchildren when I'm working, and I even did a TV feature on our set-up, promoting granny flats and multigenerational living.

I've been careful over the years to curate what I tell Mum and Dad about each other, 'supervising' visitation on the odd occasion Dad is in Melbourne. (He forgets the names of his grandkids a week later, but I am pleased he tries.) Whenever he's around, Mum falls back into a role of servitude. It beggars belief: he sits on a sun lounge by the pool, ordering tea and bowls of rice as if she's the maid. 'Mum,' I tell her, 'you don't have to do what he says.' She looks at me like I'm crazy, and I remind myself that all of this is crazy. If only I could have told the teenage girl in the mirror that it would all be okay, that the Kwa madness and my mum's schizophrenia have ended with me.

Dad breaks his neck when an IKEA shelf – not correctly bolted to the wall as per instructions – falls on him at home. He texts me: *I have broken neck. Doctors do no know what they are talking about. Want me to wear a neck brace but they are idiots. I am a doctor. Love, Dad.*

He will probably sue IKEA, but I am more concerned about his health.

I call, and he texts back. *Am busy. Magnum PI is on.*

DAD! You are eighty-three. My friend broke his neck skiing and had to wear a brace for six weeks. You must listen to the doctors.

An hour passes.

Dad replies, *I am not your friend. I am a direct descendant of the Emperor of China. I am twenty-third generation Kwa.*

EPILOGUE

WHEN MY DEAR FRIEND FOXY READ THE FIRST DRAFT OF THIS manuscript, she turned to me wide-eyed. 'Mim, how on earth did you turn out so normal?' This question got me wondering, so I've tried to weave in little insights here and there as to how I ended up fairly well adjusted.

I had a breakdown of sorts as well as a breakthrough while writing this story and excavating my past. In particular, seeing my mum every day became challenging and confronting the more memories that emerged. I'm exploring this further in a new story I'm writing, one about reconciling past trauma, forgiveness and gratitude.

Since I finished writing the last chapter of *House of Kwa*, Aunty Clara passed on in 2020 during the Covid pandemic. She was fortunate to have David, Steven and Josephine by her side.

This leaves Dad, the thirty-second child, the very last Kwa of his generation in his own Kwa strand. He's eighty-seven and still has plenty of tenant and building schemes keeping his mind active.

In Perth, Adrian and his wife, Lee, have a wonderful baby, Grayson, who brings Dad such joy when he allows it, and we all attended Jerome's wedding to Genevieve this year. This may be taken as evidence that we have pushed through our own Kwa stories alright.

When the dragon closes his eyes for good one day, I will know that tiger and predator reached an understanding of sorts and a kind of peace in the end – one that could really only come about from telling my story in order to let it go.

As I hand the brush of Kwa to my sons and daughters so they can paint their own stories, I give gentle instructions at the edge of the blank page: 'Don't hesitate to make a mark. You can always paint over it, my love, any time you like. You are not bound by history to repeat its cycle. Your story is yours, but don't forget that if you ever need it, there's a Kwa spark in you waiting to be called.'

ACKNOWLEDGEMENTS

I cannot express how deeply moved I am to have such strong and fearless women in my publishing corner. Jude and Brigitta, thank you for your support and belief in me which has frequently brought me to tears of sheer gratitude. To Kate and Barbara, your care and sensitivity with my story and empowerment of my words has been a wonderous and blessed experience. To my lovely publicist Jordan and all the dedicated Harper Collins team, I thank you for giving me this fantastic glimpse into the magical way in which your world of print lives and breathes. Thanks to Nadine for your utter care with my earliest draft and, of course, Jane for your unwavering faith from that very first call, and all those pep talks since. Andy, designer extraordinaire, thanks to you and the art team for the cover of my dreams.

To Mum and Dad, who gave me life, I am full of gratitude to you both for your love and doing the best you knew how to do. Zora, you are a lifesaver in more ways than one. Thanks to my brothers Adrian and Jerome for accepting my decision to tell my story and to David, Josephine and Steven – you are Kwa. Beloved Aunties and Paw Paw and Granddad, I could not have done without your unwavering strength. My cousin Karen, I'm so glad we reconnected after almost three decades, I am only sorry I won't ever see our dearly departed Cathy again. Matthew Kwa, thank you for your love and family trees of Kwa. Thank you Len and Kath and Robertses for not ever quite understanding Kwa but embracing me anyway.

To my besties from every chapter of my life and to dear friends who have hung closely with me to the very end of this long writing journey – Foxy, Rach, Meaghan, Georgina, Carmel and Tracey, in particular, the girls in The Band, the No 1 Melbourne Ladies Bookclub, and all who have held my hand, laughed and cried with me, walked and stretched it out and simply said, 'keep going', thank you. Jo, for always emanating light beams of love just when they were needed, George, for your brilliance coining the name *House of Kwa*, and Sherrie, I owe you special acknowledgment for checking my Chinese. Jesper, your last-minute photo is amazing.

To my high school Big Clique, Rat Pack, Scarborough, City Beach, Hale and Churchlands crews and my primary school friends, for being life rafts at a time I may otherwise have drowned, thank you – we did have fun in amongst it all. To everyone I have mentioned in this book, and to you for reading it, I fold my hands and bow.

And to John, my rock, and my kids – you are my world. I know I have been lost in my writing, thank you for supporting my healing so that I could emerge from beneath the waves to finally swim on my own.